D1286681

THE *American Democratic Tradition*:

A HISTORY

BOOKS BY THE SAME AUTHOR

The Idea of Progress in America, 1815–1860

The Decline of American Liberalism

The Civilian and the Military

THE *American Democratic Tradition:*

A HISTORY

Arthur A. Ekirch, Jr.

THE MACMILLAN COMPANY, NEW YORK
COLLIER-MACMILLAN LIMITED, LONDON

First Printing

Designed by Andrew Roberts

Library of Congress catalog card number: 63-18793

THE MACMILLAN COMPANY, NEW YORK
COLLIER-MACMILLAN CANADA, LTD., TORONTO, ONTARIO

Printed in the United States of America

IN MEMORY OF

Charles A. Beard
Vernon L. Parrington

Preface

NO ONE needs to point out the importance of American democracy in the world today. Not only in modern times but over the course of our history we have been influenced and governed by the democratic tradition. Frequently, indeed, we use democracy in such a broad sense that its history becomes virtually synonymous with American history. While it is true that much of the American past can be thought of as the unfolding of the democratic idea, that idea can hardly be understood well if it is viewed only as another approach to general history.

Democracy, though increasingly invoked as a term to describe our contemporary way of life, is also a political process and ideology of long-standing duration. For its varied historic meanings there is an extensive literature, ranging from textbooks on American government to learned disquisitions on political theory and philosophy. Professor Ralph Gabriel's *The Course of American Democratic Thought* treats certain aspects of the theory of democracy as a part of the intellectual history of the United States. Other scholars have dealt with special topics related to the American democratic tradition or have written brief interpretive essays on democracy. But there is no volume that attempts to survey and analyze both the idea and the practice of democracy for the entire sweep of American history. The present work therefore is designed to meet the need for a history of American democracy considered in terms of social theory and ideas as well as of political practice and reality.

A synthesis confined to the length of one modest-sized volume cannot pretend to be the definitive account of so large and significant a subject. I have tried, however, to give a reasonably full and comprehensive summary of the history of the American democratic tradition. This tradition, though we rightly pay due reverence to its past, has not been unchanging. Accordingly we must study the history and practice of democracy as well as its philosophy and theory. The American democratic tradition, after all, has not been static but dynamic. This has been perhaps even more true in recent years with the growing popular emphasis upon social and economic democracy. But the historian is not a prophet, and thus it may be appropriate only to point out that, despite what seem to be undoubted gains in the progress of democracy, many age-old problems remain unsolved. Yet the difficulty of achieving democracy in practice should not imply that we must yield either the traditions of the past or our hopes for the future.

For help and encouragement in doing this book I should like to express my appreciation to my fellows in the field of history, whether students, teachers, or librarians. As in all my work, I owe much to the counsel and friendship of Merle Curti, and I also wish to thank especially Professors William Neumann and Samuel Sharp for their intelligent reading and criticism of the manuscript. The final stages of the research and writing were much speeded by a full year free of teaching duties. For making this possible I wish to thank the president and trustees of the American University. Mr. Kenneth S. Templeton, Jr. of Lilly Endowment, Inc., was particularly helpful in a number of ways. I also am grateful for the care and interest with which Mrs. Patricia Hudson typed the manuscript. Finally I trust that my readers will not think me presumptuous for dedicating this volume to the memory of the two scholars of the past generation who have most influenced my own thinking and writing.

Contents

Introduction [1]

ONE
Colonial Beginnings [7]

TWO
Revolutionary Upsurge [31]

THREE

The First Great Debate [51]

FOUR

Toward a New Order [73]

FIVE

Criticism and Commentary [99]

SIX

Disruption and Disunion [125]

SEVEN

Reconstruction and Revolution [147]

EIGHT

The Triumph of Nationalism and Reform [171]

NINE

American Mission Under Arms [201]

TEN

Disillusionment and Prosperity [225]

ELEVEN

Challenge and Response [249]

TWELVE

Neither Peace nor War [277]

Notes [299]

Bibliography [317]

Index [323]

Introduction

WHEN Alexis de Tocqueville wrote his celebrated classic *Democracy in America* more than a century ago, he believed it self-evident that "a great democratic revolution is going on among us." Since that time confidence in the progress of democracy has not seriously declined in the United States. Imbued with a strong faith in the democratic idea, the American people for the most part have been convinced that the cure for the problems of democracy is more democracy. Criticism, in other words, seldom has been pushed to the point of disbelief. Instead Americans have reshaped early democratic ideals to suit later ideas and interests. Thus the liberal individualism of Jeffersonian democracy has been transformed into the centralized collectivist democracy of the twentieth century, and the diminished state favored by Jeffersonian democrats has become the powerful welfare state of the present day. In foreign affairs democracy is no longer a radical revolutionary concept, but rather an ideology of defense against communism. Yet Tocqueville's thesis still holds. No concept has been more reverenced in the United States, and Americans do not need to be reminded that men have fought and died for democracy, while free peoples everywhere have continued to try to apply its tenets in their governments.

In the United States democracy is a potent emotional symbol, acceptance of which is regarded as a test of a citizen's loyalty and patriotism. No longer considered simply as one of several species of governments, democracy has rather become a part of almost every aspect of American life and thought. The American people therefore are dangerously close to making democracy a new kind of secular religion which they believe in more as a matter of faith than of understanding.

The democratic idea itself is both simple and profound. Simple enough to be a popular credo, it is also sufficiently complex to require definition by learned philosophers. As a term, democracy may refer to a type of government, a political philosophy, or a way of life. Frequently the word is used in such fashion that it embraces all three meanings at the same time. Abraham Lincoln, describing it unforgettably in his Gettysburg Address as "government of the people, by the people, for the people," probably gave the best brief popular definition of political democracy. In more restricted terms Aristotle called it government by the many.

The word *democracy* derives from the two Greek roots *demos* and *kratia*, meaning the people or mass (the *demos*) and power, authority, or government (*kratia*). Thus it means literally the authority of the people or the people's power. The Athenians were the first to formulate a theory or philosophy of democracy and apply it in their way of life and government. Under this version of direct democracy the active citizenry enjoyed freedom of speech and assembly. In his famous funeral oration for the Athenian soldiers who had died in the first year of the Peloponnesian War, Pericles duly noted: "Our government is called a democracy, because its administration is in the hands, not of the few, but of the many. . . . All of us share in considering and deciding public policy. . . ."

To Greek democracy, the merits of which Pericles asserted, modern democratic states are still indebted. But it also had flaws which are no less significant. Most important of all was the qualification effected by the slave system. In a population that included in the fifth century B.C. some 100,000 slaves and 24,000 metics, or alien residents, plus women and children, probably only one tenth of the population—the 40,000 adult male citizens—could vote. Though all citizens were equal before the law, the Greeks did not think in terms of the modern concepts of individuality or of the supremacy of the law. In antithesis to liberal, though not to totalitarian, democracy, the individual existed in frank subordination to the state. Because Athenian democracy was undiluted by the modern device of representative government, it has little practical value as an example for large and extensive nations. Unfortunately, too, Athens could not escape from the economic problems of imperialism and land distribution, and its lack of economic democracy may have affected its political stability. Ultimately, and some would say inevitably, Athens fell prey to authoritarian government, and the rule of tyrant and king succeeded Greek democracy. Today many of the difficulties that beset democratic government in ancient Greece still remain unresolved, but it is also none the less true that the democratic creed, first formulated in Athens, continues as a modern article of faith, constantly revitalized by new interpretations, redefinition, and criticism.

Since the days of the Greek city-state, authorities have generally agreed that the most prominent feature of democracy is some form of majority rule or popular consent. If the majority does not rule, its mere acquiescence may support a totalitarian regime under a dictator, but the result is not popular self-government. At the same time, the presence of a majority that ignores minority feelings runs counter to the idea of liberal democracy as a protection of the rights of the individual and of the public. Democracy then degenerates into a species of mob rule, which is what the eighteenth-century aristocrats so feared as its inevitable outcome. Freedom of the individual in the enjoyment of his liberties may, however, conflict with the more equalitarian aspects of democracy. Historically democracy, in both its theory and practice, has given different weight to the importance of majority rule, individual liberty, and equal rights, but a democratic government in which these criteria are notably lacking is difficult to imagine.

Though democracy is often considered synonymous with such allied concepts as liberalism, individualism, or equalitarianism, it is nevertheless quite distinct from these. Its opposite is an authoritarian type of government in which the majority has no voice or rule, while the opposite of liberalism is a totalitarian state in which the individual is deprived of his liberty and individuality. If the majority refuses to tolerate minority dissent, a liberal democracy then becomes totalitarian. Though totalitarian, such a democracy is not, however, authoritarian, because the tyranny it enforces is that of the majority over the minority. In authoritarian government this tyranny is expressed by the few, or by a king or despot. On the other hand, a monarch or an aristocracy may recognize individual liberty and dissent. Such a government, though indubitably liberal, is not democratic. Finally, a totalitarian dictatorship may secure approval by plebiscite, or it may enforce a species of social and economic equality. Though equalitarian and majoritarian, such a government is, however, neither liberal nor democratic, because individual rights are overridden and because the people do not rule. Thus, though certain of these values may converge, democracy remains distinct from the other political philosophies with which it is frequently linked.

If one turns from theory to practice, democracy becomes even more difficult to appraise. Communist states deny the validity of political democracy unless it is accompanied by widespread economic democracy and a classless society. Skeptics question the extent to which any sort of democracy is actually being applied and practiced today. Certainly the modern worship of democracy often only serves to conceal the failure to realize its ideals. It is also true that many of those who venerate the ideal have been, or would be, repelled by the fact of democracy in operation; they reject the practice, though not the theory, of democracy. In the post-World War II bipolarization of the world, at least a part of the conflict between Russia and the United States stems from differing conceptions of democracy. The West emphasizes political democracy with its corollaries of majority rule and minority rights. Historically this Western democracy has also been closely dependent upon a strong middle class. In contrast many of the nations of the East, Communist and non-Communist alike, stress social and economic equality.

As democracy, both political and economic, becomes more and more a world battle cry or shibboleth, it tends to lose its older meaning as a relatively precise description of a type of government or society. Perhaps, as some authorities argue, it may better be looked upon as an ideal and aspiration or as a state of mind. That it can never be perfectly realized is not, however, reason to give it up. Whether considered the best political means to a finer life, or regarded as the highest goal that man has yet sought to attain, democracy remains worthy of belief. As a progressive and developing concept, it is probably older than any of its particular forms, whether political or economic. It remains therefore a philosophy to which complete expression has not yet been given. Flexible and adapted to change, it survives as an example of one of the noblest ideals of mankind.

CHAPTER ONE

Colonial Beginnings

THE ORIGINS of the democratic tradition belong to the history of the Old World, but the first extensive practical application of the theory was worked out in the New. Like many ideas which have later won wide acceptance, democracy was originally the hope of small numbers of radical thinkers whose views were anathema to the established political and religious authorities. Though the Greeks gave the world the limited democracy of their city-states, an example to which the American Founding Fathers often referred, the long intervening period of over 15 centuries broke the historical continuity between the democratic republics of the Ancients and the Moderns.

More timely and direct in its influence upon early American democracy was the Protestant Reformation of the sixteenth century. Secular as well as religious historians agree that the fight for religious toleration and freedom contributed much to the struggle for political freedom and democracy. In Europe there was perhaps a greater than incidental connection in the fact that those countries such as England which came closest to achieving political democracy had also experienced a religious reformation. Although the leaders of the Protestant Reformation were not personally believers in democratic government, there was a powerful incentive to nascent democracy in Martin Luther's demand that each individual enjoy freedom to seek out religious truth independent of the authority of priest or church. In Germany Luther ultimately supported a union of church and state, and at Geneva John Calvin erected his theocracy. But the more radical of the dissenting Protestants, in breaking away from Luther's and Calvin's positions, eventually were able to carry religious individuality to its logical democratic conclusions. Thus the Separatists in England adhered to the doctrine of the religious covenant or compact in which each congregation was its own master. Individuality, congregationalism, and separation of church and state were all important contributions of religious liberalism to democracy.

In seventeenth-century England religious dissent was a strong ally in the struggle for political liberty. Though independence later caused Americans to minimize their English heritage, the Mother Country's influence upon many aspects of American civilization was a decisive one. In the realm of political and religious ideas especially, the American colonials borrowed freely from seventeenth-century English radicalism. In England itself the first step in the movement toward political democracy was the achievement of Parliamentary supremacy over the Stuart kings. After the Stuarts were deposed, English liberals added the doctrine of a higher law superior to both Parliament and Crown. Acceptance of the supremacy of law, in turn, led to the concept of a government of laws instead of men and to the important idea of a constitution above the statute law. The radical left wing of the English revolutionary movement wanted to go even further in its demands, and this Leveller element, in its Agreement of the People, proposed an English constitution which would provide universal manhood suffrage, no king, and protection of the individual in his civil liberties and right of dissent. Later John Locke modified and reformulated the Leveller principles into the classic dress of the natural-rights theory—the ultimate resort of the free individual against an organized tyranny. And it was Locke, rather than the Levellers, who was foremost in stimulating American democratic theory.

By the close of the seventeenth century, John Locke's natural-rights philosophy had been translated into practical politics. The Glorious Revolution firmly established a limited monarchy and gave further protection to the civil rights of all Englishmen. In the words of Henry Bamford Parkes:

> Although the English were not a democratic people, they prided themselves on being a free people, and had acquired a deep-rooted hostility toward any form of arbitrary power. Long before the colonization of America they had become accustomed to the election of a legislative body that limited the powers of the monarchy, and they believed that every individual had certain rights and immunities which should be maintained by written laws and by an independent judiciary.[1]

Among the rights carried across the Atlantic by the early American settlers and incorporated into their colonial charters, the one of greatest practical import was that of no taxation without representation. Just as Englishmen had struggled to gain this right in Parliament, so the colonists waged a long fight in their colonial assemblies for the protection of their property against royal interference. Economic freedom accordingly took its place with political and religious freedom as part of the background of American democracy, and the rise of capitalism paralleled the overthrow of Papal authority and of Stuart kings as a major factor in the development of modern democracy.

Although the struggle for freedom—political, religious, and economic—was waged first in England, this promising heritage owed much of its later growth and strength to the unusually favorable environment of the Thirteen Colonies. As Clinton Rossiter has pointed out, "We need not go all the way with Turner—'American democracy is fundamentally the outcome of the experiences of the

American people in dealing with the West'—to acknowledge the significance of the frontier in early American history."[2] In their *Rise of American Civilization* the Beards wrote:

> It was the man fired by the passion for owning a plot of ground who led the vanguard of settlers all along the frontier from New Hampshire to Georgia; to him cheap land meant freedom, to his family a rude but sufficient comfort. . . . Moreover, these freehold farmers faced the New West, not Europe; their communities were more isolated, more provincial, more independent, more American than those along the Atlantic seaboard. Passing years but strengthened their fiber and their love of liberty, while the ties of memory and affection that bound them to the Old World faded into oblivion.[3]

Thus the frontier, or West, considered in its broader sense as the general American economy, exerted a liberalizing effect on English political and religious ideas. Because this was so, democracy was able to take a strong hold in colonial America. In the view of an early historian of Old and New England, "The first ships which reached port of refuge carried with them from Europe the seed of democracy. Sown in virgin soil, it grew vigorously."[4]

Two general factors, then, would seem to explain the origin and growth of American democracy. First was the heritage of dissent: the profound dissatisfaction of the seventeenth-century Englishman with the conditions of his political, economic, and religious life. And second was the hope that almost every grievance could be redressed in the New World environment. Along with a necessary adventuresome disposition, the average settler must therefore have needed a combination of despair with conditions in the Old World plus optimism over the future in the New to undertake the manifest risks of the long and tedious voyage to colonial America. At the outset the sheer difficulty in keeping alive necessitated a certain authoritarian rule in the various colonies, as witness John Smith's brief dictatorship in Jamestown. But in the long run, once self-preservation was assured, the vast distance from the Mother Country encouraged a large degree of autonomy and local rule. Relative independence was all the more possible because England was occupied with its own domestic and foreign problems. Isolation and neglect therefore were additional factors which help to explain the development of American democracy.

Over the colonial period as a whole, however, little real democracy existed in most of the English settlements. American colonial institutions, as befitted the times, were basically conservative and aristocratic. Royal governors or proprietors with the help of their councils held executive power in all the colonies except the two—Rhode Island and Connecticut—which were able to preserve intact their charters and autonomy down to the American Revolution. Outside the New England towns, local government was undemocratic, with administrative and judicial officials appointed by the governors. The elected colonial assemblies had the right to tax and to initiate legislation. But they were circumscribed by the veto of both the upper house, or council, and the governor. In most cases therefore the governor and council had the real power. An established church, supported by tax funds and closely tied to the colonial government, was the rule rather than the exception. In New England the Puritan Congregational Church, and in lower New York and the South the Anglican Church, enjoyed this privileged position. Yet government was probably easier, less oppressive, and more popular in the colonies than in England. And certainly the colonies of other European powers were farther from even the barest sort of self-government.

Though all free settlers had the basic personal rights and civil liberties of an Englishman, perhaps as many as one third to one half of those who came to the Middle Colonies were originally indentured servants, and in the South the Negro slave population grew to equal almost the free white population. Moreover economic freedom was qualified by various British mercantilist restrictions on colonial trade and by the increasing difficulty that the average settler had in acquiring suitable land. But it is important to note that, although the Old World class structure was carried over to the New, no feudal society or customs could take strong hold in the dynamic American environment. Change, not permanence, was the rule, and this general mobility offered almost all free inhabitants the prospect of moving upward on the social and economic scale. Thus, if not democratic in practice, the colonies did provide an attractive physical and intellectual foundation for the growth of democracy.[5]

(II)

Of all the groups of settlers who braved the passage across the North Atlantic to the area that later formed the Thirteen Colonies, the New England Pilgrims and Puritans were the most interesting and important in terms of the early development of the democratic idea. Seeking their religious liberty, they were also anxious to find in the New World greater economic and political freedom. Though the Puritans especially were far from democratic in their practice, many of their political and religious tenets were susceptible of democratic interpretation. And, despite the criticisms which some of their leaders directed at democratic government, it is possible that these Puritan worthies were unconsciously more democratic than they realized or were willing to admit.

The Pilgrims, just before their famous landing at Plymouth late in 1620, engraved upon the record of American democracy one of its most celebrated documents. Aroused by rumors that some of the less devout among them were ready to go their own independent way on leaving shipboard, and since they had no royal charter or grant of land, the Pilgrim fathers thought it prudent to draw up a civil agreement similar to their own type of church covenant. Apparently signed by all the adult males, who undertook to "covenant and combine ourselves together into a civil Body Politik," the Mayflower Compact united the colonists for their own protection. Though conferring no new liberties or privileges upon its signers, it was significant because it represented a mutual agreement in self-government and discipline in which there were no distinctions of wealth or class. It was also the first written expression in America of a social compact signed by the members of the body politic. If it was not technically a formal constitution, it was a step in the direction of self-government and constitution-making, and as such it is important in the history of American democracy.

For the Pilgrims their Mayflower Compact provided a basis of civil government that included a General Court, composed of all the freemen, and an elected governor and council. After arrangements were made to repay the English merchants who had provided funds for the overseas expedition, the Pilgrims divided their lands and property among the inhabitants, and Plymouth came close to being a political and economic democracy. Until 1638 the entire body of the freemen voted on all questions as a General Court. After that time each of the Pilgrim towns sent a committee of representatives or deputies to act for them. Only the freemen could serve as governor or deputies, but inhabitants of good character enjoyed the right to vote. Despite the development of a certain social and political hierarchy, as well as state recognition of the Congregational Church in the 1650's, Plymouth continued to approximate an independent democracy until 1691, when it was joined to Massachusetts as a part of a new royal colony.

In contrast to tiny Plymouth, the Massachusetts Bay Colony quickly became a large and prosperous settlement, the dominating influence in all New England. Armed with a land grant and royal charter, the Puritan leaders were determined to found a Bible Commonwealth in the wilderness. Favoring this goal was the fact that the charter of Massachusetts lodged all power in a General Court composed of the shareholders of the company, who were called the freemen. By agreeing that only those who desired to migrate to Massachusetts should remain shareholders, the latter were able to bring the charter with them and establish the company as the government of Massachusetts, virtually independent of all authority except the Crown in England. Since there were only 12 original stockholders or freemen in Massachusetts, a perfect oligarchy was in the making. But these freemen, who appointed themselves as magistrates, or assistants to the governor, had quickly to admit over 100 petitioning and resentful settlers as new freemen. Although the charter gave full power to the freemen, Governor Winthrop and the assistants were unwilling to allow them any political privilege except the election of new assistants as vacancies came due. Moreover, it was provided in 1631 that only members of an approved Puritan church might become freemen. Governor Winthrop's objection that the freemen were too numerous to carry on the government was answered, after a protest by many of the inhabitants, by changing the General Court from a town meeting into a representative body. The governor's assistants, who continued to be elected by the freemen, later became the upper house of the Massachusetts assembly or General Court.

Since the governor and the assistants, or magistrates, were all devout Puritans in close intellectual connection with the ministers, it was easy to turn the government into a theocracy. Originally the Puritans were dissenters who wished only to purify the Anglican Church, but the opportunities of their isolated position in America readily inclined them to pursue the independent path of their Pilgrim neighbors. Neither Pilgrims or Puritans, however, followed the Separatists in England in making the separation of church and state a dominant article of their creed. The Puritan Church accordingly, though congregational in form, was closely tied to the state, so that Massachusetts in the seventeenth century was in reality a New World model of Calvin's theocracy at Geneva. With church membership made a requirement for voting as early as 1631, an obvious foundation was established for religious interference in civil affairs. Though attendance was compulsory, church membership was not automatic or easily attained. Consent of the magistrates was necessary for the establishment of a new church congregation, and the state supported the ministers by taxation. When a dissatisfied group petitioned for removal of the civil disabilities inflicted on non-church members, the ministers and the magistrates induced both the General Court and the church congregations to approve the Cambridge Platform of 1648. Clarifying the relationship between church and state and solidifying the position of the theocracy in Massachusetts, this Platform affirmed again that it was the duty of the civil magistrates to enforce the churches' teachings and to encourage church membership or attendance. The clergy, in turn, were to continue to preach and teach religious and political orthodoxy.

Under the rule of John Winthrop and the Puritan oligarchy, neither the theory or practice of democracy was popular. Democracy in the Puritan mind was a species of mob rule. To Governor Winthrop it was ever "the meanest & worst of all formes of Governm't. . . ." And the Reverend John Cotton declared: "Democracy, I do not conceyve that ever God did ordeyne as a fit government eyther for church or commonwealth. If the people be governors, who shall be governed?"[6]

The statements of Winthrop and Cotton illustrated the lack of any general enthusiasm for democracy among the Puritan leaders. Yet, in actuality, some parts of Puritanism were quite susceptible of democratic tendencies and interpretation. As in the other colonies, the settlers were guaranteed their rights as Englishmen, local self-government prevailed in both town and church, and the compact or contract was the unchallenged device of forming new congregations and towns. Thus Puritanism preserved a measure of both individuality and democracy in the midst of the theocracy. Agriculture was the material basis for life in most of the towns, and in the distribution of lots the Puritans exercised considerable economic democracy. Certain factors, such as the amount of a man's existing property, the size of his family, and his contribution to the founding of the town, were taken into consideration, but the inequalities were not carried to an extreme. The towns also were granted a large degree of autonomy in disposing their lands and choosing their officers. Later, as newcomers had to be settled in outlying areas, the original unity of the New England village was lost, but in the beginning there was much democracy evidenced in both town and church government. Most important of all, New England economic life was conducive to the presence of a large middle class which was able to exert a democratic pressure upon the ruling oligarchy.[7]

(*III*)

The democratic leanings of the Massachusetts towns were not sufficient to satisfy Puritanism's two most distinguished rebels, Roger Williams and Thomas Hooker. Williams in Rhode Island and Hooker in Connecticut both revealed a desire to apply democratic ideas, that was in contrast to the hostile attitude of Winthrop and Cotton. Although Williams and Hooker were each respected members of the Puritan clergy and had considerable reputations even before they came to Boston, neither was content with what he found in Old or New England. In time Williams or Hooker might easily have vied with John Cotton for first place among the Boston ministers, and in Hooker's case personal rivalry may have been a factor in his decision to move on. Williams, however, had no choice. After several years of wrangling with the Massachusetts ecclesiastical authorities, he was forced to flee through the wilderness and to make a new beginning at Providence. Here he was joined by other like-minded dissidents, including Anne Hutchinson and some of her followers.

In the case of Hooker his parting was relatively amicable, although almost as sudden as that of Roger Williams. As late as October, 1635, Hooker was still so highly regarded that he was appointed by the General Court to debate with Williams and correct him in his errors. But by the following spring, when Williams was reaching Rhode Island, Hooker and his congregation received permission to remove to Connecticut, where they founded the river towns around Hartford. Since others in Massachusetts were already moving westward to the good agricultural lands of the Connecticut River Valley, economic motives undoubtedly help to explain the decision of Hooker's group to leave Massachusetts Bay.

Roger Williams' disagreement with the Massachusetts authorities was, of course, so fundamental that it hardly admitted any compromise or friendly parting. To Williams the church was a spiritual force which needed no backing from the state; their union accordingly could only be sinful. Moreover, he questioned the legality of the Massachusetts Bay Charter and the title of the company to its lands unless the Indians' rights were first satisfied. Here Williams posed problems which were without solution unless the Puritan fathers were ready to abandon the whole idea of their Bible Commonwealth. Williams, now justly hailed as one of the authors of American democracy, in his own age was looked upon as a dangerous dissident who would have subverted the whole framework of church and state in Massachusetts.

Given his radical views and severe attack upon the Massachusetts theocracy, it is not surprising that Roger Williams labored so hard to create a liberal democratic society in Rhode Island. Religious liberty, extended even to Quakers, and a land system that did not discriminate against newcomers were paralleled by the most democratic form of government in any of the colonies. At first the only political organization in the Rhode Island area was in the towns, where all householders voted regularly on the policies to be carried out. Later the suffrage was limited to property holders. In 1641 the General Court, or town meeting, at Newport declared that "the government which this body politic doth attend unto in this island . . . is a democracy or popular government. . . ." Dissension among the towns, however, persuaded Williams to secure a charter of incorporation for a united colony. In 1647, when the Rhode Island towns agreed to the confederation, their assembly stated that "the form of government established in Providence Plantations is democratical; that is to say, a government held by the free and voluntary consent of all, or the greater part of the free inhabitants." The code of laws drawn up by the assembly also listed certain rights of the people upon which the government could not encroach. Williams himself in his famous controversy with John Cotton expressed the view that the "foundation of civil power lies in the people" and that "a people may erect and establish what form of government seems to them most meet for their civil condition."[8] Under Williams' initial guidance Rhode Island continued to enjoy liberal and popular government. Like its neighbors, Plymouth and Connecticut, it could with considerable justice and accuracy be called a seventeenth-century democracy.

Farther to the west along the Massachusetts frontier, Hooker and his followers organized a community which in its democracy was between those of Rhode Island and Massachusetts. Rudimentary government was provided at first by a General Court, which in 1639 regularized its position with the adoption of the famous Fundamental Orders of Connecticut. Although the Orders were neither a modern-type constitution nor a manifesto of democracy, they did provide for a frame of government more popular than the Massachusetts theocracy. All inhabitants, irrespective of church membership, voted in their towns for representatives to the Connecticut General Court. Only freemen could be so elected to the General Court, but men of good character and loyalty, resident in the colony for one year, might be admitted by the towns to the body of the freemen. Thus the freemen were not so restricted a group as in Massachusetts. The Fundamental Orders in the guise of a constitution also put certain limits on the powers of the governor and General Court. Although Connecticut, like Rhode Island, later added a property qualification for the suffrage, it remained loyal in the main to Hooker's democratic ideas. Unlike the Massachusetts theocrats, Hooker carried the principle of the covenant and congregationalism to the logical ends of popular sovereignty and a limited governmental authority. In his famous election sermon of 1638, Hooker avowed: "That the choice of public magistrates belongs unto the people by God's own allowance."[9]

It is possible to exaggerate the differences between liberals like Hooker and Williams and the Massachusetts conservative leaders, Cotton and Winthrop. It must be remembered that none, except perhaps Williams, was a democrat by today's standards, and that all remained Calvinists in their general theology and Congregationalists in their view of church organization. Williams and Hooker made prime contributions to democratic theory and encouraged democratic tendencies in their respective colonies. But the practice of a large measure of democracy in both Rhode Island and Connecticut also owed something to the popular unrest and search for new lands that characterized the entire frontier process in New England. By the second half of the seventeenth century these internal pressures were beginning to undermine even the prestige and authority of the Puritan oligarchy in Massachusetts.

(*IV*)

Despite the power of the theocracy in early Massachusetts history, liberalizing and democratic tendencies were at work. Puritanism became less strict in its religious doctrines than the Calvinism of the Old World, and in 1662 the adoption of the Half-Way Covenant marked the beginning of its rationalization and weakening as a spiritual force. Henceforth children of members of the church were to be admitted into the congregation without the necessity of experiencing a prior personal conversion. Cotton Mather complained that the effect of this and other like measures would be "to turn the whole *Regimen of the Church* into a pure *Democracy*."[10] But, though the orthodox ministers struggled mightily, their power was waning. New settlers and immigrants encouraged the pressure of the freemen against the governor and the magistrates and added to the number of non-church members. A devastating blow was the loss in 1684 of the original charter and the transformation of Massachusetts into a royal colony. In the new charter of 1691 a property qualification for voting was substituted for the old requirement of church membership.

Actually Puritanism had weaknesses from the outset. Its emphasis upon the congregational principle of local self-government in each church deprived it of strong organizational unity, and it would have been hopelessly weak if not supported by the civil authorities during its first years in Massachusetts. To overcome this flaw and to strengthen orthodox views, Increase and Cotton Mather took the lead in suggesting a reorganization of Puritanism along presbyterian lines. Under their plan a system of church councils, or synods, would guide the ministers and impose a uniform doctrine and discipline upon the churches. Although such a system was adopted in part in Connecticut and approved by the General Court in Massachusetts, it was rejected by the British authorities. Despite this setback, the Congregational Church in Massachusetts continued to enjoy state support of its clergy from the general tax funds.

For the democratic element which believed that congregationalism in church organization should be preserved, the Reverend John Wise, minister of a small frontier church at Ipswich, Massachusetts, made an eloquent reply to the Mathers. Though he has been hailed by modern writers as an important political thinker—"the father of American democracy"—Wise remains an obscure figure. In the 1690's he was one of the few among the Puritan clergy to oppose the witchcraft persecutions, and he seems to have been active in other liberal causes. His importance, however, rests on his two works written to defend congregationalism: *The Churches Quarrel Espoused* (1710) and *A Vindication of the Government of New-England Churches* (1717). Wise justified the principle of congregationalism by analogy from political theory. Of all the types of government in the world, he concluded that democracy best fitted in with the natural rights of man. "This is the form of government which the light of nature does highly value, and often directs to as most agreeable to the just and natural prerogatives of human beings. . . ." Democracy, Wise defined as a simple type of town-meeting government in which the majority of the people ruled by adding up the ayes and noes. From this he concluded that democracy, the most natural and best form of government for either church or state, should be continued by the preservation of the congregational principle. In his words:

> . . . a democracy in church or state, is a very honorable and regular government according to the dictates of right reason, And, therefore . . . That these churches of New England, in their ancient constitution of church order, it being a democracy, are manifestly justified and defended by the law and light of nature.[11]

In his defense of congregationalism against the presbyterian ideas of a consociation held by the Mathers, John Wise made a notable plea for democracy in the institutional form of the church. But Protestant individuality and dissent, as Roger Williams demonstrated, also implied religious toleration and diversity. Moreover, in protesting an established church, dissenters became political as well as religious radicals, for only a political change or reform would result in disestablishment. If people were to have the right freely to worship, the political state should not interfere by supporting one church against all others. Although religious diversity and the multiplicity of sects and denominations increased after the Reformation, in Europe there was little toleration of religious individualism. America, too, attempted to follow an authoritarian pattern, with the Congregational and the Anglican, the two chief established churches, dominant in the greater number of the colonies. But dissenting sects, such as the Quakers and Baptists, kept up the struggle against the union of church and state. The colonies, with their need for settlers to tame the wilderness, became a haven for the religiously oppressed peoples of Europe. From the standpoint of economics and religion, toleration was thus in some measure a matter of expediency. For example, Maryland's famous Act of Toleration in 1649 was an effort to prevent an Anglican establishment which would have harmed the colony's continued existence as a refuge for Catholics. Toleration protected primarily the Catholic minority in Maryland, but the Act also pointed in the direction of the ideal America was to adopt.

Contributing in a practical way to the advancement of religious toleration was the liberal policy which William Penn was able to effect for his colony. Founded as a Quaker refuge, but attracting numerous other denominations as well, Pennsylvania made no religious discrimination. The Quakers themselves, with their simplicity, sense of equality, brotherly love, and intense religious individualism, were the most democratic of sects. Moreover, the colony was a mother to religious diversity, with German Pietists and Scotch-Irish Presbyterians stretched along the southwest frontier. Though many of the Quakers later became prosperous conservative citizens, the example of their original radical idealism and success in replacing Old World persecution with New World tolerance was not lost. Thus a virtually complete religious freedom prevailed in Pennsylvania. Although Penn's Charter of Privileges of 1701 limited residence to those who believed in God and office-holding to Christians and later to Protestants, these restrictions seemed not to have been enforced strictly nor to have given much offense.

Under Penn's twin policies of religious toleration and land grants on easy terms, Pennsylvania, the last colony settled by the English in the seventeenth century, grew the most rapidly in the eighteenth. In his Frame of Government and Charter of Privileges, Penn made clear his intentions for the colony. A legislative body of one chamber was granted powers greater than the assemblies of any other colony enjoyed, except in Rhode Island and Connecticut. A liberal suffrage was restricted only by residence and a requirement of 50 acres of land or 50 pounds worth of property. This was not difficult to meet except for Philadelphia town dwellers, since most farmers had 50 acres of land which, partly cleared, was easily worth 50 pounds. The Assembly was elected annually. Although new counties to the west had a lesser representation, this arrangement was reasonably fair and adequate until the growth of the western population after the French and Indian War. Most local county officials were elected or controlled by the freeholders of their area. Thus Pennsylvania probably came closer to political democracy than any colony outside New England.

A major reason for the rapid growth of colonial Pennsylvania in the early part of the eighteenth century was the opportunity it offered to settlers for the acquisition of land on easy terms. Here Pennsylvania provided encouragement for economic as well as religious democracy. Later, however, the Penn family became more jealous of its proprietary rights. It accordingly modified its original liberal land policy, withholding large tracts from sale and attempting to collect quitrents on the rest. "The taint of feudalism was upon the colonial system of Pennsylvania," Allan Nevins writes. "It was impossible for the later Penns to take anything but a selfish view of the great domain of which they were proprietors—to look upon it other than as an estate from which they were to wring the utmost revenue."[12] Moreover, as lands along the Delaware were pre-empted and as German and Scotch-Irish immigrants filled the southwest frontier, latecomers had to go farther south into the Great Valley of western Virginia and the back country of North Carolina.

(*V*)

Free or near-free land was the magnet that originally drew such a high proportion of permanent settlers to Pennsylvania and the other American colonies. But when the seaboard and tidewater regions everywhere became more crowded, the colonial population in its continual search for cheap land spread westward across the mountains. In tracing the course of democracy in early America, one must not overlook the practical influences of the land system and the expanding economic frontier. The experience of Virginia, first of the colonies to be settled, illustrated especially well this side of democracy. In the contrast between Virginia society in the seventeenth and the eighteenth centuries can be seen the importance of economic opportunity to the democratic idea. Thus a historian of colonial Virginia, in comparing her early history with that of New England, has written:

> Much has been said about the influence upon American life of the New England conscience, much concerning her contributions to political freedom, but her most valuable legacy has been overlooked or minimized —her essentially sound economic and social system, her democracy of labor.[13]

Both New England and Virginia at first had close ties to the Mother Country, but in each the development of self-government was a result more of the natural environment than of English ideology. In the distance from Europe and in the wide spaces of the frontier to the west were the material foundations for political independency. A Virginia governor in 1732 observed that "People remote from the seat of government are always remarkable for their disobedience."[14] In the confusion of the Commonwealth period in mid-seventeenth-century England, Virginia was virtually independent. The right of representative government, begun with the establishment of the first Virginia Assembly in 1619, was strengthened as the House of Burgesses was able to fix the principle of no taxation without representation. Suffrage was liberal, the right to vote being accorded to all freemen. Governor Berkeley's suggestion that the suffrage be limited to landholders was protested by the Assembly as an attempt to eliminate the freemen who paid only poll taxes. But in 1670 the Assembly required that the voter be a landowner or householder. In 1676 Nathaniel Bacon restored the suffrage to all freemen, but after the collapse of his rebellion the 1670 law was repassed. Bacon's Rebellion itself, whatever Bacon's intentions and whatever the discontents that inspired his followers, seems to have had little lasting effect on democracy in Virginia. The colony, however, benefited from the Glorious Revolution in England. During the next 75 years it advanced steadily in the direction of greater self-government, though not of greater democracy.

In the eighteenth century Virginia was an aristocracy, resting on the two foundations of the plantation and slavery systems. Previously, in the seventeenth century, when the Dutch controlled the slave trade, Virginia's labor force was largely limited to white indentured servants. Virginia, like New England, then also possessed a sizeable population of free farmers prosperous enough to be accounted part of a growing middle class. But, as the slave population rapidly increased after 1690, the landholdings of the large tobacco planters also expanded, and the small independent farmer was forced to migrate farther west. "The Virginia which had formerly been so largely the land of the little farmer, had become the land of Masters and Slaves. For aught else there was no room."[15] Only the large-scale producer was able to trim his costs and keep pace with the decline in tobacco prices after 1690.

In Virginia, in contrast to New England and Pennsylvania, the prospects of democracy seemed to decline in the eighteenth century. Yet, though the planter aristocracy ruled even in the House of Burgesses, this upper class was itself fairly numerous as well as liberal and enlightened. If the Burgesses added little to the power of the people, at least their running conflict with a succession of royal governors served to encourage democratic tendencies. While members of the leading families held all the important offices, the freeholders who continued to exercise the suffrage in the eighteenth century were carefully cultivated at election time. Together with the property qualification for voting went the test of membership in the Anglican Church, but this was not enforced so strictly that dissenters were disfranchised. All along the Virginia frontier these dissenters were in the majority, and their influence helped keep the ferment of political and religious democracy stirring in the Old Dominion.

Virginia's suffrage requirements were not noticeably less democratic than those of the colonies to the north. After 1736 the voter needed to own 25 acres with a house or 100 acres of unoccupied land. This latter was later reduced to 50 acres. In the case of townsmen the requirements were less strict, and sometimes they could vote without owning real property. Although land was cheap and the house could be a small cabin, it is still probable that less than one half of the white males was able to vote in Virginia on the eve of the Revolution.[16]

(*VI*)

By the middle of the eighteenth century the movement toward democracy was progressing along the three lines of economics, religion, and politics. In the realm of economic life, possession of land was the criterion of democracy. Except in the manorial system of farm tenants in New York, a feudal type of society nowhere existed in the American colonies. But although the potential opportunities to secure free land were great, the immediate desires of those who had come to America to seek their own land were not always satisfied. Accordingly there was conflict between those who already had large tracts of valuable land and those who still had little or none. This discrepancy explains in large part the class and sectional uprisings which affected most of the colonies on the eve of the American Revolution. Land-a-plenty there was on the frontier, but this land had a greater future than present value, and most of it still belonged to the Indians or the British Crown. Thus the frontiersman was land hungry, while the poorer townsmen resented the privileged economic and social position of the propertied or mercantile aristocracy.

Bacon's Rebellion and Leisler's Revolt in the seventeenth century, and the struggles of the North Carolina Regulators in the 1760's, as well as other lesser uprisings in the generation before the Revolution, were all testimony to the considerable economic discontent prevailing along the economic and geographic frontier in the colonies. Political agitation in the Middle Colonies and in the South was perhaps more severe because those colonies lacked any equivalent of the democratic safety valve of the New England town meeting. Yet, it would not be accurate to leave the impression that economic and social class lines were so strictly drawn that only violence could effect any change. The dominant note of colonial society was its fluidity. Economic opportunity was never wholly lacking, and the middle class composed the bulk of the population everywhere except in the large plantation regions of the tidewater South.

Another factor in the periodic outbursts of popular discontent was the pressure of a mounting colonial population. In both the last half of the seventeenth century and the first half of the eighteenth, there was a fivefold increase in the population. This rapid growth symbolized a shift in the balance of power from England to the colonies, and it also helped to stimulate democratic demands upon the upper-class aristocracy. Not the least of the social and economic forces behind a rising American democracy on the eve of the Revolution came from this rapidly expanding population in the Thirteen Colonies. By 1776 Philadelphia, with 40,000 inhabitants, was probably larger than any city in England except London, and the total American population stood at about 2.5 million, an increase of almost a million from the time of the French and Indian War.

In colonial religious life a number of democratic tendencies converged in the movement at the middle of the eighteenth century known as the Great Awakening. The first major evangelical crusade in America, the Great Awakening was an outgrowth of the Pietist movement in Western Europe which sought to encourage greater personal religious enthusiasm and missionary zeal among Christians.

Thus it formed a counterpart to the growing wave of religious skepticism which culminated in the eighteenth-century vogue of Deism. This skepticism and religious indifference, against which the Great Awakening inveighed, contributed nevertheless to liberty by its hostility to any religious establishment or union of church and state. The Great Awakening itself appealed both to the large numbers without any church and to members of dissenting sects like the Baptists and more radical Presbyterians. Individual Congregationalists and Anglicans were affected also, and Jonathan Edwards, the last great Puritan divine, was a leader of the Great Awakening in Massachusetts. The movement stressed the common man and his interests and provided a type of equalitarian and unceremonial religion which he could appreciate. In this way it exercised a leveling effect upon social life and relations. Cutting across denominational lines and hostile to the established churches, its methods were both opportunistic and democratic. Its popular appeal brought about a great increase in membership for the dissenting churches. In some colonies, such as Virginia, the growth of these sects as a result of the Great Awakening hastened the separation of church and state. Finally, since dissenters did not enjoy full civil liberties where an established church existed, the role of the Great Awakening in strengthening religious freedom also contributed to political democracy.

By two of the accepted tests of political democracy—civil equality and majority rule—the Thirteen Colonies did not qualify. Yet, as we have seen, in almost all the colonies the forces of political democracy were at work. In the matter of suffrage, which is a convenient if not infallible way of judging equality and majority rule, modern scholars have demonstrated that it was rather widely held—much more so than a large number of historians once thought. Albert E. McKinley, in his pioneer work on this subject, concluded that at the end of the colonial period, besides the usual requirements of law or custom which limited voting to resident free white males of the age of 21,

> a freehold of some size or value was required of voters in seven colonies: New Hampshire, Rhode Island, New York, New Jersey, Virginia, North Carolina and Georgia. In the six other colonies there were alternatives to the real estate qualification in the form of the holding of personal property or the payment of taxes.[17]

New England followed the English standard of a freehold valued at 40 pounds, or producing a 40-shilling income. In other colonies 40 or 50 acres was the average-size land holding, and 40 or 50 pounds the usual personal property required. Religious qualifications were most rigidly enforced in New England, but Quakers, Catholics, and Jews were subject to widespread discrimination. The size of the colonial electorate McKinley estimated from the scattered figures available at less than 10 per cent of the white population, and it was considerably smaller than that in some of the towns, as in Philadelphia, where only 2 per cent could vote. The number of actual voters was, of course, often much less than the number who were qualified. As McKinley pointed out:

> Property qualifications, poor means of communication, large election districts and the absence of party organization combined to make the most sharply contested elections feeble in their effects upon the community as compared with the widespread suffrage of the twentieth century.[18]

Robert E. Brown, in his study of democracy in Massachusetts, has questioned the popular view that colonial property qualifications eliminated most of the potential voters. Some incautious writers, Brown points out, have confused population and voters so that when 10 per cent of the population was qualified to vote, they assumed that only one tenth of the potential eligible voters enjoyed the suffrage. Actually, of course, in large colonial families there was an undue proportion of children. With women and children eliminated from consideration, 10 per cent of the total population could mean that the number of qualified voters was a sizeable portion of the adult white males over 21 years of age. In Massachusetts, where land was cheap and wages high, the property requirement of a 40-shilling freehold was easily met, and Brown concludes: (1) that Massachusetts was close to being both an economic and political democracy; (2) that rural areas were not so much underrepresented as indifferent to sending the number of delegates for which they were qualified to the General Court; and (3) that religious tests and tithes in Massachusettes as a barrier to voting were constantly being weakened in practice.[19]

When one remembers that the colonial period extended over more than a century and a half, it is clear that the growth of democracy in those years must have been gradual and slow. In many aspects of colonial life, subsequent attributions of democracy probably rest more on historical hindsight than on contemporary evidence. The success of the American Revolution and rise of American democracy did not necessarily mean that all colonial life and thought moved steadily toward those goals. But the Revolution did come as the culmination of a long contest between Mother Country and colonies. The democratic aspects of this conflict were most plainly outlined in America in the political struggle waged between the various royal governors and colonial assemblies. More than anything, this served to bring out the spirit of colonial democracy. Enjoying such rights as representation in popularly elected assemblies or legislative bodies, the colonists sought still more. Thus the internal dynamics of colonial life in the eighteenth century threatened a revolutionary change in relations with Britain. In the prophetic words of the conservative Pennsylvania leader Joseph Galloway in 1765, "Democratic notions in America may lead to the independence of the colonies from England."[20]

CHAPTER TWO

Revolutionary Upsurge

THE ERA of the American Revolution forms a vital part of the American democratic tradition. Without independence it is unlikely that democracy would have penetrated so many different aspects of American life in so short a time. This is not necessarily to claim that the American Revolution was primarily, or even essentially, a democratic movement. The years from 1776 to 1783 were, after all, ones in which a war was fought to gain national freedom. Yet, in the broad realms of politics and culture and of social and economic change, democracy as well as nationalism was ever an important factor during the course of the Revolution.

This twofold aspect of the Revolution was recognized by some of its leading participants. Among the Founding Fathers John Adams is on record as observing that the Revolution ended before the first shots were fired at Lexington and Concord. It had taken place "in the minds and hearts of the people. . . ."[1] On the other hand, his friend Benjamin Rush declared that, though the American war was over, this was far from being the case with the American Revolution.[2] Both men felt that the war and the revolution were not the same thing. Adams believed that only national independence was necessary to complete the revolution taking place in American life. Rush, in contrast, thought that the task of building a new democratic order still lay ahead of the American people and that the Revolution had achieved merely political separation from England.

Revolutions, whatever their final outcome, tend to encourage radical ideas, and democracy was such an idea in the eighteenth century. An historian of the period from 1760 to 1800 has recently termed these years the Age of the Democratic Revolution.[3] Most authorities agree that the American Revolution was conservative as compared with the French Revolution, and some raise the question of how much American colonial institutions were really transformed by the achievement of independence. But in the initial drive for separation from Britain, democracy enjoyed a genuine revolutionary upsurge. If for no other reason, the need to gain popular backing for the Revolution insured increasing attention to, and consideration for, the will of the body of the people. Committees of correspondence, broadsides and pamphlets, provincial assemblies, and provisional congresses, even when they were contrived by a clever radical minority, nevertheless had to appear to be democratic and to speak in the popular idiom.

The decade of political controversy that preceded the actual outbreak of Revolutionary hostilities enhanced the influence of the more radical and democratic spokesmen of the American cause like Samuel Adams and Patrick Henry. Adams was the most zealous of all the Revolutionary leaders in arguing the case for radical democracy. In an age when the rural masses were far removed from the democratic movement in Boston and a few other centers of population, Adams understood the need of propaganda and communication. The people had to be acquainted with the way their liberties were being threatened before they could be persuaded to act. Adams accordingly used the Boston town meeting as his particular forum, and through a network of local committees of correspondence helped to keep up intercolonial enthusiasm for the Revolutionary cause.

At first, American protests were conservative in nature. In their outcry against the Stamp Act and other internal taxes imposed upon them without their representation in Parliament, the Patriots stood squarely upon their rights as Englishmen. Pleading this right they enlisted much sympathy in England from Edmund Burke and his fellow Whigs. But argument over what was the proper interpretation of the unwritten British constitution was difficult to sustain or popularize. Americans, now ever more eager for greater self-government, were not content to rest their case solely on their rights as Englishmen. Whether the radical victory achieved by 1775 and 1776 was due to American sagacity, British ineptitude, or the logic or tragedy of events following 1765, continues to puzzle students of the coming of the Revolution. But, whatever the reason, the triumph of the radicals helped to ground the Revolution in democratic theory rather than in British constitutionalism. In justifying their cause, American leaders appealed not to the British eighteenth-century Whig tradition but to the more radical political dissent of the seventeenth-century revolutions and to the natural-rights philosophy as expounded by John Locke and Algernon Sidney.

In his work on American political ideas, Charles Merriam pointed out that "The theory of the state of nature, natural rights, and the contract were all steps leading up to the right of revolution. If all these premises were accepted, as they generally were, the conclusion was easy."[4] For his fellow Americans, Tom Paine argued convincingly that the right of revolution and independence was just plain common sense. Paine's little pamphlet, issued at the opportune moment in January, 1776, helped arouse the populace and stiffen the resolve of the radical leaders to push for independence even if it meant revolution. Paine rationalized the necessity of independence as well as its political justice. It was contrary to nature and the whole idea of the natural rights of man, he said, for the people of a large continent to be ruled by the king of a small island thousands of miles distant. He also presented the practical advantages of separation and the dangers and illogic of continued indecision. Moreover, by the very violence of his assault on hereditary monarchy, Paine gave encouragement to the idea of a popular democratic government.

The Declaration of Independence itself was a manifesto of democracy as well as of American nationalism. Thomas Jefferson was not a popular agitator like Paine, Adams, or Henry, and his matured concept of democratic government has to be considered in relation to a lifetime of political leadership which was just in its beginnings in 1776. In the Declaration he wrote a lawyer's brief, presenting the reasons for American Independence clearly and convincingly. Since the time for constitutional argument and protest against Parliamentary supremacy over the colonies had passed, Jefferson rested his case rather on a long list of American grievances against the British Crown. Thus the Declaration made it plain that the King was the only remaining legal tie with the Mother Country. More importantly, in the familiar opening paragraphs of the Declaration, Jefferson restated the whole natural-rights theory of the American Revolution, summing up much of the colonial position of the previous decade. Accompanying the concept of natural rights was the concept of the social contract as the necessary basis of all legitimate government. The exact nature of the contract was not spelled out, but the stress on the consent of the governed implied acceptance of the doctrine of popular sovereignty and democratic government.

The Declaration of Independence indicated that the military struggle against Britain would be carried through to a finish, and it also made clear the revolutionary political theory behind the American cause. Americans now were no longer fighting for their rights as British subjects. In formally breaking all ties with the Mother Country, the Founding Fathers were also laying the base for a more democratic political and social order. Of course, as has often been pointed out, the Declaration did not state an absolute political or economic equality. Thus men were born equal not in their natural abilities, or right to vote, or share of worldly goods, but in their equal possession of the natural right to life, liberty, and property. Consent of the governed applied to the property-holding taxpayers, and the pursuit of happiness referred to the right to use one's property without interference.

(II)

Prior to the adoption of the Declaration of Independence, the Continental Congress suggested that the former colonies establish new governments. Thus the months just before and after July, 1776, were spent not only in preparation for war but also in constitution-making. According to John Adams, the Declaration of Independence found the Thirteen Colonies at work erecting governments "as fast as children build cob houses."[5] In this transition from colony to commonwealth, the state constitutions marked the last stage in a series of steps which began with the organization of the committees of correspondence in the spring of 1773 and which had continued through a succession of provincial congresses and conventions. In 1775 provisional governments in most of the colonies had driven out the royal governors and assumed general sovereignty. Now in 1776 the drafting and adoption of written constitutions by the separate states completed the Revolutionary process. Never before had so large a group of communities decided deliberately to begin their governments under written constitutions. Even though the structure of the previous colonial governments was not always much changed by the shift to statehood, the adoption of the state constitutions was in itself a step of great revolutionary significance.

The constitutional process used by most of the states in 1776 would hardly be accepted today as an example of an ideal democratic method. Yet these first constitutions adopted under difficult circumstances survived in some instances for half a century or more with little or no change. Except for Massachusetts, which waited until 1780 to adopt its constitution, no state called a special constitutional convention and submitted the results to popular ratification. Rhode Island and Connecticut kept their colonial charters as their state constitutions. In most of the other states, special elections were held for conventions or legislatures, which then assumed both constitutional and governmental responsibility.

The novelty of the Revolutionary situation might have been expected to encourage radical innovations in the new constitutions. On the other hand, the exigencies of war and the necessity of instituting regular government as quickly as possible militated against too much experimentation. Thus, to a considerable extent, the state constitutions borrowed from colonial experience. Although the supporters of the Revolution were naturally the ones in control, they were themselves divided into various factions ranging from radical democrats to conservative Whigs. Conservatives, though desirous of governments strong enough to maintain law and order and prevent the Revolution from degenerating into anarchy, preferred to see a minimum of internal innovation in the new state constitutions. Like John Adams, they were alarmed to hear popular political arguments which confused no taxation without representation with no taxation or government whatsoever. Radical democrats, in contrast, feared that conservatives would substitute a new American despotism for the old British tyranny. "A Berkshire Man," writing in the Boston *Gazette*, complained:

> The state of our government is alarming because of . . . the tories who are everywhere crying for a new government to make men pay their debts. This was one objection we had to the old government, yet these unfeeling tories would fain bring us into the same state again. Strange that men don't understand the nature of liberty better.[6]

Democratic sentiment was strongly opposed to any authoritarian government reminiscent of British centralized power. Yet the radicals were seldom content to see the new state constitutions merely substitute American elective officials for British royal appointees. In most of the states therefore, a constitution was not adopted without some struggle between the conservative and radical points of view.

Almost none of the state constitutions was completely democratic by modern standards, yet all were far in advance of contemporary standards and instituted what were the freest governments in the world at the time. Hereditary privilege was outlawed and republican governments organized. In drafting the constitutions the framers conformed to the eighteenth-century liberal view which believed that the state should have only limited powers and that these should be divided among the executive, legislative, and judicial branches of the government. Personal and property rights were reserved to the individual and to the people. These rights were spelled out in the formal declarations, or bills of rights, which were prefixed to the constitutions of the states or were contained elsewhere in the body of the documents.

The Virginia Declaration of Rights, written by George Mason, served as a model for the other states, and it also had wide influence in France. Adopted a month before the Declaration of Independence, the Virginia Declaration gave classic expression to the same general philosophy of the natural rights of the individual. In the main the Virginia Declaration was a restatement of English principles of individual rights and liberties derived from the Magna Charta, Petition of Rights, and various arguments in justification of the seventeenth-century revolutions. It summed up the liberal theory of individual democracy which its author George Mason so well epitomized. The Virginia Constitution proper, though less liberal than the Declaration of Rights, was democratic in its tendency, even if not as advanced as Mason himself desired. For example, the Virginians refused to follow Mason in regard to the suffrage and kept a property qualification for voting.

The Pennsylvania Constitution of 1776, the most radical of all the state documents, came closest to instituting a democracy. Because so many conservatives and moderates in Pennsylvania were opposed to independence, the more radical leaders were able to gain control of the special constitutional convention which then also acted as the provisional government in the state. A single-house legislature, elected annually by all taxpayers, continued the innovation instituted by the Penn proprietary government. The executive power, much reduced by the lack of any veto over legislative bills, was granted to an Executive Council of thirteen. In Pennsylvania, as in most of the other states, the judiciary was made dependent on the legislature. A taxpayer qualification for voting, as distinct from the old colonial requirement of having a freehold, permitted as many as 90 per cent of the adult males to vote.

The Pennsylvania Constitution, though democratic in substance, was hastily written and put into effect with little regard for the views of its conservative opposition. Massachusetts, in contrast, waited until 1780 to adopt a much more conservative frame of government which was, however, subjected to widespread popular debate before it was ratified. While the Pennsylvania Constitution was supplemented by a more conservative revised version as early as 1790, the Massachusetts Constitution endured until 1820. In 1775, after the Revolutionary leaders in Massachusetts took over the posts formerly held by the Tories, they restored the old colonial charter of 1691 as the constitutional basis for the government. Mounting criticism of the charter, especially in the western part of the state, culminated in the movement for a new constitution. After a first draft was rejected in 1778, another version, substantially written in the special constitutional convention by John Adams, was referred to the towns for their consideration. A complicated process of revision carried on between the towns and the convention somewhat marred the purity of the democratic process. Nevertheless Massachusetts' Constitution of 1780 was adopted more democratically than the Revolutionary constitutions of the other states. The Constitution itself, however, was far from democratic. Subject to the most objection were a property qualification for voting, 50 per cent higher than under the colonial charter, and the continued state support of the Congregational Church.

Taken as a whole, the Revolutionary state constitutions exhibited both democratic and undemocratic features. The Founding Fathers were perhaps most negligent in failing to provide adequately for the alteration of the first state constitutions. Of the eight constitutions of the Revolutionary period that provided for change, three enabled the legislature to make amendments, but in a manner different than in their enactment of laws, while the others set up special methods. The remainder made no real provision for amendments. The constitutions reduced the powers of the governors, often by eliminating his veto, and added to those of the legislatures. The state supreme courts also lost powers, and the upper houses of the legislatures, usually appointed by the governors or councils in the colonies, were now frequently made elective. In all cases the lower houses were chosen directly by the qualified voters, and short terms of office made the representatives aware of their responsibility to the people. Thus, if sufficiently persistent, the majority of the voters could now achieve its ends in most of the states. Individual liberties were protected by bills of rights or similar restraints on the powers of government. Although the Revolution secured individual liberty, it did not result in complete religious freedom or equality for persons or denominations. Religious tests for voting and holding office continued as civil disabilities or penalties for one's private convictions or form of worship. Except in Rhode Island, New York, and Virginia, officeholders were variously required to be Protestants, Christians, or believers in God.[7]

The continuance of property qualifications for voting in all the original 13 states aroused some popular objection on grounds that anyone who fought for independence or who paid taxes should be allowed to vote. But by contemporary standards the suffrage was not illiberal. Five of the states made no changes in their colonial requirements, and the others were content merely to reduce, but not eliminate, the property qualification. New Hampshire, North Carolina, and Pennsylvania required little more than the payment of taxes, while Maryland, South Carolina, and New Jersey required a freehold worth as much as 50 pounds. On the whole, however, in an agrarian society a property qualification was not unduly burdensome, and the Revolution itself probably added to the number who could meet this requirement. To be able to hold office, as distinct from mere voting, generally necessitated additional property-holding, which often meant that only the wealthy could serve as governors or even as legislators. Representation was usually apportioned on the basis of taxable property or numbers of taxpayers, rather than on population. Thus state government was still closely tied to the institution of property, and democracy as measured by the state constitutions was far from equalitarian.[8]

The early state constitutions and laws were perhaps most disappointing to those radical democrats who wanted to interpret the rights of man as broadly and positively as possible. None of the constitutions took any specific action with respect to slavery or the rights of women. However, the simple statement in the Massachusetts Constitution that men are free and equal was interpreted by the state courts to abolish slavery. Only the "Republic" of Vermont, which was finally joined to the Union as the fourteenth state in 1791, included universal manhood suffrage and the abolition of slavery in its constitution, adopted in 1777. The state constitutions also reflected little recognition of growing humanitarian ideals, and only four made any stipulation or provision concerning education. A distinguishing feature of these first state constitutions, therefore, was their acceptance of eighteenth-century theories of limited government.

Truly no governments on earth have ever been instituted with so little authority to do ill, as those of the American states. Yet, not content with that, the framers of constitutions even limited their governments' power to do good, lest it be perverted to their hurt.[9]

(III)

While the states were coping with the problems of creating their new constitutions and governments, the Continental Congress faced the responsibilities of building a federal union and prosecuting a war for independence. Between the Declaration of Independence and the adoption of the Federal Constitution, the course of democracy was diverted from an emphasis on a negative liberty to one of more positive authority. In other words, the dissolution of British controls, a task highly congenial to radical democracy, had to be followed by the more burdensome and less pleasant corollary duty of establishing a new American central government.

The democratic and conservative forces in the American Revolution differed very sharply over what kind of central government was most desirable. From the beginning of the Revolutionary movement, Loyalist spokesmen had pointed out to the British authorities the folly of having 13 separate colonial governments, all more responsible to popular demands than to British controls. With independence, many of the more conservative American leaders also felt the necessity of some sort of strong central government to curb the rising democracy. John Dickinson, who had opposed independence to the very last in 1776, was nevertheless commissioned by Congress to draw up a plan of union. In Dickinson's first draft for a confederation, the national Congress, rather than the states, was to hold supreme power.[10] The states were to control only their imports and militia. They were to be allowed to keep their existing laws, but since nothing was said of future laws and since the militia was already subject to the discipline of the Continental Army, the sole practical restraint on Congress would have been in the matter of laying taxes and customs duties. These, of course, were natural limitations because of the circumstances of the coming of the Revolution.

The rejection of Dickinson's first draft and the adoption by Congress in 1777 of an amended and modified version of the Articles of Confederation were a victory for the democratic point of view. Under the Articles sovereignty remained with the states. The union was thus almost more an interstate or international than a truly federal union. It has even been termed a league of friendship rather than a perpetual union. Each state had one vote in Congress, and the powers of Congress, in turn, were limited largely to war and foreign relations. The states controlled their own commerce and tax revenues, subject only to requisitions by Congress. The lack of any separate executive or judicial branch, and the necessity of the unanimous consent of the states before any amendments could be made, completed what was by all odds a rather feeble government. It was, however, also one which was in accord with the reigning democratic belief that that government is best which governs least. Strong government was associated in the Revolutionary mind with British tyranny and the theory of special political privileges for favored social and economic interests. In an agrarian society the bulk of the people needed no such advantages from a powerful government. By holding most of the powers of government in the hands of the states, political authority was kept closer to the people. A centralized national government, it was felt, could more easily be swayed and manipulated by a small conservative aristocracy.

Both the original state constitutions and the Articles of Confederation belonged to the initial more democratic and less nationalistic stage of the American Revolution. Though the Articles were intended to provide a central government to help prosecute the war, they were not finally ratified until 1781. Thus from 1776 to 1781 the Revolution was carried on by a coalition of sovereign states forced to cooperate by the demands of war. Too weak to provide true national sovereignty, the Articles reflected the democracy rather than the nationalism of the American Revolution.

(IV)

The progress of democracy during the Revolution was not confind solely to politics. Impressive gains were also made in the economic, social, and cultural life of the American people. "Even during the years of fighting the State legislators were busy with the overthrow of the Establishment and the guaranty of religious liberty; the annulment of laws of entail and primogeniture in favor of a democratic system of inheritance; and the opening up, with new political prospects, of new vistas of humanitarianism also."[11] Much of this advance was a result of Revolutionary nationalism and the conscious desire to eliminate as far as possible all remnants of British influence upon American life and thought. But the Revolution also opened up new opportunities to greater numbers of the people and thus contributed to the making of a more democratic social order.

As colonials, Americans in many ways had been hindered from taking actions which ran counter to British interests and traditions. Many of their laws had been disallowed, including important legislation for issuing paper money and for curbing the African slave trade. For the colonial economy generally, the Revolution came as a relief after a decade of commercial warfare against the Mother Country. Independence offered freedom from British economic regulation and, in some cases, from British creditors. The end of mercantilist restraints made it possible to encourage American trade with the rest of the world. Business was stimulated by the wartime needs of the armies and by the inflationary opportunities for profit. Frequently the changes wrought by the fortunes of war resulted in the rise of a new conservative aristocracy to replace the departed Loyalists, but in many cases too the Revolution prepared the way for men to emerge from the obscurity of the lower social ranks into positions of economic and political power.

Particularly in regard to land tenure, a social revolution took place in almost every state. Ungranted Crown lands and the proprietary domain of the Penn family were seized by the states. Loyalist properties, including the great DeLancey and Philipse estates in New York and Lord Fairfax's lands in Virginia, were confiscated. As their estates were sold and subdivided among American Patriots, the position of the older conservative landed aristocracy was naturally weakened. In the colonial period much of the social and economic status of the upper classes had been built on large land holdings. In Virginia, for example, members of the Governor's Council were enriched by extensive land grants, while in New Hampshire the last of the royal governors, Benning Wentworth, acquired a great personal domain. Contributing to the position of the landed aristocracy were the colonial laws of entail and primogeniture, which kept large estates intact and within the same family. In Virginia one of the first measures to be passed by the new state legislature in 1776 was Jefferson's bill to repeal the law of entail. Many of the members of the Virginia Assembly enjoyed some of the advantages of entailed estates. "Yet the bill passed promptly, as if on the floodtide of democracy."[12] Primogeniture was not abolished in Virginia until 1785, but by the close of the Revolution most of the states had taken action to end their laws respecting both entail and primogeniture. The payment of quitrents also ceased.

The political and economic freedom won during the Revolution was matched in many of the states by the separation of church and state and by the spread of religious freedom. Growing religious skepticism and the vogue of Deism contributed to the undermining of the established churches' position. Although religious toleration had already made gains in the later colonial period, particular religious denominations or beliefs were still established or accorded special preferment and political influence in all of the colonies except Rhode Island. Roman Catholics especially were subject to various discriminations. After the Revolution, in New England outside Rhode Island, the Congregational Church continued to enjoy its position as the state church. Contributing members of other churches, however, were generally exempted from the payment of the Congregational Church taxes. Because of its continued close ties with the Mother Country and its English origins, the Anglican Church was vulnerable to Patriot resentment and quickly lost its established position and prestige in the South.

In Virginia, even before the Revolution, Anglicans were in a minority, and there was strong pressure for disestablishment from the Baptists and other dissenters moving into the Great Valley west of the Blue Ridge. In the Virginia Declaration of Rights, James Madison was able to substitute for George Mason's clause protecting religious toleration the more clear-cut statement that "All men are equally entitled to the free exercise of religion." For the next 10 years, spurred on by the petitions of the Baptists and other dissenting sects, the supporters of religious freedom sought to pass a law which would fulfill the promise of the Bill of Rights. In 1779 Jefferson drew up a measure for religious freedom which failed of passage. But, in the same session of the legislature, George Mason was able to secure approval of his bill ending tax support for the Episcopal Church. Meanwhile, sentiment developed for a general assessment or tax for the support of all churches. After such a measure was narrowly defeated, Madison was able to bring forward Jefferson's old bill of 1779, which then became law in January, 1786. This famous statute denounced religious coercion as hypocrisy and provided that no man should be forced to attend or support any form of worship or suffer discrimination because of his religious opinions. The Virginia law was the cornerstone or model of religious freedom in other states, and in the Old Dominion itself the only remaining vestige of the late Anglican establishment was the guaranty to the Episcopal Church of its existing properties.[13]

(V)

In quickening the separation of church and state, the Revolution was helping to transform American cultural and intellectual life. Although the war brought no new ideas to the fore, it accelerated and popularized such older doctrines as the natural-rights philosophy and the humanitarian feelings associated with the eighteenth-century Enlightenment. Intellectual losses suffered by the removal of cultivated and learned Tories were balanced by gains in the growth of intellectual democracy and an American culture. As David Ramsay pointed out in his pioneer *History of the American Revolution*, "It seemed as if the war not only required, but created talents."

In the course of the developing conflict with the Mother Country, Patriots realized the need of popular support. If the common man's help was to be gained, he had to be educated in the issues at stake and promised some of the fruits of victory. In Revolutionary propaganda therefore lay the beginnings of a mass culture in America. The people were encouraged to read the Patriot pamphlets and newspapers, including Tom Paine's *Common Sense* and *Crisis*. Many of the Founding Fathers sincerely believed that, in a republic, culture and education should be more widely diffused. If the political system was to rest on a broad electorate, its members should be well-informed. Although there was public support for education in the

New England towns, elsewhere schooling was largely controlled by church or private groups. The Revolution, however, stimulated plans for a state system of education, and in 1779 Jefferson proposed his comprehensive blueprint for public education from the primary school through the university. Education, he felt, was one way of insuring democracy by providing to the common people a necessary instrument to cope with the aristocracy. Jefferson earlier had also introduced a public library bill. Others, like Benjamin Rush in Philadelphia and Timothy Dwight in Connecticut, took an interest in developing educational opportunities for girls, and the Quakers and other reformers of a humanitarian persuasion sought to make a start in formal education for Negroes in America.

Although ideas were not lacking, little could be done until after the Revolution. The war itself worked a disaster upon many schools and colleges, destroying or putting to military purposes their buildings and equipment. Teachers joined in the fighting, and, like many of the Revolutionary soldiers, their intellectual horizons were widened by contact with the men of other colonies or states. But there remained sizeable difficulties in the way of establishing even the beginnings of a truly democratic culture. And the plans of Jefferson and others had to wait the coming of peace. Probably the greatest incentive which the Revolution itself offered was in generating a patriotic and nationalistic concern over the state of American education and the arts. This presently resulted in a literature which was both American and democratic in its outlook and sympathies. Freneau's poetry, Jefferson's *Notes on Virginia*, and Mercy Warren's plays in verse were early examples of the defense of democracy in American literature.

Although the state constitutions usually contained a bill of rights or similar statement of the natural rights of man paralleling the assertions of the Declaration of Independence, these were mostly claims of the individual to be protected from his government. The purpose of the constitutions was not to expand the realm or powers of government, and thus education, for example, received little mention. Yet the Revolutionary era did witness a growing humanitarian and democratic concern over such unfortunates as Negro slaves.[14] The Founding Fathers were not unaware of the contradiction between the words of the Declaration of Independence that all men are created equal and Negro slavery. The similar phrase of George Mason's in the Virginia Bill of Rights provoked the opposition of conservative slave owners, who resented its implications. Before the Revolution, however, various colonies had attempted to limit or forbid the further importation of Negro slaves, only to see these laws vetoed in England. Delaware, in its Constitution of 1776, was the first of the states to forbid the importation of slaves. Two years later, in Virginia, Jefferson's bill to cut off the slave trade was passed, and soon after the close of the war all of the states except South Carolina and Georgia either abolished or put limits on the slave trade.

To emancipate the Negro slaves already in America was more difficult than to outlaw the slave trade. Massachusetts and Rhode Island had colonial measures placing certain restrictions on slavery, and Vermont abolished it in its Constitution of 1777. Most interesting was the forthright ruling of the court in Massachusetts that the state constitution, in declaring all men born free and equal, precluded the continuance of slavery. Elsewhere in the North plans for gradual emancipation began with the Pennsylvania law of 1780 and the Connecticut and Rhode Island measures of 1784. Under these statutes slave children were to receive their freedom on reaching adulthood. In Virginia gradual emancipation was discussed and favored by Washington, Jefferson, Patrick Henry, George Mason, Richard Henry Lee, and James Madison, but the moment for action passed and sentiment gradually changed. Nevertheless, at the Federal Constitutional Convention, Southerners joined the North in denouncing the foreign slave trade, while leaving slavery itself as a matter for the states to decide.

Almost as miserable as the Negro slaves and in some ways in a much worse state were the wretches confined to American prisons in the eighteenth century. Although crime and hence its punishment was seemingly less an occurrence in the New World than the Old, harsh and barbaric penalties were often exacted of those convicted of even minor offenses. In this the colonies followed the criminal and penal code of Britain, and only in Pennsylvania under the influence of the proprietor and the Quakers was colonial practice toward criminals dictated by humanitarian feelings. The Revolution offered an opportunity to make American penal laws conformable to republican justice, but reform took place slowly. Virginia began the study of its laws as early as 1776 but made no revision until 20 years later. The Pennsylvania reforms and system of prison administration subsequently became a model for other states. Particularly a matter of concern was the illogical imprisonment of debtors, whose indefinite incarceration, of course, precluded any chance of their earning enough to repay their obligations.

(*VI*)

For those who were discontented with their economic and social status at home, so long as they were freemen, there was ever the hope of moving farther west to seek a new start in life. Since the time when Roger Williams and Thomas Hooker had led their followers from Massachusetts, the frontier seemed to offer greater opportunities for democracy than could easily be found along the seaboard. Even the years of the War of Independence did not slow down this westward movement. In fact, the ending of all British controls over the trans-Appalachian West only excited American interest in the possibilities of speculation or settlement.

Many of the large-scale speculators had little feeling for democracy, but the need to attract settlers often forced concessions susceptible of democratic interpretation. On the New England frontier the Vermonters adopted a constitution with universal manhood suffrage which was more democratic than that of any of the original 13 states. On the frontier of Virginia and North Carolina, the settlers along the upper reaches of the Watauga River in the 1770's formed themselves into an association which established universal manhood suffrage and complete religious freedom. And under the Articles of Confederation, Jefferson's committee on the western lands drew up plans for the national domain which provided both political democracy and economic opportunity. The 50-acre freehold qualification for voting imposed by Congress in both the Ordinance of 1784 and the Northwest Ordinance, though more strict than the requirements of the older seaboard states, was no great practical barrier to the suffrage in the virgin West. Since land titles frequently could not be cleared, the suffrage requirement was often ignored, and town lots were also made the value equivalent of the 50 acres.[15]

In the fact of the West itself and its attachment to the original 13 states was a tremendous promise for the future of an agrarian-type democracy based on individual ownership of property. Moreover, the West and the frontier were a force for democracy as multiple participation, in the sense that new communities attracted people into government. Thus the winning of the West was not the least of the democratic gains of the Revolutionary era.

Finally, the Revolution was not only of national and American importance, but it was recognized also as an example to the world. If the United States was able to keep its independence, it would demonstrate the virtue and practicality of a republic and popular government. As Benjamin Franklin pointed out to one of his French correspondents, "Establishing the liberties of America will not only make that people happy, but will have some effect in diminishing the misery of those, who in other parts of the world groan under despotism, by rendering it more circumspect, and inducing it to govern with a lighter hand."[16] Both liberal French philosophers and radical English Whigs joined in their praise and hopes for America, while Washington called himself "a Citizen of the great republic of humanity at large," and Tom Paine later pointed out in the *Rights of Man* that the American Revolution promised a new era to the human race. Franklin, Paine, and Jefferson all maintained a considerable cosmopolitan and international outlook, and Jefferson, like Franklin, termed a "just and solid republican government . . . a standing monument and example for the aim and imitation of the people of other countries. . . ."[17]

CHAPTER THREE

The First Great Debate

THE CLOSE of the American Revolution marked the beginning of the first great debate on the nature of the American government. The differing concepts of democracy revealed in the discussions over the state constitutions and Articles of Confederation continued to prevail in the sessions of the Constitutional Convention at Philadelphia in the summer of 1787. Indeed arguments over democracy seemed now to reach a new intensity. The Founding Fathers divided into Federalists and Anti-Federalists, as John Adams, Alexander Hamilton, Thomas Jefferson, James Madison, and Tom

Paine all offered their varying interpretations of the meaning of democracy.

Idealogical differences in this era were sharpened not only by the domestic difficulties of the infant United States, but also by the diplomatic problems which grew out of the French Revolution. In the turmoil abroad Americans saw in exaggerated form both the desirable and undesirable features of democratic government, and political leadership in the United States did not hesitate to draw analogies from the course of events in Revolutionary France. Though American democracy continued to grow in the late eighteenth and early nineteenth centuries, the adoption of the Federal Constitution and reaction against the radicalism of the French Revolution ushered in a period of conservatism. Popular democracy was subordinated to the leadership and control of an upper-class aristocracy, while the very word *democracy* was seldom used except in an unfavorable sense. Even Jefferson and his associates preferred to regard themselves as republican aristocrats rather than as leaders of a mass democracy, while many of the Federalists were openly critical of any leveling or equalitarian tendencies in the United States. With John Adams, the author of the Declaration of Independence agreed that "there is a natural aristocracy among men. The grounds of this are virtue and talents." There was also, Jefferson admitted, "an artificial aristocracy, founded on wealth and birth, without either virtue or talents. . . ."[1] But though men were unequal in their person, property, and abilities, Adams and Jefferson affirmed that they were equal before the law and before God and in their possession of those inherent natural rights specified in the Declaration of Independence.

The state constitutions put into effect during the American Revolution provided a mechanism for majority rule, even though an aristocracy controlled some of the state governments. Property qualifications for voting were not so stringent that legislatures were not responsible ultimately to a considerable electorate. This was especially the case in elections for the lower houses of the legislative bodies, to which the upper chambers, governors, and state judiciary alike were able to offer little constitutional check. Although the suffrage was far from universal, it was sufficiently widespread to enable many of the state governments to be considered democratic. It was this relative democracy in the states in the decade after 1776 which aroused the fears of many of the Founding Fathers. When state legislatures, amenable to popular agrarian influences, issued paper money to help debtor farmers pay their taxes and mortgages, conservatives took alarm for the safety of their property. In Rhode Island the paper money forces captured control of the state government, and in Massachusetts the same forces were behind Shays' Rebellion.

In the early stages of the Revolution, Patriot leaders often exhibited an enthusiasm for democracy that was in marked contrast to their views a decade later. Alexander Hamilton, for example, in a letter to Gouverneur Morris in 1777, deprecated the fears of democracy:

> That instability is inherent in the nature of popular government I think is very disputable; unstable democracy is an epithet frequently in the mouths of politicians. . . . When the deliberative or judicial powers are vested wholly or partly in the collective body of the people, you must expect error, confusion, and instability. But a representative democracy, where the right of election is well secured and regulated, and the exercise of the legislative, executive, and judiciary authorities is vested in select persons, will, in my opinion, be most likely to be happy, regular, and durable.[2]

John Adams, on the other hand, was dubious from the start of governments in which full powers were entrusted to the legislatures.[3] And Edward Rutledge advised John Jay to secure for New York a constitution providing a strong executive, for, he said, "a pure democracy may possibly do, when patriotism is the ruling passion; but when the state abounds with rascals, as is the case with many at this day, you must suppress a little of that popular spirit."[4]

By the time of the Constitutional Convention and under the alarm generated by the Shaysites, criticism of popular democracy became much more general. Theodore Sedgwick, later a member of Congress from Massachusetts, wrote to Rufus King: "Every man of observations is convinced that the end of government, security, cannot be attained by the exercise of principles founded on democratic equality."[5] In the opening speech to the Convention at Philadelphia, Governor Edmund Randolph of Virginia told the assembled delegates: "Our chief danger arises from the democratic parts of our constitutions. . . . None of the constitutions have provided a suffi-

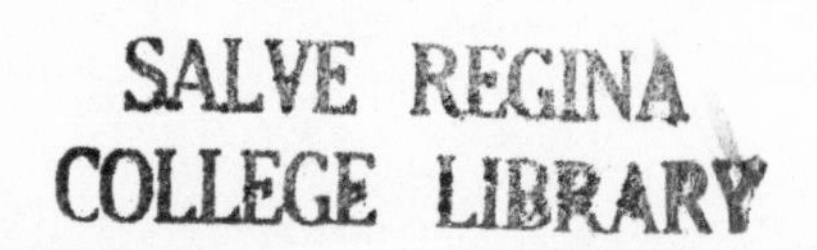

cient check against the democracy." Randolph, in tracing the political troubles of the country to their origins, later declared that "every man had found it in the turbulence and follies of democracy."[6] Elbridge Gerry of Massachusetts expressed the view that "the evils we experience flow from the excess of democracy." General Henry Knox voiced the opinion that the Convention had come together to "clip the wings of a mad democracy," which "sweeps away every moral trait from the human character." To substantiate Knox's view, Alexander Hamilton at the Convention called for a President and Senate elected for life. "Can a democratic Assembly," he asked, "who annually revolve in the mass of the people, be supposed steadily to pursue the public good? Nothing but a permanent body can check the imprudence of democracy. Their turbulent and uncontrolling disposition requires checks." Gouverneur Morris wanted a Senate of wealthy aristocrats to "keep down the turbulency of democracy," while Charles Pinckney moved "that the first branch of the national Legislature be elected by the State Legislatures, and not by the people." James Madison also favored a Senate in which the members would enjoy a long term in order to counteract the instability of democracy.[7]

(II)

Conservative dissatisfaction with the radical democratic tendencies exhibited in some of the states after the Revolution helps to explain the call for the Constitutional Convention. Even more than the weaknesses of the Articles of Confederation, this dissatisfaction brought the delegates together at Philadelphia. The technical deficiencies of the Articles in the matters of regulating commerce and securing revenue could have been corrected in time if these had been the only problems. But mere revision and amendment of the Articles offered little prospect of providing peace and security for the United States. What was necessary, Jefferson pointed out, was "a government, which should go on of itself, peaceably without needing continual recurrence to the state legislatures."[8] The 1780's were difficult postwar years, and the government of the Articles could hardly be blamed for the inevitable economic readjustment that ensued. But the Articles did bear the brunt of the ill feeling of those who desired a political reformation along more conservative, nationalist lines. A stronger national government would better defend property rights, and it would also be able to protect individuals against the majoritarian and popular concepts of democracy growing in the states.

Despite the attacks on the workings of democracy in the states, the members of the Constitutional Convention still favored popular government and democracy as principles. There was recognition of the danger that, as George Mason put it, "we should incautiously run into the opposite extreme." Although admitting some excesses and injustices from democracy, he believed "the genius of the people is in favor of it, and the genius of the people must be consulted."[9] Except in the isolated case of Alexander Hamilton, who may have preferred a monarchy, the delegates were agreed upon the desirability of keeping a republican form of government. As Gottfried Dietze has pointed out, the Constitutional Convention had no intention of instituting some form of monarchy or aristocratic government as an antidote for democracy. "The Fathers accepted popular government as the very premise for their deliberations. Their problem was how to prevent too much democracy. It was democratic absolutism that was feared. . . ."[10] In the debate concerning the House of Representatives, though some of the delegates felt that the state legislatures would choose better qualified members, the Convention recognized the practical wisdom of James Wilson's advice that "one branch of the Legislature ought to be drawn from the people, because on the great foundation of the people all Government ought to rest." Madison, in concurring, argued that popular election "would inspire confidence, and . . . induce the Government to sympathize with the people."[11]

The Founding Fathers gathered in the Convention at Philadelphia were ready to accept the compromise of a federal republic in which democratic majoritarian principles, rather than being discarded completely, would be subject to some limitation. Neither a popular nor a despotic authority could flourish in a federal system dividing power between the states and the central government. Within the latter there would be the mutual checks and balances exercised by the executive, legislative, and judicial branches of the government. The Constitution accordingly was faithful to eighteenth-century concepts of democracy in its protection of the individual in his personal and property rights. A pure democracy like that of ancient Greece or the New England town meeting was unthinkable in an extensive federal nation. And a radical democracy, akin to that of some of the states, was also regarded with hostility. Unbridled popular rule the Constitution hoped to forestall with the checks of a Senate, Electoral College, appointive judiciary, and Presidential veto power. At the same time the Constitution provided that the House of Representatives should be chosen by the people of the several states and that new states should be admitted into the Union in full equality with the old. In granting no exclusive powers to special classes or interests, and in placing no federal restrictions on the suffrage, which was left in the hands of the states, the Constitution kept the way open for the growth of economic and political democracy in the United States.

In the great debate over the ratification of the Constitution, neither its supporters or opponents took an unqualified democratic position. While the Federalists or nationalists frankly desired a stronger central government with its checks on the popular majoritarian democracy of the state legislatures, the Anti-Federalists had almost as little confidence in the virtue or ability of the people. Termed by a recent writer "Men of Little Faith," the Anti-Federalists opposed the Constitution not because they were modern-day democrats. Rather they feared a large consolidated national government and the perversion of democracy by aristocratic leaders and military heroes. They did not believe that the system of representative government under the Constitution would make possible the achievement of a satisfactory democratic republic.[12]

James Madison, who more than any other person deserves the distinction of having been the chief architect of the Federal Constitution, contributed also to its defense as co-author with Hamilton and Jay of *The Federalist* papers. Here Madison distinguished between a democracy and a republic, and in the course of his famous discussion of the role of factions and interests in the government, he argued that in a pure democracy there was "nothing to check the inducements to sacrifice the weaker party or an obnoxious individual." On the other hand, a republic refined and moderated popular passions so that:

> The two great points of difference between a democracy and a republic are: first, the delegation of the government, in the latter, to a small number of citizens elected by the rest; secondly, the greater number of citizens, and greater sphere of country, over which the latter may be extended.

A republic Madison defined as "a government which derives all its powers directly or indirectly from the great body of the people, and is administered by persons holding their offices during pleasure, for a limited period, or during good behavior." Within the American Republic, he stressed the importance of popular elections. "Who are to be the electors of the federal representatives?" he asked.

> Not the rich, more than the poor; nor the learned, more than the ignorant; not the haughty heirs of distinguished names, more than the humble sons of obscurity and unpropitious fortune. The electors are to be the great body of the people of the United States. They are to be the same who exercise the right in every State of electing the corresponding branch of the legislature of the State.[13]

(III)

Conspicuous by their absence from the Constitutional Convention, because they were in Europe at the time, were John Adams, Jefferson, and Paine, all of whom had strong convictions regarding an ideal form of government. Although Adams himself was in England, his writings, particularly his *Defense of the Constitutions of the Government of the United States*, had considerable influence on the delegates at Philadelphia. Adams, who had grown more conservative during the Revolution, now modified his earlier belief in the self-sufficiency of a representative government responsive to the popular will. His *Defense*, written chiefly in justification of the conservative Massachusetts state constitution of 1780, advanced his theory of a mixed government in which some of the characteristics of monarchy, aristocracy, and democracy would all be represented.

A republic conformed to Adams' notion of mixed government,

although republics varied from "the smallest and most popular," to "the larger and more aristocratical," and finally to "the largest and most monarchical." In any case, he believed that a "simple and perfect democracy never yet existed among men." Simple democracies tended toward tumults and disorders.

> We may appeal to every page of history we have hitherto turned over, for proofs irrefragable, that the people when they have been unchecked, have been as unjust, tyrannical, brutal, barbarous, and cruel as any king or senate possessed of uncontrollable power. The majority has eternally, and without one exception, usurped over the rights of the minority.

There was no stable basis of government in unlimited democracy, just as there was "no freedom nor justice in a simple democracy for any but the majority." Equally disastrous to public liberty were other types of simple governments, such as an absolute monarchy or an aristocracy of wealth. Within Adams' ideal republic or mixed government there had to be one branch closely tied to the people and responsive to their will through frequent elections, "a more general privilege of voting," and small districts in which the suffrage was confined to residents. "There can be no free government," he declared, "without a democratical branch in the constitution."[14]

Adams agreed with the classic position of the American Revolutionary Patriots that the people were the best keepers of their own interests and liberties, but he denied that "they are the best keepers, or any keepers at all, of their own liberties, when they hold collectively, or by representation, the executive and judicial power, or the whole and uncontrolled legislative. . . ." Liberty was best preserved when the lower house of the legislature, representing the people, was checked and balanced by an upper house, by a judiciary, and by an executive holding the veto power. Such a mixed government would provide a republican balance between aristocracy or monarchy and democracy.[15]

Adams, like Jefferson, had conflicting feelings with regard to the new American Constitution. Although content with the Articles of Confederation, and at first inclined to regard the Constitution as too aristocratic, he approved its adoption. In the light of his concept of a mixed government partaking of some of the characteristics of democracy, aristocracy, and monarchy, he believed that the House of Representatives should be more democratic and closer to the people, while the elective Senate and President should, in the opposite way, be chosen for life. Adams thus seemed to continue to hold monarchical and aristocratic ideas, a widespread assumption on the part of his political enemies which he bitterly resented. As he explained some years later in his *Letters to John Taylor:*

> You say, sir, that I have gravely counted up several victims "of popular rage, as proofs that democracy is more pernicious than monarchy or aristocracy." This is not my doctrine, Mr. Taylor. My opinion is, and always has been, that absolute power intoxicates alike despots, monarchs, aristocrats, and democrats, and jacobins, and *sans culottes.* I cannot say that democracy has been more pernicious, on the whole, than any of the others.

Adams continued:

> Democracy has never been and never can be so durable as aristocracy or monarchy; but while it lasts, it is more bloody than either. . . . Remember, democracy never lasts long. It soon wastes, exhausts, and murders itself. There never was a democracy yet that did not commit suicide.[16]

Although he never relented in his attacks on a simple popular democracy, Adams did become reconciled sufficiently to the republicanism of the American government to serve loyally as its second President.

Thomas Jefferson, later Adams' great political adversary and his successor as President, like him accepted the basic constitutional arrangements worked out at Philadelphia. In many ways a republican aristocrat and eighteenth-century liberal rather than a radical democrat, Jefferson valued tradition and the evolutionary process, even though he was not averse to the occasional tonic effect of such popular upheavals as Shays' Rebellion and the French Revolution. But he was not a radical agitator like Sam Adams or Tom Paine, and in Virginia during the Revolution his chief contributions to democracy were his constructive efforts in regard to religious equality, educational opportunity, and a more liberal suffrage. At the very outset of the Revolution, in discussing the type of constitution that would be desirable for Virginia, Jefferson announced that he favored the indirect election of the Virginia Senate through the votes of the popularly elected lower house of the legislature. "I have ever observed," he wrote, "that a choice by the people themselves is not generally distinguished for it's [sic] wisdom. This first secretion from them is usually crude and heterogeneous. But give to those so chosen by the people a second choice themselves, and they generally will chuse wise men." Although Jefferson, as John Adams, thus had some doubts over the wisdom of establishing an unchecked popular democracy, he was no more sanguine of the integrity of an aristocracy of wealth, and he opposed therefore a property qualification for the Virginia Senate. "In general I believe," he added, "the decisions of the people, in a body, will be more honest and more disinterested than those of wealthy men; and I can never doubt an attachment to his country in any man who has his family and peculium in it."[17]

In respect to the Federal Constitution, Jefferson deferred in the main to the judgment of his friend Madison who was on the scene, but he also wrote from Paris giving Madison his opinion of the merits and defects of the document. Jefferson liked the organization of the government into three major branches, each checking and balancing the others. He approved the popular election of the House of Representatives and its power to levy taxes, but to the executive veto he would have added also some kind of judicial veto power. Although Jefferson approved the Constitution in general, he also offered some strong objections. First and foremost was "the omission of a bill of rights." The need for such a bill of rights was consistent with Jefferson's own philosophy as stated in the Declaration of Independence and also with the Declaration of Rights which prefaced the Virginia Constitution. To Jefferson government, no matter how perfect, was subservient to the liberties of the people, for, as he well knew, governments tended to encroach upon the individual's freedom either by coercive laws or by naked violence. Accordingly a bill of rights was ever a necessary protection for the individual. Jefferson's second objection related to the lack of any clear principle in the Constitution providing for a rotation in office. This, he feared, might lead to a President continually re-elected to a life term in office.[18]

In the conclusion of his long letter to Madison acquainting him with his views of the Constitution, Jefferson could not refrain from offering a restatement of his essentially agrarian view of the limited role of government. "I own I am not a friend to a very energetic government. It is always oppressive." His experience in Europe strengthened his opposition to monarchy and his belief in the principle "that the will of the Majority should always prevail." As long as agriculture remained the principal object of the American people, and as long as there remained sufficient vacant lands, the corruption that he saw as a result of the piling-up of people in European cities would be avoided. Jefferson had a greater faith than Adams in democracy and in the virtue of the people if they were kept free of such corrupting influences. But he also recognized that a pure and simple government without checks and balances could degenerate into despotism. Thus in 1789, as the new government was being organized, Jefferson expressed the opinion that

> The tyranny of the legislatures is the most formidable dread at present, and will be for long years. That of the executive will come in it's [sic] turn; but it will be at a remote period. I know there are some among us, who would now establish a monarchy. But they are inconsiderable in number and weight of character. The rising race are all republicans.[19]

Jefferson placed his basic political trust in the judgment of the people if they remained free of a consolidated government or an industrialized society.

> Our country is too large to have all its affairs directed by a single government. Public servants at such a distance, and from under the eye of their constituents, must, from the circumstance of distance, be unable to administer and overlook all the details necessary for the good government of the citizens; and the same circumstance, by rendering detection impossible to their constituents, will invite the public agents to corruption, plunder and waste.

To this end of keeping government close to the people, he emphasized the importance of local political units. He admired the democracy of the New England towns, and he included a similar system of local government in his suggested plans for organizing the Northwest Territory. In Virginia he urged the adoption of a type of local government extending down through the counties to the wards, which were units based on the old Anglo-Saxon institution of the hundreds. Like Cato, he told one correspondent he could only conclude every bit of advice on government with the injunction, "divide the counties into wards," and he depicted as his ideal a society in which

> Every State again is divided into counties . . . ; each county again into townships or wards, to manage minuter details; and every ward into farms to be governed each by its individual proprietor. Were we directed from Washington when to sow, and when to reap, we should soon want bread.[20]

The Adams and Jefferson theories of democracy were put to the test of practical politics after 1789. Although both Federalist supporters and Anti-Federalist critics of the Constitution united at first behind the Washington administration, a renewed political division soon sprang up over Hamilton's financial measures. In general the Federalists became more conservative and aristocratic, while their opponents espoused the popular democratic view of most political questions. Madison, who broke away from his original strong nationalism, and Jefferson, following his resignation from Washington's Cabinet, became the leaders of a new party, the Republican, which henceforth opposed the Federalists.

(*IV*)

In the states the 1790's were a decade of relative progress in democracy. In contrast to the conservative policies enforced by the Federalists in the national government, the democratic tendencies of the American Revolution were continued in many of the states. At the same time some of the first state constitutions were now revised on the grounds of certain technical deficiencies. Jefferson, for example, complained in his *Notes on Virginia* because too much power was granted to the legislature at the expense of the other branches of the state government. This was a general characteristic of the Revolutionary constitutions which was gradually corrected. In Pennsylvania, the most conspicuous case of plenary legislative authority, the new Constitution of 1790 substituted a bicameral legislature for the former single house and also provided a single executive with a limited veto power. Any concentration of power, Jefferson believed, was "precisely the definition of despotic government." And the fact that it was exercised by a large membership was no help, because "one hundred and seventy-three despots [the number of Virginia legislators] would surely be as oppressive as one." Jefferson summed up his criticism of this part of the Virginia Constitution with the assertion, "An *elective despotism* was not the government we fought for. . . ."[21]

In a somewhat different way Jefferson's concern over an elective despotism was expressed in the complaint that the early state constitutions did not sufficiently apply the liberal principles stated in their bills of rights. Specifically, limitations on the suffrage were displeasing to those who had fought for their freedom from Britain and now found themselves in some instances governed by a native aristocracy. John Bach McMaster pointed out in his *History* that "During the ten years which followed the inauguration of Washington eight constitutions were made or amended, and by almost every one the rights of man were extended."[22] Since the Federalists controlled the machinery of government, including the legislatures in most of the states, the Republican opposition was eager to revamp the state governments by constitutional changes.

Liberalization of the requirements for voting, plus the factional strife of Federalists and Republicans, generated increasing interest on the part of the voters in the late 1790's. The determination of who should vote was, of course, a state and not a federal matter until the adoption of the Fifteenth Amendment after the Civil War. The secret ballot, though not unknown in the colonial period when elections were mainly *viva voce*, first came into more general use after the Revolution and then only in some of the states, notably New York, New Jersey, Maryland, and Kentucky. In some states aliens probably voted; others tried to exclude naturalized citizens from the suffrage.

Although in Virginia after the Revolution, Jefferson estimated that one half the potential voters were disqualified by property tests, this was not true in some of the northern states. Figures for Massachusetts and Pennsylvania in the 1790's indicate that about 18 per cent of the white population was qualified to vote and that this included the overwhelming majority of the white males over 21. In New York in 1790, from 65 to 70 per cent of the adult males could vote for members of the lower house, but only half that number for senators and governor. Despite the limitations of property or tax payment, the qualified voters were almost as numerous as they would have been with universal white manhood suffrage. There were, however, geographic discriminations against certain areas within the states and additional limitations on voting for the governors or members of the upper houses of the legislatures, which further restricted the average person's suffrage. But the point is that voting was often more limited by indifference than by law. Thus to 1798 it is estimated that only 5 per cent of the New England population voted, but by the turn of the century the figure rose to 8 per cent without any modification in the suffrage requirements.[23]

The chief changes in the qualifications for voting that were made by the states after the Revolution were the elimination of religious tests and the substitution of tax payment as an alternative to the ownership of property. Some states, particularly those where the frontier influence was strong, went even further in liberalizing their suffrage. For example, the new states of Vermont and Kentucky came into the Union with universal manhood suffrage. New Hampshire, in successive constitutional revisions, moved from a property qualification to simple tax payment and then to virtually no restriction on manhood suffrage. Most of the older states still required at least tax paying or militia duty, but Tennessee, when it was admitted as a state in 1796, insisted that voters possess a freehold. Ohio, however, required only the payment of county taxes, which might be commuted by work on the roads. In the South both South Carolina and Georgia made substantial revisions of their old constitutions following the federal Constitutional Convention. Although South Carolina resisted the demands of the frontier back country for a fairer distribution of representation in the legislature, the property qualifications for holding office were somewhat reduced, and the religious test of Protestantism was dropped entirely. Indeed, the new South Carolina Constitution granted perfect freedom of worship, declaring that "The free exercise and enjoyment of religious profession and worship, without discrimination or preference, shall forever hereafter be allowed within this state to all mankind. . . ." While South Carolina retained a property qualification for voting with a tax-paying alternative, Georgia in its revised constitution lowered the qualifications for voting to simple tax paying and residence. At the same time, however, it raised the qualifications for holding office.[24]

Increasing attention to the political rights of the common man was paralleled by a growing concern over his social and economic needs and status. Thus the years around the turn of the century witnessed the rise of a broad movement for humanitarian reform. In part this reform movement reflected the continuance of the humane ideals of the eighteenth-century Enlightenment. But even more it drew support from the religious revival which took place after 1800. A multitude of voluntary associations sprang up in the first quarter of the nineteenth century, founded by religious and business-minded reformers who believed that, though poverty and evil were misfortunes which could not be eliminated, they might be alleviated through well-organized Christian charity. The social reform movements of the period were conservative as well as religious in motivation in the sense that they were a result of upper-class direction and leadership rather than of popular democratic pressures. In some ways the whole notion of humanitarian reform was an anti-democratic abandonment of the concepts of progress and perfectibility for the alternative philosophy of palliating evils and ills regarded as inevitable. Thus colonization for Negroes, prisons for criminals, and almshouses and hospitals for the poor and diseased were all essentially compromises with ideal notions of a democratic equality which might eliminate slavery, crime, and poverty. These charitable endeavors continued to be more popular with the upper-class aristocracy than with the working people, whose leaders stressed equal rights in regard to voting, property, and education as the solution to their ills.

Particularly shocking to democratic believers in a simple and virtuous republican form of government was the development in the new nation of a variety of social and class distinctions. The Society of the Cincinnati, a self-perpetuating hereditary organization of Revolutionary War officers founded in 1783, provoked a storm of criticism on the grounds of its undemocratic and militaristic nature. The Cincinnati revived the old fears, inspired by a mixture of fact and rumor after the American Revolution, that a small group of officers might attempt a military coup and establish a monarchical government over the states. In Europe as well as America, the Cincinnati was looked upon as an anomalous institution and a strange departure from the declared ideals of the new nation. At home its opponents included the two Adamses, Elbridge Gerry, John Jay, and Thomas Jefferson. Jefferson, for example, believed it an undemocratic organization, incompatible with the Revolutionary spirit of liberty and equality. Washington, although he accepted the presidency of the Cincinnati, suggested fundamental changes in its constitution designed to keep it out of politics and to minimize the hereditary feature of its membership.[25]

In Philadelphia, the capital of the United States in the 1790's, a Republican court developed around the President and Mrs. Washington. John Adams thought that Washington should be addressed as "His Majesty, the President." Without going that far, Washington himself nevertheless assumed a ceremonial dignity which democrats considered hardly compatible with the head of a republican government. Once when Mrs. Washington found a spot on her wall just above a sofa, she is supposed to have reproached her niece for entertaining "a filthy democrat."[26]

In contrast to the society of Philadelphia, in western Pennsylvania, far removed from the Federalist social and political aristocracy, democracy reared its head in the form of bitter protests against the hated excise tax on whiskey. Western farmers and distillers took matters into their own hands by refusing to pay the tax and forcibly resisting its collection. If this lawless action seemed to conservatives a demonstration of the worse side of popular democracy, to radical democrats the determined action of Hamilton and the Federalists in suppressing the revolt appeared to be based mostly on their desire to exhibit the power of the national government over the people.

(*V*)

More important at this time to democracy than domestic politics was the ideological crisis brought on by the French Revolution and the French government's request for American aid. At first, Americans hailed the storming of the Bastille and early revolutionary steps in France as a replica of their own recent revolt. But as the Revolution widened into a general European war, marked by the execution of the King and Queen and the institution of the Reign of Terror, conservative American opinion shifted. Federalists looked with horror upon the course of the Revolution abroad as an example of unchecked popular democracy, culminating in violence and despotism and the destruction of life and property. Edmund Burke's *Reflections on the French Revolution*, published in 1790, became a model for conservative attacks on democracy, and its position was quickly reflected in a wide range of American writing. William Cobbett, the English emigrant journalist better known as "Peter Porcupine," and John Fenno, editor of the Federalist *United States Gazette*, savagely attacked radical democratic ideas. Joseph Dennie of the Philadelphia *Port Folio* also lent his magazine to criticism of democracy, and in New England the celebrated group of poets known as the Hartford, or Connecticut, Wits took up the cudgels for anti-democracy and for political and religious orthodoxy. Thomas Green Fessenden, the Maine lawyer and writer, in his volume *Democracy Unveiled* warned his readers against the principles of the French Revolution.

Of the individual Americans who supported the radical democracy of the first years of the French Revolution Tom Paine was by all odds the most important. Forced to flee from England and increasingly denounced in America as a radical atheist, Paine found a temporary home in France, where he became a member of the revolutionary National Convention. Thus he managed to carry on his political agitation in three countries within the space of a generation and to live through two full-scale revolutions. Before the French Revolution degenerated into the Terror, Paine defended democracy against the attack of Burke's *Reflections* with the publication in 1791 and 1792 of the two parts of his own *Rights of Man*. In this work he continued the assault on monarchy and justification of revolutionary change which he had begun in *Common Sense*. Accusing Burke of confounding pure democracy and representative government, Paine pointed to the American example of representation engrafted upon a simple democracy as "a system of government capable of embracing and confederating all the various interests and every extent of territory and population. . . . What Athens was in miniature," he declared, "America will be in magnitude."[27]

Paine in the 1790's was a convinced democrat. Governments, he maintained, grew out of the people and were sustained in their authority by majority rule. Basing the suffrage on property holdings to the exclusion of the majority of the people, he argued, would only compel the latter to unite and seize political control. Along with equality of political rights, he advocated government support of social and economic justice. Finally, as a Deist, Paine maintained that democracy was the best form of government because it was the most natural government, the one that best fitted in with the laws of nature. It was possible and desirable because men were by nature rational and good and acted in their own best interests.

In full agreement with Paine in his apologia for democracy were a number of Democratic-Republican Societies, the first of which was organized when President Washington issued in 1793 his Proclamation of Neutrality denying American aid to the French Republic. The Societies, however, were not just an outgrowth of the French Revolution but had as their forbears the English clubs founded to commemorate the Revolution of 1688 and the Sons of Liberty and other radical organizations in both England and America. In the United States, unlike France, the issue of the 1790's was not between a monarchy or a republic, but between the conservative republicanism of the Federalists and the radical republicanism of the Jeffersonian Republicans or Democrats. It was the principles of the latter, as well as those of the French Revolution, which were defended by the Democratic-Republican Societies. For the Jeffersonian Anti-Federalists the societies were a means of organizing a political party to oppose the intrenched Federalists, who controlled the administrative and judicial machinery of most of the local and state, as well as national, governments.[28]

The great debate over democracy was given a new dramatic intensity therefore by the bitter division of American opinion over the French Revolution. Washington was openly critical of the Democratic-Republican Societies, and in his Farewell Address he earnestly pleaded that his countrymen avoid the dangers of excessive factionalism at home and alliances abroad. However sound this advice, it seemed also to be a parting Federalist thrust at the Jeffersonians. In the succeeding Adams administration the crisis in foreign relations led to the undeclared naval war with France and to the passage of the Naturalization, Alien, and Sedition Acts. These laws extended the residence period before an alien could become a citizen from five to 14 years, provided for the deportation of dangerous aliens in peacetime and their imprisonment in war, and made it an offense to indulge in public criticism of the President and Congress. The measures were anti-democratic in their violation of traditional individual liberties and in their effort to suppress or weaken the political opposition. Thus they transgressed both minority rights and the will of a potential majority. But in the Kentucky and Virginia Resolutions, Jefferson and Madison effectively defended the democratic position, and the two sets of Resolutions became a rallying principle in the election of 1800 which brought Jefferson to the Presidency.

(*VI*)

Jeffersonian democracy in the eyes of the Federalists was synonymous with French Revolutionary Jacobinism and atheism. As the Democratic-Republicans made election gains even in New England, the stronghold of Federalism, the dismay of the conservative leaders was complete. In Connecticut Noah Webster denied the doctrine of popular sovereignty. Expansion of the suffrage, he feared, corrupted good government. While all men should have the equal protection of the laws, he did not believe that they should have equal power to make the law. In Massachusetts Fisher Ames, the most vocal of the Federalist political leaders, echoed John Adams' earlier criticisms of democracy. In discussing the recent democratic changes in France, and in the United States under Jefferson, Ames remarked bitterly: "Our country is too big for union, too sordid for patriotism, too democratic for liberty. What is to become of it, he who made it best knows. Its vice will govern it, by practising upon its folly. This is ordained for democracies. . . ." Comparing ancient Rome, Revolutionary France, and the United States, Ames argued that democracies degenerated inevitably into military tyrannies. Like Adams, he believed that all simple governments were despotisms, "and of all despotisms a democracy, though the least durable, is the most violent."[29]

From the Louisiana Purchase in 1803 to the close of the War of

1812, the unhappy New England Federalists flirted with the idea of seceding from the Union and forming some kind of Northeastern Confederacy. Toward the close of Jefferson's second administration, in their hostility to his embargo policy, the Federalists organized a number of Washington Benevolent Societies. Each applicant for membership in these societies was asked to take an oath to preserve the Constitution of the United States "against the inroads of despotism, monarchy, aristocracy, and *democracy*," and to be faithful to the principles of the Washington and Adams administrations. The member was then given copies of the Constitution and Washington's Farewell Address.[30]

Despite all this furor, it is probable that the Federalists in their dismay and the Republicans in their rejoicing exaggerated the significance of what Jefferson termed "the great revolution of 1800." Indeed, Hamilton was the more correct in his prediction that "Mr. Jefferson's character warrants the expectation of a temporizing rather than a violent system."[31] Although Jefferson in office did not overthrow the whole Federalist program, he did make important changes along the lines of his own theories of agrarian democracy and republican simplicity. His famous assault on the judiciary, of which the Federalists made much, was well in accord with prevailing democratic sentiment. In the states, as well as in the national government, Federalist judges with their life tenure were in a position to thwart the will of the voters. Accordingly the Democratic-Republicans supported the growing movement to place constitutional limitations on office-holding, and Jefferson himself adhered to his stated view that two terms should be the limit on the Presidency.

Jefferson's major contribution was that he turned American government and society once again in a democratic direction. In his Inaugural Address he pointed to the strength of America as a rich and rising nation, and he asked his countrymen to

> bear in mind this sacred principle, that though the will of the majority is in all cases to prevail, that will to be rightful must be reasonable; that the minority possess their equal rights, which equal law must protect, and to violate would be oppression.

Spelling these rights out in detail, Jefferson proceeded to summarize the essential features of a liberal democratic government—equal justice, limited power, and freedom of the individual in all his pursuits. Indulging in his famous conciliatory remark, "We are all Republicans, we are all Federalists," Jefferson further declared: "Let us, then, with courage and confidence pursue our own Federal and Republican principles, our attachment to union and representative government."

Despite Jefferson's fond hopes of tranquillity and felicity in his administration, the foreign situation continued to provoke domestic discord and to involve Jefferson himself in measures which were hardly consonant with his own liberal and democratic principles. The unrelenting Federalist opposition gained new electoral support from the growing sectional dislike of Jefferson's embargo and foreign policies. Equally unhappy were some of the old-line Jeffersonian leaders in the South, figures like John Randolph of Roanoke and John Taylor of Caroline. To such agrarian believers in limited government and strict constructionism, the Democratic-Republicans were coming dangerously close to the Federalist theory of a nationalistic consolidated government. Although not radical democratic levelers, Taylor and Randolph and their group did not believe that the government should bestow its favors on any special interest and thus produce an inequality. Agriculture they did not regard as such a special interest, because a nation of small agrarian property owners needed no extra governmental protection. Moreover, a limited government could not provide the economic support to build an industrial order. Wealth, John Taylor agreed with his Federalist foe John Adams, " 'is the great machine for governing the world.' Hence wealth, like suffrage, must be considerably distributed, to sustain a democratick republick. . . ."[32]

Although Jefferson himself had much sympathy in principle with such views, he was forced by the exigencies of war and office to modify some of his most cherished convictions. As his successors among the Democratic-Republican Presidents, aided by Chief Justice Marshall and the Supreme Court, moved ever farther in a nationalist direction and away from the original philosophy of the Jeffersonian Republicans, a political and economic revolution seemed to be taking place. Manufacturing and machinery were making inroads upon an agrarian society. Encouraged by the growth of a nascent industrialism and moving frontier, a new democratic order was coming into being to influence the course of American political and social life in the era from Jackson to Lincoln.

CHAPTER FOUR

Toward a New Order

IN THE Middle Period of American history, roughly the years from the War of 1812 to the Civil War, a new democratic order gradually took form. This was an era of expansion in which the nation pushed its borders to the Pacific and began to people the Mississippi Valley. Immigrants added to the growing native population, helping to furnish a needed labor force for factories as well as farms. Exalted by the sweep of progress, the ferment of reform seemed to touch every aspect of American life and thought by the 1830's and '40's. Science, education, religion, and politics—all felt the impress of democratic ideas, while American literature and culture enjoyed its first renaissance.

The age of Jackson and the triumph of democracy are usually regarded as simultaneous and synonymous events in American history. For this view there is, of course, much justification. In the second quarter of the nineteenth century in the United States, for the first time the people could be said to rule. Colonial leanings toward democracy, already quickened by the Revolutionary and Jeffersonian eras, now approached fulfillment in the Jacksonian revolution. In comparison with the democracy of the Jeffersonians, that of Jackson and his followers was more radical and equalitarian. The Jacksonians, as Arthur Schlesinger, Jr., has pointed out, "moderated that side of Jeffersonianism which talked of agricultural virtue, independent proprietors, 'natural' property, abolition of industrialism, and expanded immensely that side which talked of economic equality, the laboring classes, human rights and the control of industrialism."[1]

This shift from an eighteenth- to a nineteenth-century version of democracy created certain problems. Along with its democracy, progress, and reform, the Jacksonian era also witnessed a crude economic materialism, intolerant nationalism, and instances of mob rule. These aspects of American life were what led Tocqueville and other observers of the passing scene to offer their critical judgments of United States democracy. The illiberal side of Jacksonian democracy was fully apparent in the attitude of the administration and the American people toward such minority groups as the Indians, immigrants, Catholics, and abolitionists. Perhaps Jacksonian democracy, like other successful mass reform movements, depended too much on the subordination of individual rights to the majority will. In any event there was an evident ruthlessness in the way in which the Jacksonians identified democracy with nationalistic demands and carried it forward under the banners of manifest destiny and reform.

Under Jefferson, American democracy had been limited by the liberal individualist tenets of the eighteenth century. Its ideal society was one of small independent farmers plus an intellectual planter aristocracy. As Jefferson made clear, such an agrarian society had no room for a population of urban masses, the inevitable accompaniment of the rise of manufacturing and an industrial economy. Elevated to national power after 1800, Jefferson and his successors were forced increasingly to modify, and even to abandon, much of their liberal agrarian philosophy. In its place, in the years after the War of 1812, an era of Republican commercial nationalism arose to serve as a kind of interlude before the triumph of Jacksonian democracy. In other words, the Jeffersonian notion of a simple agrarian economy with its minimal government yielded first place to the more positive needs of commerce: tariffs, a navy, internal improvements, a national bank. In the long run, however, these Whiggish policies proved unsatisfactory to all the major economic groups in the country except the business community in the northeastern part of the United States. As the different regions developed special sectional interests, the economic nationalism of the Era of Good Feelings fell apart. In its place Southern cotton planters, Western frontier farmers, and Eastern workingmen accepted the new political alignment sketched out by the Jacksonian politicians. Despite the frequent protests and disaffections on the part of some of the varied Jackson following, the Democratic party managed to keep alive its heritage and hold together, much better than its Whig opposition, until the coming of the Civil War.

The appeal of Jackson's program is easier to understand if it is considered, not in terms of labor or farmers versus capital, but as a program for the lower middle classes, whether urban or rural. While Jackson, unlike Jefferson, accepted industrialism and the support of the urban workingman, this did not mean that the Jacksonians gave up entirely the goal of an agrarian society. However, the agrarianism of the Jacksonian Democrats was broad enough to include small businessmen, petty traders, and prosperous artisans, as well as independent farmers. This large and growing segment of the population stood to gain most from the Jacksonian war on monopoly and privilege. With the resources of the West available for exploitation, and with manufacturing entering upon a century of expansion, the lower middle class could afford to be capitalist in its inclinations and hopes for the future. Jacksonian laissez faire and equal rights were closer to the needs and desires of the great mass of the people than the Whiggish economic theories of Henry Clay or John Quincy Adams. Although Clay and his nationalist school of later Jeffersonians sought to make the old Hamiltonian Federalist program popular by broadening its economic base, the Jacksonian philosophy had a greater appeal in an America that was still young and expanding.

Andrew Jackson became the symbol of his age, but the symbol, John William Ward writes, "was not the creation of Andrew Jackson from Tennessee, or of the Democratic party. The symbol was the creation of the times. To describe the early nineteenth century as the age of Jackson misstates the matter. The age was not his. He was the age's."[2] Jackson united in his own heroic image the democratic values prized alike by frontiersmen and workingmen, but the origins and victory of this modern-type democracy in 1828 can also be explained in more prosaic terms. As Wilfred Binkley notes in his account of American political parties:

> It was the depression of the twenties that had provided the seed-bed of what has since come to be known as the Jacksonian movement. Keen political observers perceived deep-seated stirrings of both the rural and urban masses accentuated by the prevailing hard times. A profound conviction that the ruling class had betrayed the people's interests was taking possession of the common man. A new species of politicians expert in canalizing mass movements began to emerge and sweep the horizon in search of a national leader.[3]

(II)

In the political sphere Jackson was the beneficiary and not the creator of an aggressive democratic upsurge. This rising political democracy, in turn, encouraged reform movements which affected the social and economic life of the mass of the American people. In many of these changes Jacksonian democracy played an important role, but the rise of the common man politically was the necessary prelude and not the aftermath of Jackson's Presidency. Thus Marvin Meyers is able to say:

> Jacksonian Democracy is rightfully associated with "the rise of the common man"; it is wrongfully identified with the fight for the acceptance of the principles of politicial democracy, which had been fought and won before Jackson's party came on the scene.[4]

The decade before Jackson's election in 1828 was especially significant for the growth of democracy. New popular pressures associated with industrialism and urban labor, plus the continuing influence of the radical individualism of the West, helped to speed a political revolution. The extension of the suffrage, creation of more equal election districts, popular choice of Presidential electors, and adoption of new or revised state constitutions were all characteristics of an age that was forcing politicians to devise new techniques of manipulation in order to influence public opinion.

During the period before Jackson's national triumph, a bitter battle for constitutional reform was fought in many of the states. Hard times following the Panic of 1819 and the political demands of the returning war veterans encouraged democratic tendencies, but the hold of intrenched conservatism in the seaboard states was also strong. Connecticut in 1818 adopted a constitution which liberalized the suffrage and separated church and state but at the same time retained hostages to conservatism in the form of the requirements of good character plus either the payment of taxes, ownership of property, or service in the militia. Massachusetts and Virginia both resisted the movement for universal suffrage in their constitutional conventions and kept tax-paying or property qualifications for voting. The Virginia Constitutional Convention of 1829 was also disappointing to the democratic forces in that state because of its failure to provide for greater representation of the populous western counties. Everywhere in the states of the old colonial South, the western back country areas were exerting pressure for democratic reforms, but the growing Southern sensitivity over the slavery question was a barrier to political change. In Virginia it was feared that a more democratic and representative suffrage would result in legislation for gradual emancipation. In the South free Negroes had not voted as a matter of custom and social pressure, but after the 1830's, outside New England, they began to be excluded by statute in the North as well as the South.[5]

In all of the state struggles over constitutional revision during the 1820's, the democratic movement won its most clear-cut victory in New York. Although the old Federalist aristocracy had been a minority in the state since 1801, it still dominated certain sections and continued to wield extensive powers through its control of the judiciary. An especial Federalist stronghold was the Council of Revision, made up of all the judges of the state supreme court, the state chancellor, and the governor. This unique body was able to veto or revamp bills passed by the legislature. In 1820 it sought unsuccessfully to avert or postpone the call for the constitutional convention due to meet the following year. In a famous appeal to this convention to retain the old aristocratic order of things, Chancellor James Kent warned the delegates of the dangers of democracy. Profoundly distrustful of the supposed virtue of the people, Kent feared that universal suffrage would merely encourage "the poor to covet a share in the plunder of the rich." "The tendency of universal suffrage," he declared, "is to jeopardize the rights of property, and the principles of liberty." But despite the learning and eloquence of the Chancellor, the New York Constitution of 1821 swept away virtually all restrictions on the suffrage and reduced the property qualifications for holding high state office to a simple freehold. Kent himself was forced into political retirement by the abolition of the Council of Revision, in which he had been a leading conservative voice.[6]

In 1826 the few remaining limitations on full political democracy were eliminated by further changes in the state constitution, and universal manhood suffrage in the Empire State became a fact but for one curious exception. In New York, slaves when manumitted often had some property and thus qualified for the suffrage, usually voting for their former Federalist masters. When the property requirement was removed for the whites, it was kept for Negroes despite the protests of old Federalists like Peter Jay. The Negro vote was now, of course, less important, but it continued to favor conservative candidates. The Democrats meanwhile remained opposed to Negro suffrage, chiefly because of the hostility of their labor supporters.[7]

In the Ohio and Mississippi Valleys a tier of new states was admitted to the Union after the War of 1812. Although the constitutions of these states were more democratic than those of most of the older states along the Atlantic seaboard, it was particularly in the area bordering the Ohio, "the valley of democracy," that the new liberal tendencies were carried furthest. The Northwest Ordinance did not prescribe democracy in the early stages of territorial government, but it was democratic in the way it provided for the subsequent easy transition to full statehood. The Pennsylvania and Kentucky constitutions of the 1790's served as models for the Ohio and Indiana constitutions. Indiana, settled by squatters and small landowners, adopted the most democratic state constitution and, together with Illinois, Alabama, and Missouri, provided at the outset for universal manhood suffrage.[8]

By 1820 liberalization of the remaining restrictions on white manhood suffrage had been carried to the point where in most of the older states the simple payment of taxes was accepted in place of a property or religious qualification. Connecticut in 1818, Massachusetts in 1820, and New York in 1821 all shifted from a freehold to a tax-paying requirement, and the freehold as a qualification for voting remained only in North Carolina, Rhode Island, and Virginia. In the latter state the restriction became more burdensome as the small farmer tended to sell out his land holdings to the large planter. Even eligible voters, however, frequently failed to avail themselves of their privilege until political partisanship revived following the one-party rule of the Era of Good Feelings. Voting therefore was often more a result of the pressures of rival political parties and better modes of transportation than of eased suffrage requirements. In 1823 in Pennsylvania, which required only the payment of taxes, the creditable number of 154,000 persons voted out of 208,000 eligibles. By this time many of the states had such a trifling tax requirement that the change to universal manhood suffrage added comparatively few names to the voter's rolls. In New York in 1827 the extension of voting from the ratable basis to full manhood suffrage increased the enfranchised by only 15 per cent over the large number who could already vote under the new constitution of 1821. Eased requirements for voting, however, were often applied only to choosing members of the lower house of the state legislature or the federal House of Representatives. When universal suffrage permitted the average voter to extend his choice to include the higher state offices, it became a more important democratic device. This was also true when it was accompanied by the ending of geographic discriminations against frontier areas, and when it permitted the vote to long-term leaseholders or owners of mortgaged property who had formerly not qualified as freeholders.[9]

In most of the states the fight for a more liberal or nearly universal suffrage was won before Jackson's election to the Presidency, but the process of a democratic revision of the various states' constitutional machinery continued into the 1830's and '40's. In the South between 1830 and 1837, there were new or revised constitutions in seven of the states. Alabama's democratic constitution was now matched by that of Mississippi, which also established universal manhood suffrage. Tennessee abolished its requirement of a freehold for voting, and the coastal states of Maryland, Virginia, and North Carolina made important changes in their constitutions. By mid-century the state and local county governments of the South had achieved considerable democracy, with governors and lesser officials subject to popular election. Only the older states of Virginia and South Carolina were able effectively to resist most of the more drastic political changes. By 1850 the remnants of property qualifications for voting had been abolished in all states save North Carolina, while low tax restrictions on the suffrage were still found in only six of the states. Religious tests applied to Catholics were also modified or repealed. In New York the Constitution of 1846 took an important step toward economic democracy by abandoning the peculiar system of feudal land tenure on some of the large estates in the upper Hudson River Valley. This remnant of the Dutch patroon system had occasioned the bitter anti-rent wars of the early 1840's. The New York Convention also debated the question of married women retaining their rights to personal property—a first step in the feminist crusade for economic and political equality. Two years later the Married Women's Property bill became law.[10]

In Rhode Island in this same period, popular dissatisfaction at the failure of the state to make any revision of its old charter government, dating from colonial times, resulted in the adoption of a People's Constitution with universal suffrage. A violent struggle then ensued between the conservative state government and the popular party led by Thomas Dorr. Although the Dorrites were suppressed, their demands finally achieved recognition in 1843 when Rhode Island gave practical universal suffrage to native citizens. Naturalized citizens, however, still had to meet a property qualification. This type of discrimination spread in the 1850's as anti-immigrant feeling reached its peak. Massachusetts and Connecticut both instituted literacy tests as a device to help exclude naturalized citizens from voting. On the other hand, Wisconsin and Michigan offered the vote to aliens who had declared their intention of becoming citizens. Thus in the West the immigrant who was scorned in the East was made doubly welcome.[11]

(III)

Widening the suffrage under the new and revised state constitutions adopted in the 1820's and '30's was a notable democratic achievement. Less obvious, but hardly less important in determining the future course of American democracy, was a series of more subtle political changes which occurred in the Jacksonian period. A new concept of executive versus legislative power, changes in the method of choosing Presidential electors, the rise of nominating conventions, and the redivision of political parties again into two major contending organizations were some of the devices which helped to outline the political boundaries of the new democratic order.

The constitutions of the new states after the War of 1812 provided for an elective governor with a limited veto power. The early American fear of a strong executive authority had diminished, and there was now a counter tendency to make the governor, elected by all the voters, rather than the legislature, chosen by districts, the defender of popular rights. President Jackson also acted on the premise that he had a mandate from the entire electorate and was thus more representative than Congress of the interests of the nation as a whole. His use of the veto and appointing powers and his criticisms of the Supreme Court illustrated his positive conception of the Presidential office. At the same time the demand grew in the states for the periodic election of new judges and for the end of lifetime judicial tenure. Thus the democratic upsurge of the twenties and thirties partly modified the system of checks and balances and the traditional relations of the various governmental branches with the electorate. The concept of indirect representative government was weakened in favor of a more thorough popular democracy. Proposals for this type of change in the federal government included a single Presidential term, a direct popular vote for President, and the exclusion of former members of Congress from appointive offices.

Although these suggested ideas for amending the Constitution failed, the people did gain the right to choose directly the members of the Electoral College.[12]

In the first years of the Republic, Presidential electors were usually selected by the state legislatures. Although the Constitutional Convention seemingly desired to check democracy in part by interposing the Electoral College between the people and the President, it is not certain that they expected the further indirection and check of the choice of electors by state legislatures instead of by the voters generally. The Constitution prescribed that members of the House of Representatives should be chosen by persons entitled to vote for the most numerous branch of the state legislatures, but it did not fix the qualifications for voting in Presidential elections. This matter was simply left in the hands of the states, which adopted an extraordinary variety of methods for choosing members of the Electoral College. Some states were divided into districts in which the people were allowed to vote for individual electors. In others legislatures nominated a slate of electors, while in some states the two methods were combined, with a portion of the electors voted upon in local districts and the remainder picked at large either by the people or by the legislatures. Ultimately, of course, if no Presidential candidate received a majority of the electoral vote, the decision rested with the House of Representatives, voting in the undemocratic fashion of one ballot for each state regardless of its size or population.

The evils of this system, or lack of system, were as annoying to the politicians who had to cope with them as they were to the mass of the citizenry whose will was at least in part thwarted. Thus the complexity of the method of voting often obscured the real popular choice, and if it had not been for the development of the two political parties of Federalists and Republicans, few Presidential candidates would have been likely to receive a majority in the Electoral College. From this confusion there emerged first the general ticket in which the whole slate of electors was chosen either by the people or the legislature. Although such a system meant the complete loss in the Electoral College of the minority votes in the various states, it at least prevented a minority from choosing most of a state's electors because of inequable electoral districts or political maneuvering in the legislature. The second reform came when the legislatures bowed to the people's demand that the voters be allowed to choose the electors directly. By 1824 only six states still permitted the legislatures to make this choice, and in 1832 only the single state of South Carolina clung to the original method.[13]

An allied political change, which was hailed as a democratic victory in the Jacksonian era, was the abolition of the caucus system and the substitution of the convention as a means of nominating party candidates. On a local level, conventions or meetings had long been used in the North to put forward candidates. Otherwise the aspirant himself or a friend might present his name for public consideration. On the national scene the Federalists and Anti-Federalists in Congress each met in caucus to suggest its Presidential candidate, who then became by custom the party's nominee. The caucus or some similar system of suggesting candidates was necessary to avoid an excessive number of office-seekers which would prevent any candidate from receiving a majority or even a large plurality. Moreover, as the states began to give up the district choice of candidates in favor of the general ticket, state-wide nomination, either in caucus or convention, became desirable. As early as 1800, in Pennsylvania, representatives from the various towns were sent to county conventions to nominate candidates, but on a state and national level the legislative caucus continued to prevail. However, it was rapidly falling into disfavor as an undemocratic device. Typical of the new feeling toward the caucus was the editorial comment in 1816 which complained:

> The people are no longer anybody in this famous land of liberty. They are taken to the market like oxen and like them bartered away. Sixty-five member of Congress usurp the power to make a President, and to give an exclusive right to Virginia in the Chief Magistrate. It is unnecessary to appoint electors; for if a caucus nomination is to be obligatory, electors are no more than puppets. . . . Members of Congress nominate the President, and in case of no election by the electors, members of Congress elect him: so that first and last a President is made by members of Congress. And this is called a democracy![14]

In national politics "King Caucus" was overthrown in 1824. Since the Republicans were the only nation-wide party in James Monroe's second term, if their members in Congress had been allowed to decide his successor, there again would have been no contest. The intense personal rivalry of several aspirants to the White House intervened at this juncture, and the caucus was accordingly ignored in favor of nominations in state legislatures or in popular mass meetings. By 1832 this system in turn was succeeded by the formal national nominating conventions. Party conventions from the local and state to the national level now came to be regarded as a means of insuring the doctrine of popular sovereignty and of widening the people's power of effective choice. At the same time the adoption by the parties of national platforms helped to educate the voters and lessen the degree of secrecy in the political process.

In the enthusiasm for rule by the people, even the spoils system was hailed by Jacksonians as a democratic device. They justified, or at least rationalized, appointment by patronage on the theory that one man was as good as another, and in a democracy all deserved an equal chance to gain a government position. Nothing could be more equlitarian than a rotation of offices, and, if this was the goal, the spoils system was logically less open to objection than the aristocratic method of permitting a permanent tenure in the civil service. No one, Jackson declared in his first annual message to Congress, had a property right to a government position.

During Jackson's Presidency the old Democratic-Republican party split into the two new rival groups of the Democrats and the National-Republicans, or Whigs. The latter, likening Jackson to a monarch and calling him King Andrew the First, took the name of the historic English party opposed to royal prerogative. Jackson's critics found democracy, in the sense of the protection of minority rights, sadly defective under a President who encouraged the forcible removal of the Indians to the Far West and who denied abolitionists the use of the mails. On the other hand, Jackson's personalized concept of his high office and the great popularity of his important policies with the majority of the people could be interpreted as democracy of a different sort. In any case, Democrat seemed a better description of Jackson's party following than the old Jeffersonian term Republican.

One measure of Jackson's popularity, as well as of the new interest in politics generated by a more liberal suffrage and well-defined political parties, was the increase in the popular vote for

President. The aggregate vote for all candidates rose rapidly after 1824, when Adams, Jackson, Clay, and Crawford polled only 356,000 ballots. In both 1828 and 1832, Jackson and his opponents together drew more than a million persons to the polls, and in 1836 the total vote was almost a million and a half. Thus in the 12 years in which Jackson's name was actively involved, the electorate increased by well over a million voters, while in the next decade an average of over two million persons voted in the Presidential years. Between 1828 and 1848 the popular vote trebled, while the population did not quite double.

As President, Jackson pursued policies that were both popular and consistent with his own interpretation of democracy as majority rule and limited government. In his veto of the bank recharter bill Jackson criticized the Bank of the United States as an aristocratic and monopolistic sectional institution. Against South Carolina's states' rights and nullification of the tariff, he threatened the use of force to support the will of the majority and the sovereign power of the nation. But the South, with its distrust of centralization, could approve Jackson's general concept of limited government. His cautiousness in respect to further projects for canals and roads at federal expense, although seeming to oppose a traditional Western interest, proved popular in the long run. Western farmers favored free land to preserve democratic opportunity rather than expensive internal improvements necessitating a large federal budget. Landowners feared taxes for improvements they did not want, and they also distrusted banks and accepted Jackson's hard money policy.

Internal improvements at government expense were susceptible of democratic support only insofar as they filled a real public need which could not be supplied by private capital. By the close of Jackson's Presidency this was no longer the case. The state and federal governments' aid had encouraged inflation and the overbuilding of canals, while the railroads were soon to supply a competitive means of transportation. Since the railroad was not a public conveyance in the same sense as a road or river, public support for its construction could more easily be questioned. Finally the Panic of 1837 called a halt to further immediate governmental support for internal improvements and gave belated justification to Jackson's conservative economic ideas.

Among the radical left wing of the Jacksonian movement, laissez faire and hard money were already popular doctrines. The *Working Man's Advocate* and Loco-Foco Democrats stressed the achievement of equal rights and believed that governmental activity should be confined to the abolition of monopoly and privilege. Although Jackson as President showed little interest in labor, many of the intellectuals and reformers who, in default of any strong organization of labor, spoke for the workingmen's interests had aims similar to those of the administration.

State economic policy in the period did not deviate markedly from Jackson's negative program regarding internal improvements. Democrats emphasized equality of economic opportunity. They supported free banking legislation and general incorporation laws designed to make it easier for anyone to begin a commercial enterprise. As the Handlins point out in their study of Massachusetts, "Democratic unwillingness to confine the corporation to a favored few had dispersed it among many holders and that in turn had separated it from the state."[15] Outside the field of transportation, which was looked upon as vital to agriculture in the West, laissez faire prevailed in most economic matters in the United States before the Civil War. The Jacksonians, in their hostility to monopolies and economic privilege, made a partial return to the original agrarianism of Jefferson.

(IV)

In the Middle Period a full-scale retreat to Jeffersonian agrarianism was, however, impossible. Jacksonian democracy differed from its Jeffersonian antecedents in that it had to adjust its principles to the growth of a vigorous industrialism. Though machines and factories were not unknown in the preceding generations, technology did not pick up much momentum until the era between Jackson and Lincoln. Science, and particularly the practical application of scientific knowledge to the building of machines and the fashioning of what came to be called technology, had tremendous importance for democracy. In their *Rise of American Civilization* the Beards called attention to the coincidence, and even probable causal relationship between scientific progress and the rise of democracy in the United States as well as Europe in the second quarter of the nineteenth century.

More than that, science pointed the way to progressive democracy in its warfare against starvation, poverty, disease, and ignorance, indicating how classes and nations long engaged in strife among themselves might unite to wring from nature the secret of security and the good life. It was science, not paper declarations relating to the idea of progress, that at last made patent the practical methods by which democracy could raise the standard of living for the great masses of the people.[16]

Contemporary writers and scientists, reviving the admonitions of Sir Francis Bacon, stressed the ways in which technology could be of practical benefit to mankind. In the free institutions of the United States some saw an especial incentive to the inventor. Thomas Ewbank, an English immigrant and businessman who became Commissioner of Patents in the United States, particularly insisted upon the social significance of science and invention. In any conflict of science and religion he proposed that the latter should yield, and he also predicted that technology would ultimately make Southern slavery obsolete. Although few went as far as Ewbank, the great possibilities of science were sufficient to disarm most of its potential critics. Social and religious reformers and labor spokesmen, it is true, denounced the autocratic discipline of the machine system and the loss of individuality which accompanied factory toil and life in the city, but, if industrialism threatened the American workingman with the slums and degradation already so apparent in England, it also offered new opportunities along with the risks. Only an expanding economic system could provide the bulk of the citizenry with the chance to rise quickly on the social and economic scale. In America by the 1830's a growing industrialism, in conjunction with the westward movement, supplied the best outlet for continued economic and social progress.[17]

Edward Everett and Daniel Webster were only the two most eloquent of the public men who defended the democracy of the new industrial order. In their talks before groups of young mechanics and tradesmen, and in their more formal patriotic addresses, Everett and Webster stressed the opportunities being opened up by the machine age. Improved printing presses, turning out cheap books and newspapers, made possible for the first time in history a truly mass culture. At least in theory, the advantages of industrialism were available to all. The poor boy, it was argued, could become an inventor or factory owner more easily than he could become a landed proprietor, except, perhaps, in the more remote regions of the West. Even the corporation was pointed to as a democratic device which opened the way to a more diversified ownership of property.

Labor spokesmen, though differing from their business counterparts in their analyses of industrialism, nevertheless agreed that the use of science and machinery offered the common man the means to a fuller life. At first, however, a change was necessary in the existing social and economic order. Control of industry by a small minority prevented the mass of the people from realizing the democratic possibilities inherent in scientific progress. Utopian Socialist followers of Robert Owen and labor spokesmen in the Northeastern states stressed the importance of equal rights in politics, in education, and in the ownership of land. When Owen's son, Robert Dale Owen, a leader in the labor cause, was accused by a correspondent in the *Working Man's Advocate* of being an enemy of technological progress, he replied that the fault was not in machinery but in its perversion under the contemporary, commercialized economic system. In his pamphlet *Wealth and Misery* the young Owen wrote:

> I see that the immense modern powers of production *might be* a blessing, but that they *are* a curse. I see that machinery, instead of aiding the laborer, is brought into the market against him; and that it thus reduces his wages and injures his situation.[18]

As even radical thinkers discarded Utopian agrarian notions which they knew bore little reality in an America being rapidly transformed by the effects of science and technology, it is not surprising that democracy made its peace with the forces of the machine age.

(V)

In the midst of the changes in American life taking place under the impact of Jacksonian politics and the technology of a rising industrialism, the new democratic order was also being affected by an extraordinary variety of plans for social reform. Human miseries and ills which had been corrected or alleviated in an agrarian society by individuals or local church congregations now needed the attention of organized, and even professional, charities. Accordingly there were societies for the care of orphans, the blind, the deaf, and the insane, and for the redemption of juvenile offenders, criminals, and prostitutes. Religious reform was encouraged by a Sunday School Union, Home Missionary Society, and Bible and Tract Societies, while the evils of war, slavery, and drunkenness were brought under the organized attack of a number of different groups of zealous reformers. Fad or fancy, practical or impractical, few of these hopeful reform schemes was able to attract the attention or support of a majority of the American people. But, whatever the realities, reformers were undaunted in their belief that their respective programs offered the way to the salvation of mankind.

Although the relationship of reform and democracy was not always clear or compatible, there was merit to Tocqueville's view that democracy, by destroying the barriers of class and privilege, fostered a general feeling of compassion for all members of the human race. Reform programs at the same time provided important new goals for democracy, while reformers themselves often served as the conscience of society. Yet there was little that was democratic in the methods the reformers used to advance their schemes. The true reformer refused to accede to popular inertia or accept the will of an indifferent majority. Instead he felt compelled to agitate and crusade for his ideas. Often impractical and part of a small minority, the reformer was a radical before he was a democrat.

In their ideological origins democracy and the reform movement borrowed from common roots. From the eighteenth-century Enlightenment and the example of Christianity, reformers drew their confidence in the progress and perfectibility of man and his importance as an individual possessing a soul and enjoying certain natural rights. An enlightened humanitarianism and Christian charity were also reinforced by romantic and utilitarian notions of individuality and self-interest as stimuli to self-culture and self-improvement. Finally the rise of labor and the common man to economic and political power provided an important impetus to reform.

Many of the major reforms which enlisted widespread support had as their over-all purpose the completion or perfection of American democracy. Equal rights for women, freedom for the Negro, and public education for children were all looked upon as reforms intimately connected with the realization of democracy. In the case of labor, much of the reform agitation was directed against what were felt to be the undemocratic discriminations which prevented its organization in trade unions and which continued to exact militia service and imprisonment for debt. On the left wing of the labor movement, the Utopian Socialist followers of Robert Owen and Charles Fourier sought a complete reformation of society. Their communitarian experiments in socialist living were offered as laboratories of social reform, the success of which would point the way to a more perfect democracy. Although most of the reformers believed that the democratic institutions of the United States provided the best environment for testing their schemes, some became bitterly disillusioned. Majority rule was not always sympathetic to the ideas or rights of an unpopular minority. Thus the radical wing of the antislavery movement encountered widespread hostility in the North as well as in the South until the eve of the Civil War. William Lloyd Garrison and some of his fellow abolitionists felt compelled to follow a course of non-cooperation and of non-violent resistance to a government in which the democratic majority refused to extend freedom to the slave.

Historically the church and the school were two of the most vital agencies in encouraging or retarding social change. Education offered the lower classes of society a means of improvement. In the Jacksonian era the workingmen and farmers, who now possessed the ballot, used their political power to press for state systems of free common schools. From the beginning of the American Republic, the Founding Fathers had realized the connection between an educated electorate and good sound government. Jefferson, of course, was famous for his interest in seeing Virginia provide a comprehensive plan of education surmounted by a state university, but he was not alone, as Federalists and Republicans alike encouraged the establishment of a national university, state support of education, and attention to that phase of education so neglected in the colonial era —the formal training of girls and young women.

However, except in the founding of new colleges with state support in the South and by religious denominations everywhere in the United States, for a quarter of a century there was little response to the calls for educational expansion and reform. Outside New England even elementary education continued to be looked upon as a private voluntary matter. Wealthy aristocrats with liberal notions of reform contributed to the support of private or denominational charity schools. Self-culture and self-education were carried forward by societies for diffusing useful knowledge, by lyceum lecture series, and by mechanics and workingmen's institutes. In New York City the well-known Free School Society, established in 1805 by members of some of the leading Protestant denominations, assumed responsibility for the elementary schools, administering the public funds contributed by the city and state and making no discrimination between the children of the rich or poor.

By the 1830's popular pressures for more equal opportunities in education were receiving the added backing of able reformers who urged the adoption of state-wide systems of tax-supported schools. In England education was controlled by the aristocracy, while on the Continent both Napoleonic France and Prussia had subjected their class-conscious education to the dominion of the state. In the United States too, a growing American nationalism united with Jacksonian democracy in encouraging government control of education, but the federal system and democratic insistence on equality prevented either a nationalistic or class domination of education. Under the Constitution public education was a matter for the separate states, and in both the industrial East and agricultural West plans for reform were carried through in the 1830's.

Horace Mann and Henry Barnard, as state superintendents of education in Massachusetts, Rhode Island, and Connecticut, revamped the old district school system. State funds and supervision, minimum standards, and the better training, education, and remuneration of the teachers were among their important reforms. Mann especially believed that an improved system of education was vital to American democracy and social stability. He accepted as eternal truth that "In a republic ignorance is a crime; and that private immorality is not less an opprobrium to the state than it is guilt in the perpetrator." In his Annual Reports he portrayed "education as means of removing poverty and securing abundance." Mann was not a socialist or advocate of violence or revolution, but he seemed radical to many conservatives in his insistance that the wealthy classes had a responsibility for the support of genuine public education. To those who opposed the necessary state taxes, he retorted that education was "the great equalizer of the conditions of men,—the balance wheel of the social machinery. . . . It does better than to disarm the poor of their hostility towards the rich; it prevents being poor."[19]

Mann's appeals for education stressed its widespread and even contradictory character as a universal panacea. Wealthy proprietors, threatened by the leveling effects of universal suffrage, were urged by such influential conservative spokesmen as Daniel Webster and Edward Everett to support public education in order to prevent further radicalism. Mann himself, though not blind to the evils of industrialism, stressed the importance of education in the inculcation of nationalism and patriotism and in the maintenance of the economic status quo. His colleague Henry Barnard, in his *American Journal of Education*, observed that, by lending their help to public education and other reforms, men of wealth began

> to feel the luxury of doing good, to see that a wise endowment for the relief of suffering, the diffusion of knowledge. . . and the spread of religious truth is in the best sense of the term a good investment—an investment productive of the greatest amount of the highest good both to the donor and his posterity, and which makes the residue of the property from which it is taken both more secure and more valuable.[20]

Conservative self-interest in educational reform was matched by the enthusiasm of a wide variety of labor spokesmen who made the cause of public schools their own. Although some were suspicious of upper-class support of public education, most of the labor press and leadership accepted tax-supported free schools as a necessary prerequisite to a more democratic social order in which labor might rise to full economic equality. Edward Channing noted that the leaders in the movement for free public schools in the two industrial states of New York and Pennsylvania were the Utopian Socialist radicals Robert Dale Owen and Frances Wright.[21] In Pennsylvania poorer communities, even with the promise of state aid, were unable or unwilling to establish public schools, and indigent parents were often reluctant to take the pauper oath necessary to their children's education under state support. Prodded by the speeches of Thaddeus Stevens, who resembled Mann in his advocacy of complete democracy in education, Pennsylvania adopted a public school law in 1834. New Jersey followed with a statute allowing the districts to act and in the 1840's ended all distinctions between tuition and free pupils. In rural areas of New York the rate bill, under which parents of school-age children paid a special tax, continued until 1867. In New York City, Catholic Church protests against the role of the Free School Society, a Protestant group, resulted in 1840 in the stipulation that no sectarian school should receive public funds. Although this satisfied the opponents of religiously dominated education, it was disappointing to those who had hoped to see parochial schools receive state aid.

Elsewhere in the nation educational reform moved more slowly. The South lagged badly behind the rest of the country in accepting the idea of education as a public responsibility. In the West Michigan took the lead with an ambitious plan in 1817 which proposed a full program of education from the primary school to the university. "But, far too frequently," as Frederick Jackson Turner noted, "the new Western commonwealths paid only lip tribute to the relations between liberty, democracy, and the public schools."[22] In 1837 Ohio established a common school system and sent Calvin Stowe to Europe, in the footsteps of Horace Mann, to study foreign methods of education. Throughout the Old Northwest there was strong support for the concept of democracy in education. Like the reformers and workingmen in the older states of the East, democratic leaders in the West accepted education as a universal panacea. Robert Dale Owen, who settled in Indiana, where he became a Congressman and leader in the public school movement, asserted this typical philosophy of education and democracy:

> They who govern should be wise. They who govern should be educated. They who decide mighty questions should be enlightened. Then, as we value wise government, as we would have the destinies of our kind shaped by an enlightened tribunal, let the schools of the people, and the teachers who preside in these schools, and the system that prevails in these schools, be our peculiar care.[23]

But public tax support for a completely free system of common schools did not come in the West until the 1850's. In higher education the section was more generous, and it was in the North Central States of the Middle West that the state university first achieved its characteristic modern form. At the same time Oberlin College, founded in the 1830's, became the first private or state institution to open its doors in full equality to women and Negro students.

(*VI*)

In American religion in the Middle Period the separation of church and state was everywhere completed, although, to be sure, church properties continued to be exempt from taxation and certain other state ties remained. In New England the Congregational Church was disestablished. The Connecticut Constitution of 1818 guaranteed freedom of worship and provided that no person should be obligated to support a church not of his own choice. Massachusetts in 1833 amended its constitution, placing all sects on an equal footing of voluntary support, a provision which the state supreme court decided prevented any establishment. By this time religious tests for holding office were also being abandoned, although a few such disabilities, chiefly in the South, prevailed until the Civil War era.

Democracy in religion was manifest in the weakening of the old Calvinist doctrines which limited the promise of salvation to the few who were the elect of God. Unitarianism, having made deep inroads upon Congregational New England, offered strong church backing for radical individualism and social reform. Under the pressures of Jacksonian democracy and the rise of technology, people increasingly were encouraged to discard theories of supernatural intervention and to look with more favor upon science and politics as agencies for social betterment. Thus democracy seemed to contribute to a growing secularization of American religious life and feeling. Yet, at the same time, organized religion gained in membership and influence compared to the era of skepticism and hostility which had characterized the American Revolution. On the frontier the home missionary movement sought to redeem the West from its so-called barbarism. Churches which were democratic in their organization and which made provision for considerable control by the laity won increasing numbers of adherents. As Turner pointed out, "The sects which were most flourishing were those that best adjusted themselves to the rural conditions of an expanding people and represented its democratic and emotional spirit."[24] Helped by revivals and camp meetings, Methodists and Baptists and, to a lesser extent, Presbyterians dominated the frontier and provided a certain leaven of religious reform in the midst of the materialist concerns of the typical pioneer. Evangelical religion particularly encouraged support for both education and the antislavery movement in the West, while small radical sects developed religious communities similar to those of the Utopian Socialists.

The churches' emphasis upon Christian charity and humanitarian endeavors of all kinds was much less radical than the socialist insistence upon a complete and revolutionary change in society. Accepting the fact of evil and the limitations of human nature, conservative Christian thinking stressed the need for a moral reformation and the temporary alleviation of ills and suffering which could never be permanently eliminated in the temporal and physical world. Although the religious influence upon reform was fundamentally conservative, Christianity and democracy also stood upon common ground in many of their hopes for the future. Ralph Gabriel has suggested a number of parallels between the democratic faith and Christianity: for example, belief in the concepts of a fundamental law and of the free individual and a confidence in progress and the sense of mission or destiny. In more extravagant terms a contemporary religious writer and reformer, the Baptist minister Elias L. Magoon, offered his version of a synthesis of science, religion, and democracy, which he called Republican Christianity. "The present," he said, "is an age auspicious for humanity, inasmuch as good books are every where multiplied, benevolent institutions are springing up of every kind, and the divinest enfranchisement is rapidly embracing all our race."[25]

In some circles evangelical Christianity was looked upon as a threat to traditional American doctrines of the separation of church and state. The failure of religious reformers to convert their fellow citizens led them at times to demand the passage of censorious or coercive legislation: laws against drinking, blasphemy, Catholics, or Sunday mails. This increasing aggressiveness aroused the fears of radical democrats and occasioned a rise of anti-clericalism in the Jacksonian movement. Whig political sentiments were strong among the Protestant clergy and many humanitarian reformers. And in contrast to the time of the American Revolution, when it seemed that Christianity was in danger of being secularized by the new American nationalism, there now appeared to be some prospect that evangelical Protestantism would dominate the new democratic order.

The notion of a Christian Protestant party in politics attracted the attention of conservative Whigs seeking to counteract infidelity and the radical influence of Jacksonian democracy. In a curious work published in England in 1839 as *A Voice from America to England by an American Gentleman*, Calvin Colton, the close friend and biographer of Henry Clay, united his conservative Whig politics with an argument for introducing a stronger religious influence into American life. Decrying the fact that the United States had become a direct democracy, though it had been constituted as a representative republic, Colton went on to plead for some relaxation of the rigid separation of church and state in America. Although he did not reject religious freedom in principle, he held that "it behooves every Christian State to honour religion, and to provide for its support; that, if there be any interest of the State, which demands more tender care than another, it is that of religion; that a nation 'without God' cannot prosper; and . . . will fail to accomplish its most desirable destiny."[26]

It was true that among the radical Jacksonites there were many of the noted religious skeptics and unbelievers of the period, including the Owen Utopian Socialist family and Abner Kneeland, the defendant in a celebrated trial for blasphemy in Massachusetts. But it was also true, as the Jacksonians argued, that religion was a personal matter and that American tradition accepted the separation of church and state. Some of the Jacksonians, in response to the challenge of their Whig religious critics, went further and maintained that true Christianity was democratic. Thus Orestes Brownson, the radical reformer, supported many of his political positions by reference to religion, and George Bancroft, the historian, declared: "The cause of democracy is the cause of practical Christianity."[27]

As the furor over infidelity waned, many Protestants turned their wrath against Catholics and immigrants. Older well-established Protestant denominations were startled as large numbers of Irish and German immigrants swelled the strength of the Catholic Church from one-half million communicants in 1830 to a million and a half in 1840 and twice that number in 1850. In the 1850's this anti-Catholic and anti-immigrant feeling reached its peak. Mob violence and rioting were paralleled by the effort to secure state and federal laws discriminating against foreigners and naturalized citizens on grounds of their race or religion. By the mid-fifties this potential blot on American democracy had won the backing of the substantial numbers of voters who enrolled under the banners of the short-lived Know Nothing party. In Massachusetts, when nationalist pressures led to legislation against the naturalized citizen, Carl Schurz, a recent refugee from the Revolution of 1848 in Germany, made reply. At Faneuil Hall, Boston, "the cradle of American liberty," he defended the democratic concepts of liberty and equality as expressed in the Declaration of Independence. To the objection that the immigrants were unfitted to rule or hold office, Schurz retorted that nothing would better prepare them than experience. The toleration of liberal democracy, he believed, was the best weapon against fanaticism.[28]

In the age of Jackson there was already some danger of democracy itself becoming virtually a mass religious faith, but the nation and federal government as symbols of loyalty and patriotism still had to contend for popular backing with the separate states. This was the case especially in the South. Elsewhere in the United States, moulded by the various forces compounded of Jacksonian democracy, of science and industrialism, and of religion and reform, a new democratic order was being achieved. In the democracy of this Middle Period in American history, there was still an equable balance between agriculture and industry, as well as between the majority will and minority rights. Nationalism continued to be challenged by the states' rights doctrines of the South. And democracy, despite its mass support, was not suffered to escape the criticisms of sympathetic, and sometimes also hostile, observers.

CHAPTER FIVE

Criticism and Commentary

THE GROWTH of a new democratic order in the United States inspired both critical and sympathetic commentary. English and European visitors published serious or gossipy books based on their often hasty observation of the American political scene and customs, while native authors also were moved to try to interpret the democratic tradition. Rising far above the level of most of this literature was Alexis de Tocqueville's *Democracy in America* with its penetrating and leisurely analysis of the meaning of American free institutions. Yet, at least one American author achieved a study of democracy which deserves to rank with Tocqueville's much more celebrated volumes. This was Frederick Grimké's now-forgotten work entitled *Considerations upon the Nature and Tendency of Free Institutions.*

The extensive literature concerning American democracy indicated a serious interest in the future of free institutions. Tocqueville and other foreign observers saw a lesson for their own countries in the American experience, while Americans themselves often wrote and thought in terms of the world-wide spread of democracy. In the 1840's the doctrine of an American mission was defined primarily in terms of territorial growth. Manifest destiny, a phrase first used by the editor of a Democratic magazine, became a popular slogan embracing American interests in the Far West. The United States, it was assumed, was an oceanbound republic, carrying American freedom and democracy to the more benighted Indian, Mexican, Spanish, and British peoples on the North American Continent.

Until the 1830's, ideologies of territorial expansion and democracy were seldom linked. The Revolutionary and Founding Fathers had feared that the liberties of the citizen would soon be dissipated if the bonds of the Republic were spread over too great a territory. They believed that free institutions should expand by the peaceful workings of the American example rather than through the extension of American sovereignty. Jefferson, however, suggested as early as 1795 that a republic covering a large area might avoid the local schisms and partisan concerns of a smaller country. From the ensuing interplay of widespread and differing sectional interests a more perfect democracy might result.[1] American uncertainty over the merits of territorial growth was further modified with the Purchase of Louisiana, until finally all remaining apprehensions disappeared in the midst of the strong American desire for Oregon, Texas, Cuba, and California. Though a considerable degree of national imperialism and exploitation was not lacking in the concept of manifest destiny, it was also true that in the thirties and forties territorial expansion was regarded as an avenue toward a greater economic and political freedom. Manifest destiny in part was the romance of the agrarian small farmer, and Oregon, it was said, must be occupied by pioneers who needed homes and would extend the area of free institutions. The westward movement offered the individual new opportunities as well as release from the political and economic restraints of the older society east of the Mississippi. In this sense, then, Americans were able to relate territorial expansion with democracy.[2]

Although the pursuit of manifest destiny implied a concern only for the political freedom of the United States, the concept of an American mission also embraced the belief, popular in the Middle Period, that democracy was destined to become the political ideology of all nations. In their Fourth of July addresses, patriotic orators reminded their audiences that the Revolution and Declaration of Independence had struck what were merely the first blows for freedom and liberty in the world. Looking back on these years from the vantage point of his later residence in England, Thomas Low Nichols, an American expatriate, recalled that the sentiments celebrated openly on the Fourth of July were entertained at all times by Americans.

> Ours was the model Government of the world; our institutions were the model institutions, our country the model Republic. . . . We read it in our books and newspapers, heard it in sermons, speeches, and orations, thanked God for it in our prayers, and devoutly believed it always.[3]

George Bancroft, in his patriotic and popular *History of the United States*, emphasized that the Revolution had been fought to advance the natural rights of all nations. "The authors of the American Revolution," he wrote, "avowed for their object the welfare of mankind, and believed that they were in the service of their own and of all future generations."[4]

Although the French Revolution disappointed American democrats by degenerating into the Napoleonic military despotism, revolutions abroad continued to nourish American hopes of the world-wide growth of democratic ideals. The successful establishment of sister republics in South America strengthened the belief that political freedom was growing and would spread in time from the New to the Old World. It is true that the Monroe Doctrine, in underlining the distinct political interests and system of the Western Hemisphere, pointed up the contrast between Europe and America. But unofficially Americans continued to take an interest in the struggles of the Greeks, Irish, Germans, Italians, French, Poles, and Hungarians for national freedom or republican institutions. The revolutions of 1848 especially elicited expressions of American sympathy. Radical democrats in the United States, aided by the pressures of foreign patriots, attempted to secure some form of American intervention, or at least financial aid, for European peoples in revolt. The American reputation abroad was described in somewhat exaggerated fashion in 1851 by a writer in a radical English newspaper who exclaimed:

> An American force in the battlefield of Europe, raising the standard of Universal Democracy, would call forth every People of the Continent in hope, courage, and irresistible numbers. Floating in that field, "the star-spangled banner" would strike terror and despair into the heart of old Despotism, conscious of its doom. Its very coming would be victory.[5]

In the United States, however, prevailing official policy and general popular belief adhered to the doctrine that America could contribute best to Old World struggles for democracy by demonstrating the success of its free institutions at home. As Secretary of State in 1850, Daniel Webster, although refusing to consider American aid or intervention in Europe, made no apology for America's inner feelings.

> Certainly, the United States may be pardoned [he declared], even by those who profess adherence to the principles of absolute government, if they entertain an ardent affection, for those popular forms of political organization which have so rapidly advanced their own prosperity and happiness, and enabled them in so short a period, to bring their country, and the hemisphere to which it belongs, to the notice and respectful regard, not to say the admiration, of the civilized world.[6]

On the whole the Democratic party in the United States took a more lively interest in promoting American ideologies abroad than was the case with their Whig political rivals. Immigrants to the United States seemed to gravitate naturally to the party of Jefferson and Jackson. The Jacksonians welcomed the newcomers and attacked the nativist agitation which was already beginning in the 1830's. Jacksonian democracy itself was not without some international significance. On both sides of the Atlantic the thirties saw major political changes. The Revolution of 1830 in France and the Reform Bill of 1832 and Chartist agitation in England aroused the interest and sympathy of the Jacksonians. On the left wing of the party the workingmen's associations, led by the followers of Robert Owen, gave an international cast and outlook to the Jacksonites, while

Jeremy Bentham, the most celebrated of the English intellectual radicals, looked with favor upon Jackson's administration of the United States government.

English Chartists and spokesmen for the working classes freely urged British adoption of certain features of American democracy. They admired especially manhood suffrage, freedom of the press, religious toleration, and public education. Surprisingly, English radicals were not alienated by aggressive American nationalism in respect to Canada or Oregon. In the absence of any serious threat of war between Great Britain and the United States, they remained enthusiastic believers in the idea that American democracy was to liberate the world. The chief concern of the English radicals therefore was their fear lest democracy in the United States be corrupted and overcome by the growing industrialization of the country.[7]

(*II*)

At this auspicious time in the world's history, in the spring of 1831, a young French aristocrat arrived in the United States, ostensibly to study the prison system, but in fact to observe and analyze American democratic society. Of curious foreign visitors there was no lack in the United States. Like locusts they descended upon the land to record their impressions in the inevitable travel books for which there was an everlasting market because of the American fondness for reading about themselves. Many of the travelers wrote from their own preconceived prejudices of America. Thus the first British accounts in the early nineteenth century reflected a Tory distaste for the American republican experiment, while a later generation of English authors was more liberal and sympathetic. Many believed that democracy, as judged by universal suffrage and frequent elections, had not worked well in practice. They feared the evils of the party system and the tyranny of public opinion. American public education and separation of church and state attracted more friendly comment, but all writers deplored the situation of the Negro. On the whole, according to a careful student of the English travelers' accounts, the opponents of democracy seemed to exceed its friends.[8]

Despite an interest in American party politics, few foreign visitors paid much attention to the principles behind the democratic political system. In this regard Tocqueville was the great exception. Though his books revealed his own liberal aristocratic convictions, they showed too his desire to achieve a broad understanding of the wider significance of his chosen subject. "I confess," he wrote, "that in America I saw more than America; I sought there the image of democracy itself, with its inclinations, its character, its prejudices, and its passions, in order to learn what we have to fear or to hope from its progress."[9]

The feature of democracy that captured Tocqueville's immediate attention was the growth of the principle of equality, which, he declared, had all the characteristics and inevitability of a providential fact. With the advantages of the old order of things destroyed along with the power of the landed aristocracy, modern society faced the problem of learning to adjust to, and purify, the new forces of democracy. Tocqueville had no doubt that democracy characterized the basic social conditions of the American people. Yet, as a liberal aristocrat who prized personal freedom above all other values, he was concerned by the contradiction which he discerned between the democratic stress on equality and the preservation of individual liberty. "In a democratic community," it was his opinion that "individuals are very weak, but the state, which represents them all and contains them all in its grasp, is very powerful. Nowhere do citizens appear so insignificant as in a democratic nation. . . ." "It is easy to foresee," he predicted, "that the time is drawing near when man will be less and less able to produce, by himself alone, the commonest necessaries of life. The task of the governing power will therefore perpetually increase, and its very efforts will extend it every day." Although he believed that democratic communities had "a natural taste for freedom . . . , for equality their passion is ardent, insatiable, incessant, invincible; they call for equality in freedom; and if they cannot obtain that, they still call for equality in slavery." This love of equality led constantly to the desire for a still more complete equality of conditions. In an aristocratic society, in which inequality was commonplace, differences did not strike the eye, but in a democracy even the slightest distinction was unbearable.[10]

In strange juxtaposition to this love of equality, Tocqueville noted the American fondness for acquiring wealth. Fortunately, he believed, the wealth circulated so rapidly in the United States that it was "rare to find two succeeding generations in the full enjoyment of it." In American economic life equality stimulated the competitive spirit and the desire to become rich. In addition, the vast natural resources of the West offered a perfect opportunity for aggressive exploitation. Thus Americans were able to fashion the high standard of living and the accumulation of material goods which ever since Tocqueville's time have provoked both envy and criticism. But Tocqueville also saw in the early American development of techniques of mass production an eventual threat to democratic equality. While craftsmen in an aristocratic society could produce carefully a small number of articles for a limited market, a democratic population demanded the manufacture of an ever-larger amount of goods of lesser value.

> When none but the wealthy had watches, they were almost all good ones; few are now made that are worth much, but everybody has one in his pocket. Thus the democratic principle not only tends to direct the human mind to the useful arts, but it induces the artisan to produce with great rapidity many imperfect commodities, and the consumer to content himself with these commodities.[11]

The mass production of articles, Tocqueville believed, involved a paradox in a democratic society. While the people demanded more material goods, their manufacture in large quantities destroyed the independence of labor and created a new and more brutal aristocracy. "In proportion as the principle of the division of labor is more extensively applied," he noted, "the workman becomes more weak, more narrow-minded, and more dependent. The art advances, the artisan recedes." At the same time the economic advantages of large-scale manufacturing attracted the investment of capital and encouraged the rise of a new class of wealthy factory owners. This manufacturing aristocracy, though still small and confined to a few, was "one of the harshest that ever existed in the world" and the most serious potential danger to the preservation of a democratic equality of conditions.[12]

Despite Tocqueville's criticism of American materialism, he admitted that the richness of the New World environment helped to maintain democracy in the United States. "New wants are not to be feared there, since they can be satisfied without difficulty," he wrote. "It is in America that one learns to understand the influence which physical prosperity exercises over political actions, and even over opinions which ought to acknowledge no sway but that of reason. . . ." Yet, in the last analysis, he did not believe that the physical environment was the determining factor in Anglo-American democracy. South America also enjoyed "inexhaustible riches" but "has been unable to maintain democratic institutions." The success of these institutions in the United States, he attributed, "to the laws themselves and the customs of the people. . . ." The author of *Democracy* therefore devoted a major share of his analysis to the theory and practice of the American political and social system.[13]

American government and society, Tocqueville emphasized, was dominated by the principle of majority rule. To the Frenchman this power of the majority was manifested most clearly in popular control of the government and the press. Like Jefferson, he feared all arbitrary power whether of the many or the few. "I care but little to know who oppresses me," he wrote, "and I am not the more disposed to pass beneath the yoke because it is held out to me by the arms of a million men." Democratic insistence upon equality and hatred of privilege caused an emphasis upon uniformity. By legislation and the pressure of public opinion the individual was coerced.

> I know of no country in which there is so little independence of mind and real freedom of discussion as in America. . . . The more equal the conditions of men become and the less strong men individually are, the more easily they give way to the current of the multitude, . . . individuals seem of less and society of greater importance; or rather every citizen, being assimilated to all the rest, is lost in the crowd, and nothing stands conspicuous but the great and imposing image of the people at large.

In democratic states the old words *despotism* and *tyranny* were inappropriate. The power of democracy was more subtle. "The will of man is not shattered, but softened, bent, and guided; men are seldom forced by it to act, but they are constantly restrained from acting." Thus Tocqueville concluded that "in the democratic ages which are opening upon us, individual independence and local liberties will ever be the products of art; that centralization will be the natural government."[14]

In the political institutions of the United States the power of the majority was expressed most clearly in the federal Congress and in the state legislatures. Unlike many other European observers of the American scene, Tocqueville was less alarmed at the supposed weaknesses of the government or the excessive liberty in the country than "at the inadequate securities which one finds there against tyranny." If ever the free institutions of the United States were destroyed, he declared, the event would be attributable to the omnipotence of the majority, "the complete subjection of the legislature to the will of the electoral body, and the concentration of all the other powers of the government in the legislative branch."[15]

Yet, despite his pessimistic fears over this power of the majority and over the tyranny of public opinion, Tocqueville also recognized that there were strong influences which mitigated the possibility of despotism in the United States and which operated to maintain the democratic republic. In theory he did not believe that majoritarian democracy and individual liberty could be reconciled. In practice he was inclined to admit that America during the 1830's had achieved a workable compromise. Thus, while he feared the tendencies of American democracy, he also revealed much sympathy for some of the practical adjustments that were being executed in the United States. Throughout the two volumes of his *Democracy* therefore, he carried on a running argument between the two opposing themes of the inevitability of equality and democracy and the need to check its more dangerous trends.

Tocqueville devoted considerable attention to those institutions which, he believed, might exercise some check on the power of the majority. In some of his judgments he inevitably went astray, particularly in his evaluation of the Presidency. Coming to the United States in 1831, he failed to discern the significance of Jackson's expansive conception of the powers of his office. On the other hand, most of Jackson's successors before the Civil War lived up to Tocqueville's description of the weaknesses of the executive, and Tocqueville was certainly correct in his observation that it was the lack of serious foreign troubles in the United States which contributed to the feebleness of the executive branch of the government. Also interesting was his view that this weakness in the President eased the peaceful transition from administration to administration. The change from a strong President, he believed, might be much less easily accomplished, but he concluded: "Whatever the prerogatives of the executive power may be, the period which immediately precedes an election, and that during which the election is taking place, must always be considered as a national crisis. . . ."[16]

Although Tocqueville failed to appreciate the role of the political parties, which were just beginning to revive again in the United States, he noted that the privilege of re-election made every President cater unduly to the will of the majority during his term of office. "The principle of re-eligibility renders the corrupting influence of elective government still more extensive and pernicious. It tends to degrade the political morality of the people and to substitute management and intrigue for patriotism." As checks upon the majority he stressed local government, the exercise of judicial review, and the right of the people to form themselves into all kinds of political and voluntary associations. To Tocqueville this right of association was "almost as inalienable in its nature as the right of personal property. No legislator can attack it without impairing the foundations of society," he warned.[17]

Finally Tocqueville saw as the ultimate threat to democracy in the United States the creation of a vast empire and the danger of war. "All the passions that are most fatal to republican institutions increase with an increasing territory," he declared. "It may therefore be asserted," he added, "that nothing is more opposed to the well-being and the freedom of men than vast empires." War was ever a calamity which reduced "nations to the wretched alternative of being abandoned to ruin by defeat or to despotism by success." While the general population of a democracy desired peace, a democratic army might easily lend itself to a movement for war or to the ambitions of a military despot. In other words, the very martial enthusiasm which made democratic armies formidable fighting forces also made them a threat to civil institutions. "After all, and in spite of all precautions," he concluded, "a large army in the midst of a democratic people will always be a source of great danger."[18]

Although Tocqueville wrote his celebrated work for his French compatriots, *Democracy in America* also gave Americans a thoughtful view of their government and society in the opening stages of the great political upheaval under Andrew Jackson. To the Jacksonians much of Tocqueville's antithesis of equality and liberty seemed unreal, but with many American critics the general outlines of Tocqueville's analysis found much favor.

(*III*)

The American democracy with which Tocqueville was so fruitfully preoccupied through the 1830's also attracted the attentions of the rising school of native American writers. The plea of Emerson and others for an American literature and culture independent of that of England was answered in part in the growing discussion of American political institutions. Although Emerson complained that the Democrats had the best principles and the Whigs the best men, a goodly share of the leading intellectuals of the Middle Period were found in Jackson's party. According to the list compiled by Arthur Schlesinger, Jr., in his *Age of Jackson,* Hawthorne, Bryant, Whitman, Cooper, Bancroft, and Irving, among others, were all at some time Jacksonians. Jackson's successor, Martin Van Buren, offered government positions to George Bancroft and several of his literary colleagues, while the *Democratic Review* in 1837 proclaimed that the "vital principle of an American national literature must be democracy."[19]

During Jackson's Presidency the leading literary and political magazines were in the hands of his opponents, and it was not until 1837 and 1838 that two new monthly journals, the *Democratic Review* and the *Boston Quarterly Review,* gave Democratic writers a sympathetic medium for publication. The cover of the *Democratic Review* carried the banner "The best government is that which governs least," and its editorial introduction praised Jackson's party for its opposition to consolidated government. The *Democratic Review* was more than an unofficial party organ, however. Numbering Hawthorne, Thoreau, and Whitman among its contributors, the magazine quickly achieved a high measure of literary and intellectual distinction. The theory as well as practice of democracy was the subject of careful articles and reviews, but in the forties the magazine's concept of democracy became more and more narrowly tied to the doctrine of territorial expansion. Its editor was probably the first to use the term *manifest destiny*, and the magazine as a whole was imbued with an ultra-nationalistic faith in the American mission.

The *Boston Quarterly Review*, edited by the mercurial Orestes Brownson, a religious reformer and Jackson leader in Massachusetts, was more the personal vehicle of its founder. Although recognizing the importance of individuality, Brownson called upon the Democratic party to unite with the forces of organized reform. The Democratic party, he admitted, was "an imperfect embodiment of the great idea of progress," but it was the Whigs who were explicitly "the anti-progress party." In a famous article which discussed the laboring classes in terms of a war between operatives and employers, or labor versus wealth, Brownson urged the government to come to the aid of labor by the destruction of banks, monopolies, and hereditary property. Answering the question, "But what shall government do?" Brownson declared:

> Its first doing must be an undoing. There has been thus far quite too much government, as well as government of the wrong kind. The first act of government we want is a still further limitation of itself. It must begin by circumscribing within narrower limits its powers. And then it must proceed to repeal all laws which bear against the laboring classes, and then to exact such laws as are necessary to enable them to maintain their equality. We have no faith in those systems of elevating the working classes, which propose to elevate them without calling in the aid of government. We must have government and legislation expressly directed to this end.[20]

By the late thirties Brownson was becoming increasingly critical of majority-will democracy. His emphasis on social justice and minority rights foreshadowed his later belief in the religious nature of reform and his sympathy for a states' rights position. Disillusioned completely with the voice of the people, as reflected in the Whig election triumph of 1840, Brownson expressed his dissatisfaction with a democracy based on individual liberty in contrast to positive authority. Democracy, he felt, was not a feasible form of government. Although satisfactory as an end or goal, democratic or popular government was not the best means to this end. He now proclaimed as his motto, "Liberty only in and through Order," and in 1844 he became a convert to Catholicism.[21]

Though refusing to resign their individuality to the dictates of either church or state, like Brownson many of his transcendentalist friends in New England were skeptical of democracy. Ralph Waldo Emerson and Henry David Thoreau were notorious for their denial of politics and reform, and transcendentalism itself was too mystical and individualistic a philosophy to have great appeal for the Jacksonian masses. Yet, as Merle Curti points out,

> there was much that was democratic in it. The exaltation of man, of all men; the doctrine that all power, all wisdom comes from nature, with which man must establish an original and firsthand relationship; the relegation of books to a secondary place in the hierarchy of values; the insistence that instinct is good and must be obeyed rather than curbed in accordance with conventions and authority—all these ideas were closely related to the democratic impulse.[22]

Although he remained personally aloof, Emerson understood that popular hopes of betterment were being awakened in the political tumults of the 1830's. But the sage of Concord also suggested that true democracy was not

> that ill thing, vain and loud, which writes lying newspapers, spouts at caucuses, and sells its lies for gold. . . .
>
> Democracy, Freedom, has its root in the sacred truth that every man hath in him the divine Reason, or that, though few men since the creation of the world live according to the dictates of Reason, yet all men are created capable of so doing. That is the equality and the only equality of all men.

In his essay on *Politics* he deprecated the importance of the state as compared with the individual or nature. There was a limit, he declared, to what could be done by law. Nature was despotic and not disposed to yield its authority to any democratic protest. Yet, he pointed out that all persons enjoyed equal rights in their identity with nature, and "This interest of course with its whole power demands a democracy." Property rights were, however, obviously unequal, and Emerson and his fellow transcendentalists were gravely concerned over the effects of industrialism in creating still further inequalities in man. Democracy, Emerson admitted, was the best form of government for the United States because it fitted in with the spirit of the times, but he cautioned: "Every actual State is corrupt, Good men must not obey the laws too well."[23]

Even more than his friend Emerson, Thoreau was an uncompromising advocate of individual freedom who scorned the ways of society and the state. The dissent with the industrial and political order which he expressed in *Walden* and in his essay *Civil Disobedience* is justly famous. "I heartily accept the motto,—'That government is best which governs least'," he wrote, conceding that he also believed "That government is best which governs not at all." The individual's conscience directed him to obey a higher law than that of the state, and the citizen therefore should not resign his conscience to the legislator or to a majority of his fellow citizens. "Any man more right than his neighbors constitutes a majority of one already," while "Law," he declared, "never made men a whit more just." Although Thoreau admitted that the "progress from an absolute to a limited monarchy, from a limited monarchy to a democracy, is a progress toward a true respect for the individual," he asked: "Is a democracy, such as we know it, the last improvement possible in government? Is it not possible to take a step further towards recognizing and organizing the rights of man?" With the concept of an American mission, Thoreau had no patience. As he complained to a friend early in the 1850's:

> The whole enterprise of this nation, which is not an upward, but a westward one, toward Oregon, California, Japan, etc., is totally devoid of interest to me, whether performed on foot or by a Pacific railroad. It is not illustrated by a thought; it is not warmed by a sentiment; there is nothing in it which one should lay down his life for, nor even his gloves,—hardly which one should take up a newspaper for. It is perfectly heathenish,—a filibustering *toward* heaven by the great western route. No; they may go their way to their manifest destiny, which I trust is not mine.[24]

Like Thoreau, Herman Melville questioned the direction of American democracy. In *Mardi*, one of the more philosophical and less popular of his novels, he drew upon his experiences in the South Seas of the Pacific to fashion an allegory of the fate of the American

Republic. A prophet of doom in the mythical kingdom of Mardi warned the people that they were forgetting the lessons of history. It was merely the error and conceit of the age to believe itself something special and eternal. Civilization itself, Melville felt, was no friend of freedom, and monarchies might be better for some nations. In any case, he wrote, "It is not the prime end and chief blessing, to be politically free." Most valuable of all to a nation were youth and an expansive range of free territory.

> Free horses need wide prairies; and fortunate for you, sovereign kings! that you have room enough, wherein to be free. And, may it please you, you are free, partly because you are young. Your nation is like a fine, florid youth, full of fiery impulses, and hard to restrain; his strong hand nobly championing his heart. On all sides, freely he gives, and still seeks to acquire.

Thus Melville summed up his feelings regarding the manifest destiny of American democracy.[25]

(*IV*)

Generally speaking, the democracy which was winning the increasing support of the majority of the American people in the Middle Period found almost as little favor with most writers as it did with Melville. Since the days of those staunch upholders of Federalist conservatism, the Connecticut Wits, democracy had been a popular subject for literary satire. Even a Jeffersonian like Hugh Henry Brackenridge, author of *Modern Chivalry*, complained in friendly fashion of the excesses of democracy. Brackenridge refused to accept the philosophy that because democracy gave every man equal protection under the laws, he had to exercise an equal voice in making the laws. Jacksonian democracy was subject still more to the attacks of Whig and Southern writers who shared Calhoun's hostility to a democracy based on a numerical majority. Only William Gilmore Simms, the Southern counterpart of James Fenimore Cooper, was bold enough to affirm in an unusual burst of optimism in 1839:

> I am a Democrat of the Jackson School, a State rights man, opposed to Tariffs, Banks, Internal improvements, American Systems, Fancy Rail

Roads, Floats, Land Companies, and every Humbug East or West, whether of cant or cunning. I believe in the people, and prefer trusting their impulses, than the craft, the cupidity & the selfishness of trades & Whiggery.[26]

Of the major novelists of the period, James Fenimore Cooper devoted the most systematic attention to the theory and practice of American democracy. Though nominally a Democratic supporter of Jackson, his politics and philosophy wavered uncertainly in the wake of the popular upheavals of the thirties and forties. Cooper was always a rather aristocratic type of democrat, as befitted the son of a wealthy Federalist landowner with large estates in central New York. He was also a staunch individualist, the creator of the strong and self-reliant Leatherstocking. But, as Ralph Gabriel has pointed out, Leatherstocking was not a primitive barbarian who flouted law and order. "I know we live in the woods," Cooper made Leatherstocking say, "and are thought to be beyond human laws,—and perhaps we are so, in fact, whatever it may be in right,—but there is a law, and a law-maker, that rule across the whole continent. He that flies in the face of either, need not call me friend."[27]

In addition to the considerable amount of his social philosophy which found its way into his novels, Cooper was also the author of two general books in which he aired his concept of democracy. In the *Notions of America Picked Up by a Travelling Bachelor* (1828), Cooper defended his country against the usual British visitors' criticisms by impersonating an Englishman who gave a favorable view of the United States. The secret of the progress of the United States was its adherence to the principle of individuality and the great practicality of the people in developing their natural resources. Americans were reformers, not revolutionists, who desired to see their ideas of government spread to Europe by peaceful example. In general Cooper expressed satisfaction with popular American institutions—for example, the extension of the suffrage and common schooling.

During the first half of the 1830's Cooper was abroad, and *The American Democrat*, published in 1838 after his return, gave a critical picture of the changes which had taken place at home in his absence. Though he complained that a real equality of political and civil rights did not exist in the United States, he felt that the tyranny of public opinion was more social than political. "America occupies a middle place in the scale, wanting most of the higher tastes, and excelling in that species of civilization which marks ease and improvement in the middling and lower classes."[28]

Much of Cooper's irritation was directed, not at Jacksonian Democracy, but at the new rising commercial class which he identified with the Whig party. In *The American Democrat* and in his novel *The Monikons* (1835) he attacked the stake-in-society theory that government should be founded on the representation of property. As a landowner he reserved his principal criticism for the business class of merchants and manufacturers. But in the 1840's, as landed property, including his own estate on Otsego Lake, was threatened by the anti-rent disturbances in New York, Cooper became more conservative and hostile to democracy. His ideal was ever the rural pastoral countryside of landed squires and hard-working farmers. "As a champion of the land, Cooper had rejoiced at the Jacksonian attacks on business; but now demagogues were extending the attack, under the same rallying cries, to the land itself. Would not their victory destroy the foundations of property the nation over?" Thus in his later years his disillusionment with popular democracy became intense. He denounced the disposition to confuse change with true progress, and he saw no hope in either extreme reform or extreme conservatism. "Neither course is in the least suited to the actual wants of society, and each is pernicious in its way." Noting that the telegraph sped truth and falsehood alike, Cooper expressed his conviction that in an age of progress, individuality was lost and law was disregarded.[29]

(V)

Compared with the novelists, the political writers of the Middle Period were more partisan and predictable in their discussion of democratic tradition and practice. George Bancroft, one of the most scholarly and dependable of the Jacksonites, placed no reservations on his faith in popular democracy. He was confident that the Democrats were the "party of progress and reform," the leaders in the "struggles for universal education and universal suffrage." In a scholarly oration, "The Office of the People in Art, Government, and Religion" (1835), Bancroft measured progress in terms of the intellectual advance of the common mind. It was the duty of democratic government to encourage this progress by promoting the general welfare and providing for the happiness of the mass of the people. Over a decade later Bancroft returned to this theme in a famous address before the New York Historical Society. Progress was the law of man in which each individual contributed "some share toward the general intelligence." In true democratic fashion, he maintained that progress therefore depended upon "the totality of contemporary intelligence." The United States, he concluded, had a divine mission to spread the principles of freedom and help achieve the unity of the human race.[30]

Richard Hildreth, Bancroft's rival historian and a radical Whig in his politics, took a less romantic view of the American democratic tradition. His *Theory of Politics*, published in 1854 but written over a decade earlier, was a realistic utilitarian study in comparative government. The rise and fall of ancient democracies and the inequality of man made him discount the notion of the partisans of Rousseau's *Social Contract* "that there exists in the numerical majority of the people an exclusive right to control the community." Hildreth also noted that democratic principles did not necessarily secure a democratic administration of the government. The chief advantage of democracy was that the pleasure of governing was not confined to the few. Thus the pain of obeying was compensated by the pleasure of commanding. Even the votes of a minority had some influence in a democracy, and when a majority performed a tyrannical act, it fell into the danger of ceasing to be a majority. Meanwhile the ballot box provided a means of peaceful change. Hildreth recognized that, in practice, the actual administration of affairs in any system of government would be undertaken by a few men, but he also believed that democratic governments were hostile to monopolies and to censorious restrictions and prohibitions. The chief dangers to American democracy stemmed from the English common law, from mystical ideas, and from the institution of slavery. Its salvation lay in the rise of the working class.[31]

Hildreth's rather surprising labor sympathies were carried much further in the literature of Fourierist socialism, of which Parke

Godwin's *Democracy Constructive and Pacific* was a good American example. Godwin took the typical socialist position that under the existing society democratic principles no longer prevailed in fact. "Your absolute liberty," he wrote, "is only an absolute abandonment of the unarmed and destitute masses to the charity of the well-fed and well-armed few." Accordingly a socialist regeneration of industrial society was necessary if political democracy was to accomplish its mission.[32]

Ranged against socialism, conservative political theory was well represented by Francis Lieber, a refugee from Germany in 1827 who became the author of the first systematic works on political science in the United States. Lieber had little sympathy for what he felt was Bancroft's rose-colored view of the progress of democracy. In his major work *On Civil Liberty*, which he published in 1853, he maintained that rule by the propertyless masses, or "democratic absolutism," was the very antithesis of liberty. True liberty was embodied in institutions, the main function of which was to protect the rights of the minority. Like Tocqueville, Lieber feared the great powers of a democratic popular majority, and his *Civil Liberty* ardently defended the concept of limited government. Until he became embroiled in the nationalism and bitterness of the Civil War era, Lieber was a passionate devotee of personal liberty who admired the American federal system and English common law as bulwarks for the protection of the free individual against the democratic masses.

The popular impact of much of the literature devoted to analyzing American democracy is difficult to evaluate, but in 1841, when an obscure citizen George Sidney Camp completed a small volume called *Democracy*, Harper and Brothers thought it worthy of inclusion in their Family Library and later brought out a second edition. In 1852 the book was also published in South America in a Spanish translation. Camp made frequent reference to Tocqueville's *Democracy in America*, and indeed his own work was in some ways an abbreviated account of the Frenchman's famous study. But he went further than Tocqueville in stressing the role of Christianity in the progress of American democracy. "Faith," said Camp, "is as necessary to the republican as to the Christian, and the fundamental characteristic of both."[33]

(VI)

Camp's slender book, though it showed the influence of Tocqueville, did not rival *Democracy in America* as an original and thoughtful commentary. In the Middle Period the only work which could pretend to vie with the distinguished French visitor's volumes as a systematic analysis of American democracy was Frederick Grimké's *Considerations upon the Nature and Tendency of Free Institutions.*[34]

Although he was the older brother of the famous abolitionist sisters Sarah and Angelina, Frederick remains a rather shadowy figure. Like his sisters, he left South Carolina and settled in the North, becoming a judge in the Supreme Court of Ohio in the 1830's. In 1842 he retired from this position to devote himself to study and writing, and six years later he published the *Considerations.* Written in a sober legal style, the massive book can hardly be said to have achieved widespread popularity. Terming the volume "a wheat-stack, not a loaf of bread," a contemporary writer in the *North American Review,* in an extended notice of the work, testified rather grudgingly to its significance. Despite its stylistic defects, Grimké's book had some use as a text, and in 1856 a second edition was published with the inclusion of a new introductory and concluding chapters.

The major portion of the *Considerations upon the Nature and Tendency of Free Institutions* was devoted to a detailed analysis of the theory and practice of the American government. Democratic representative institutions were defended, not only as a desirable ideal, but also as the best means yet ascertained of preserving political authority without the loss of individual liberties. The United States' historical experience was fitted into the background of European civilization, and throughout the work there was careful consideration of the fundamental problems of a democracy, with Grimké essaying the role of critic and prophet. Even today many of his conclusions have a vitality and force which make them no less deserving of attention than the writings of Tocqueville or Lieber. Especially interesting were some of Grimké's predictions as to the future course of

American democracy, in which he forecast the filling-up of the West and the increasing importance of labor.

Grimké adhered steadfastly to the principle of majority rule. Against the political opponents of Andrew Jackson who continued to protest that minority rights were being endangered by a popular despotism, he asserted that "whenever a majority is competent to take care of its own interests, it will also be competent to take care of those of the minority." He explained that this was true because in practice majority rule provided its own restraints. Among these were the system of checks and balances within the government and, more importantly, the check of "the power out of government"—the moral force of the community reflected in the "elevation of the lower orders, the formation of a great middle class," and "the creation of a genuine public opinion." Grimké assumed that the constant trend in a republic was toward the development of a large middle class and that this class might be said "fairly to represent the interests which are common to the whole society." With no fixed aristocracy and with "unbounded freedom of thought and action," individuals would pass continually back and forth from majority to minority.

> It is then correct to say, that in a country where free institutions exist, all the great interests of the minority will be inclosed in those of the majority; that the public men who conduct the one party will, in no important respect, be different from those who conduct the other, and that the great variety of opinions which divide the community will not in the long run, and in the general upshot of human affairs, affect fundamentally or even sensibly the well-being of the state.

To the apprehension, frequently expressed by conservatives, that free institutions would result in political anarchy or in the tyranny of the mob, Grimké replied that in a free society such as a democratic republic, there was less opportunity for conflict between the government and the people, because the government was more amenable to fluctuations in the popular will, and at the same time its authority was reinforced by the weight of the public opinion which created and maintained it. Citing the popular election of the President as an illustration, he asserted that the chief executive enjoyed greater prestige as the representative of the whole people than he would as the choice of the Electoral College. During the forties, while Grimké was engaged in writing his treatise, the Presidency was occupied by men not otherwise especially talented. Therefore it was not surprising that he felt the system of popular election to be the cause of the selection of average men who would be disposed to carry out the people's mandate instead of moulding it to suit their own purposes.

Universal suffrage, Grimké admitted, increased the proportion of ignorant voters. Yet in the United States it had not culminated in any sudden burst of unwise laws, and in the "honesty of purpose" which he associated with the common people he discerned a check on the self-interest of the aristocratic minority. Although no system of elections was perfect, the solution, Grimké averred, was not a return to the "notion of a property qualification . . . derived from feudal institutions," but rather the education of the electorate and the diffusion of property.

Like Tocqueville, Grimké believed that the principle of equality "found a natural support in America" and that it had not "been the creature of the laws."

> The leading fact in the history of American civilization, undoubtedly consists in the very equal distribution of the landed property of the country. And this is owing to the circumstance in which the country was found when it was settled by Europeans. The population was so thin, and so entirely below the standard of European civilization, that it quickly disappeared, and left the whole field of enterprise open to the whites. This is a fact quite new in the history of society.

With the growth of population, however, the influence of free land was weakened, while the gulf between the very rich and the poor was widened. Grimké therefore, in anticipation of later American developments, posed the problem of whether or not political institutions should be used to promote a broader diffusion of property. In the United States, he felt, this was one of the functions of democracy. "The laws, the character of the government, may do much toward either promoting or preventing the disparity of estates. And it is one reason why free institutions are preferable to any other, that they contribute to produce this last effect." Although a complete leveling was undesirable and incompatible with the progress of civilization, Grimké in an important passage ably called attention to the great advantage of believing in "the maxim that all men are equal."

> First. Because to teach and to act upon it is the only way of attaining equality, to the extent to which it is actually attained. Second. Because it is not in the power of government to make anything like an accurate discrimination between the inequalities of different men. . . . Third. Because the principle of equality may very well be recognized as the rule among men as citizens . . . although as individuals there may be great and numerous inequalities between them. The utmost which the citizen can demand is that no law shall be passed to obstruct his rise, and to impede his progress through life.

Grimké embraced in large measure a liberal laissez-faire conception of the state, with its powers limited to the preservation of equal opportunity for all. In his philosophy he adhered to the Jeffersonian tradition, and his *Free Institutions* was closer in point of view to the writings of John Taylor than to any other American treatise on politics. Political democracy, with majority rule and universal suffrage, he believed should be reinforced by a social democracy based on the widest possible diffusion of property and education. He did not, however, wish to see the sovereignty of the people erected into a nineteenth-century counterpart of ancient absolutism. Although he wrote that "the greater the proportion of the population, by whom political power is exercised, the greater will be the probability that the laws will be just and wise," he also shared the Jeffersonian distrust of a centralized all-powerful national state. "There is no power on earth," he observed, "the people no more than the prince, which can be conceived to be absolved from the eternal principles of justice," and he went on from this to conclude that

> the American people have been scrupulously jealous of their own power; that they have endavored to guard against the idea that might gives right; and have thus given to the term "sovereignty of the people" an interpretation which it has received in no other commonwealth, either of ancient or modern times.

At the close of his volume Grimké turned to the question of the future of free institutions and their probable effect upon Europe. American freedom, having enjoyed the advantages of relative geographic seclusion and a large middle class, was, he believed, now capable of exercising "a more marked influence upon European institutions than it is possible for Europe to exert upon American institutions." As the discoveries of "Newton transferred the principle of gravity to the whole material universe," so the example of the United States proved "first, the practicability of conferring the electoral franchise upon the great body of the people; and secondly, of making all the political departments elective." Grimké concluded that the true mission of American democracy was to spread its influence through such peaceful agencies as immigrant letters and travel books. War and military institutions, he asserted, had been the traditional means by which popular liberties were abridged. Therefore he warned the United States against any inclination to military pursuits, pointing out that while "no nation ever was endowed with such a capacity for doing good; none has ever been endowed with such a capacity for inflicting evil."

Grimké and Tocqueville, the first major commentators upon American democracy, died within a few years of each other as the Civil War was disrupting the Federal Union. Although neither foresaw that great struggle, Grimké witnessed its beginnings, and he also placed on record his criticisms of the anti-democratic extremists in both the North and the South.

CHAPTER SIX

Disruption and Disunion

THE CIVIL WAR, the greatest war and most dramatic event in American history, also marked the disruption of American democracy. It is true that violence and civil strife were not typical of American society or government and that democracy, after all, survived the four long years of fighting. But in the struggle of North and South the future of democracy frequently seemed in doubt, and, whatever the outcome of the war, democratic traditions and institutions appeared bound to be affected, abroad perhaps almost as much as at home. Though the Confederacy lost its bid for independence, the Negro slaves gained their freedom and the Union was preserved.

It was these achievements that enabled Abraham Lincoln and Walt Whitman to see the ultimate democratic significance of the war years despite the terrible carnage of over a million casualties on the two sides.

The outbreak of the Civil War indicated, at least temporarily, the failure of American democracy. Although Northern newspaper editors affirmed that free institutions could survive secession and a split in the Union, democracy in terms of the consent of the governed and of majority rule had met defeat. A large minority had withdrawn its consent from the federal government, and the majority was attempting to work its will by force of arms. "By any definition," Ralph Gabriel observes, "political democracy had, for the time being, lapsed. . . . Responsibility for the disaster rested with the American people. No outside nation was involved."[1] Along these same lines Avery Craven has written:

> The secession of the Southern states and Lincoln's call for troops to crush "rebellion" completed the breakdown of the democratic process. Men ceased to tolerate differences, to discuss their problems, and to compromise the clashes. The rule of the majority was no longer accepted. Bullets took the place of ballots; soldiers the place of statesmen.[2]

The virtual collapse of democratic government in the United States prevented agreement upon some kind of peaceable compromise. Even though the Congress and the Supreme Court still functioned, their prestige had been greatly sapped in the course of the protracted sectional controversy over slavery. A succession of weak Presidents between Polk and Lincoln helped to make possible the mistakes of what has been called "a blundering generation," while the possibility of positive executive action was further diminished by the confusion of the transition from Buchanan to Lincoln. If the former's policies were indecisive, the latter's were perhaps too unyielding. In any case, by April 1861, neither North nor South could understand the other's point of view. Intimately related with the failure of democracy was the breakdown of effective communication between the two sections. Despite the many historic common ties that bound the American people together, North and South had become almost two separate cultures or civilizations. "One might think," a contemporary authority on the Constitution wrote, that the two sections of the country . . . would each find its complement in the other. That as the cotton-fields of the South, the grain-fields of the West, the mills and workshops of the East, supplied mutual wants, so the conservative element of Southern society would give moderation and stability to Northern democracy, which, in return, would import something of its own spirit of movement and progress to the aristocratic and oligarchic tendencies of the South. So it happened until a recent period of our history.[3]

Each of the two sections, in its own way, believed that it was fighting for freedom and democracy. Thus both North and South offered their variant interpretations and definitions of the democratic tradition. The South accepted a version of democracy which it likened to that of ancient Greece—a society of equals superimposed upon a slave class. To Southern leaders, ever fond of pointing out the parallels between secession and the American Revolution, political freedom meant the right of national self-determination. But to Northern statesmen, the continuance of American democracy required the preservation of the Union and some assurance of respect for the principle of majority rule. By 1861 both North and South held strong convictions in regard to freedom and democracy, but neither section was able to feel that its basic institutions were secure against the political attack of the other.

Involved, of course, in their contradictory concepts of democracy were the equally conflicting Northern and Southern views of the Constitution and slavery. Against the South's states' rights and state sovereignty, the North placed the doctrine of the Constitution as the creation of the people of the United States as a whole. Even more important to the fate of democracy was the way in which it had become intertwined with the slavery question. While Northerners increasingly felt concern over the moral issue, Southerners believed that their rights included the expansion of slavery. Despite the succession of compromise agreements that had been worked out, the events of the generation before the Civil War showed the weakness of democracy in dealing with a matter that involved the fundamental structure of society.

(*II*)

Slavery itself was never in harmony with American institutions. From the beginning it was an anachronism in a free and expanding society. Consequently it had to be rationalized as a means of Christianizing and civilizing its victims. Though it gradually gained economic strength and importance in the American colonies, it was also attacked, most notably by some of the devout Quaker leaders. At the same time, to many enthusiastic believers in the ideals of the eighteenth-century Enlightenment, slavery seemed incompatible with the doctrine of the natural rights of man. When the natural-rights philosophy was invoked to justify the colonial cause in the American Revolution, the question of the Negro slaves' rights to liberty also arose. Tom Paine thought that since slaves "are not convicted of forfeiting freedom, they have still a natural, perfect right to it. . . ."[4] Although Jefferson's statement condemning the British for the slave trade was stricken from the final draft of the Declaration of Independence, there was strong complaint against the inconsistency of a Declaration which proclaimed the rights of man and ignored the enslavement of the Negro. Anthony Benezet, the leader of the Quakers' crusade against slavery, declared:

> If these solemn truths uttered in such an awful crisis, are *self-evident;* unless we can show that the African race are not men, words can hardly express the amazement which naturally arises on reflecting that the very people who make these pompous declarations are slave holders, and, by their legislation, tell us, that these blessings were only meant to be the *rights of white men,* not of all *men;* and would seem to verify the observation of an eminent writer: "When men talk of liberty, they mean their own liberty, and seldom suffer their thoughts on that point to stray to their neighbors."[5]

Defenders of slavery were quick to point out that the Declaration asserted equality only for those who were members of the body politic. But the moral, if not political, conflict of slavery and the natural-rights philosophy could not be explained away so easily. Many of the Founding Fathers, in the South as well as the North, condemned the institution of slavery and took steps to encourage gradual emancipation. Although its ultimate abolition in the North, like its preservation in the South, was largely a matter of economics, the moral issue of slavery became increasingly important with the growth of democracy in the United States. Americans tried to ease their conscience by stopping the foreign slave trade and by supporting plans for colonizing emancipated Negroes in Africa. In Christian churches and among humanitarian reformers, antislavery sentiment was never stilled. Even the South, as William F. Cash pointed out, "in its secret heart always carried a powerful and uneasy sense of the essential rightness of the nineteenth century's position on slavery."[6] But the wavering conscience of the nation concerning slavery was not really aroused until the struggle over the admission of Missouri and the rise of the militant abolitionist movement highlighted its significance.

The abolitionists in all the years before the Civil War were ever only a small minority, even in the North, but they were responsible for keeping fixed before the nation the paradox of the existence of slavery in a democracy. Although there were societies and individuals calling for the end of slavery prior to 1831, William Lloyd Garrison's founding of the *Liberator* in that year gave the abolition movement its particular radical flavor. Garrison and his followers, in their demands for some plan of immediate abolition, refused all compromise with slavery. Their position was as simple as the Declaration of Independence and its "life, liberty, and the pursuit of happiness," which they insisted belonged to the Negro as well as to the white man. Since Garrison believed that the country had abandoned the natural-rights philosophy of the Declaration in favor of the protection of slavery under the Constitution, he proposed to follow a policy of passive resistance and non-cooperation in his relations with the United States government. This intransigent stand he later dramatized in the famous episode of his address at a Fourth of July meeting called in 1854 to protest the return of the escaped Anthony Burns to slavery. After burning copies of the hated Fugitive Slave law and of the federal decision in the Burns case, Garrison held up before his audience a copy of the United States Constitution. Branding it "a covenant with death and agreement with hell," he turned it to ashes, exclaiming, "So perish all compromises with tyranny!"[7]

Less violently than Garrison, other opponents of slavery at this time also questioned the democracy of a nation that kept the Negro in bondage. Richard Hildreth entitled his inquiry into the slaveholding system in the United States *Despotism in America.* The United States, he pointed out, was described as an experiment in democracy, with the assumption usually that the experiment was succeeding. This, he argued, was not true, because the aristocrats of the South practiced the worst sort of despotism in the form of Negro slavery. Hildreth also disputed the liberalism of the Founding Fathers in regard to slavery, making the comment on Jefferson that "The democracy which he preached at home, was democracy among the aristocrats. . . ."[8] Theodore Parker, the radical Unitarian minister, in a discourse in 1855 contrasted the great possibilities of the United States with the dark realities imposed by the slave system. "What opportunities—and what a waste of them," he declared. "Has any nation more deserved rebuke? A Democracy, and every eighth man a slave! Jesus the God of the Church, and not a sect that dares call Slavery a sin!"[9]

Militant and uncompromising abolitionists like Garrison forced the slavery question into the open. While such individualistic reformers as Emerson and Thoreau held aloof at first, and while the Jacksonian Democrats avoided the abolition of slavery as the great untouchable issue, the radical antislavery agitators gradually aroused the American conscience. By invoking the natural rights of the Negro slave, the abolitionists identified their cause with democracy, even though they themselves were impatient of democratic procedures and of the majority's indifference to their crusade. Among the more moderate antislavery church leaders, the Reverend William Ellery Channing was typical of those who defended the right of the abolitionists to be heard, though deploring their fanaticism. Channing agreed with the abolitionists that slavery, in its violation of the fundamental rights of man and of his equal moral nature in the sight of God, was a threat to democracy. Slavery, he declared, in his survey of its evils and weaknesses, "is a strange element to mix up with free institutions. It cannot but endanger them. It is a pattern for every kind of wrong."[10] By their own willingness to suffer martyrdom for exercising their rights to free speech and a free press, Garrison and his colleagues finally were able to impress upon the

North the conviction that liberty for the abolitionist minority also involved the question of the general liberty of all Americans.

Frequently Garrison was hated, almost as much in the North as in the South. Even within the antislavery movement there were many who questioned his uncompromising methods. Not all abolitionists, in other words, were willing to admit that the Constitution was a slaveholder's document which precluded any effective contrary political activity by the antislavery forces. Unlike the Garrisonites, many of the antislavery reformers were ready to use the traditional democratic means of political parties, petitions, and the ballot to achieve their ends. But, whatever its methods, the abolitionist movement was able to gain little success or influence until the crisis of the 1850's. With the emergence of the Republicans, antislavery for the first time enjoyed major party support. Though not abolitionist in its tenets, the Republican party opposed the expansion of slavery in the territories. As the South had long recognized, if slavery could not expand and grow, it would gradually die out. Thus the South responded to every challenge, whether from Garrison and the abolitionists, or from Lincoln and the Republicans, and the Northern attack on slavery was met by the proslavery arguments of Calhoun and his fellow Southern spokesmen.

(III)

In the South slavery never lacked ardent supporters. First defended as a necessary evil that would eventually yield to the forces of progress and civilization, slavery in time was asserted to be a positive good—"the most safe and stable basis for free institutions in the world."[11] The turning point in Southern thinking occurred between Jefferson's death in 1826, the Virginia Constitutional Convention of 1829, and the legislative debate concerning slavery in 1832. A year earlier the Nat Turner slave revolt and the founding of Garrison's *Liberator* also helped to arouse Southern feelings. Under the intellectual and political leadership of John C. Calhoun, the South repudiated the natural-rights philosophy of Jefferson and the Revolutionary generation. Calhoun frankly rejected all democratic notions of the equality of man. Civilization and progress, he said, depended on an inequality, while government arose from man's social needs and for the protection of his private property. Calhoun desired the kind of democracy that had flourished in ancient Greece—a government of the free citizens over and above the slave class.

As a sound basis for democracy, Calhoun denied alike the liberty and equality of the abolitionists and the majority rule of the Northern masses. Distrustful of an all-powerful central government, "a great national consolidated democracy," he defended state sovereignty and minority rights as checks upon the majority. Thus he opposed Jacksonian democracy and the Mexican War because he feared that they would strengthen the nationalizing tendencies of the government. As long as the United States remained a federal republic, slavery could continue to be a state matter, but once nationalist doctrines gained ascendancy, slavery and the labor system of the South would become equally the responsibility of the North. Only the maintenance of states' rights would keep slavery a local issue and the United States a federal union.[12]

As his final plan to preserve slavery within the United States, Calhoun developed his doctrine of the concurrent majority, an elaboration of South Carolina's nullification of 1832 and an original contribution to political theory. To the power of the numerical majority, Calhoun proposed to add the check of what he called the concurrent majority. In practice this would amount to some form of state nulilfication or temporary veto over federal laws. Thus a measure opposed by all the Southern states could never secure final approval. In the United States Senate in the years before 1861, Calhoun's theory was often applied to protect Southern interests, and after the Civil War the concurrent majority operated in the check that strong organized minority groups and economic-interest blocs were able to interpose to prevent or secure desired legislation. That his concurrent majority would impede the workings of democracy in the sense of popular sovereignty was, of course, part of its merit in the eyes of Calhoun and the South. But Calhoun also maintained that his scheme would tend "to unite the most opposite and conflicting interests, and to blend the whole in one common attachment to the country. By giving to each interest, or portion, the power of self-protection, all strife and struggle between them for ascendancy, is prevented. . . ."[13]

Historians still differ seriously in their judgment of Calhoun, their views colored perhaps by the weight which they attach to the role of minority rights or majority will in a democracy. Thus there is a wide gap between the evaluation of Calhoun as an agitator, "the Marx of the Master Class," and the assertion that he ranks with Thoreau in his support of the individual against the state. Perhaps most correct is Parrington's conclusion that Calhoun's states' rights doctrine was the last defense of an older decentralized type of agrarian democracy. But in associating his principle with the doomed institution of slavery and in "championing a Greek democracy Calhoun affronted the latent idealism of America, and the harm he did to agrarian democracy was incalculable."[14]

In the decade after Calhoun's death at the time of the Compromise of 1850, the debate over slavery frequently seemed to turn on economic matters. Conceivably if the pace of the territorial expansion of the United States could have been slowed, the slavery question might have been solved peaceably with the passage of time. But the dynamism of industrial society and the continual advance of the frontier precipitated the issue of the expansion of slavery. Two differing labor systems, the free labor of the industrial North and the slave labor of the agricultural South, competed for the control of the West. Southern spokesmen, outraged by the abolitionists' attacks on their peculiar institution, compared it favorably to what they termed the "wage slavery" of the Northern capitalists. George Fitzhugh, a leading proslavery publicist in the fifties, used the conservatism of the Southern way of life as the basis for his attacks on democracy. Slavery alone, he believed, provided the social and economic controls necessary to ward off a coming revolution from the class of landless factory operatives in the North. In his picturesquely entitled volume *Cannibals All! or, Slaves Without Masters*, Fitzhugh denounced both liberty and democracy. The one encouraged the weak to attack the strong, while the other offered a false equality to all.

On the floor of the United States Senate in 1858, James H. Hammond, possessor of Calhoun's old South Carolina seat, advanced his famous "mud-sill" theory of democracy. While the Senator pointed with pride to the power and prosperity of his section, he noted that "the greatest strength of the South arises from the harmony of her political and social institutions. . . . In all social systems," he explained,

> there must be a class to do the menial duties, to perform the drudgery of life. . . . Such a class you must have, or you would not have that other class which leads to progress, civilization, and refinement. It constitutes the very mud-sill of society and of political government; and you might as well attempt to build a house in the air, as to build either the one or the other, except on this mud-sill. Fortunately for the South, she has found a race adapted to that purpose to her hand. . .

The South's slaves were black, Hammond declared, but the North had its wage slaves, who fortunately had not yet learned to use to the full their privilege of voting, although they were already clamoring for free homesteads. "Transient and temporary causes have thus far been your preservation," he warned the North. "The great West has been open to your surplus population, and your hordes of semi-barbarian immigrants, who are crowding in year by year. They make a great movement, and you call it progress. Whither? It is progress, but it is progress towards vigilance committees."[15]

In terms of both democracy and practical politics, the most effective reply to Hammond came from Lincoln and the Republican party. Like the Southern spokesmen of the fifties, Lincoln and the Republicans saw the essential conflict as one between free labor and slavery. In Parrington's words, Lincoln amalgamated idealism and economics. To do this was no easy task, and Lincoln's success in the endeavor was a test of his political skill. Though a Jeffersonian democrat in many of his beliefs, he was a Whig and Republican in his economic nationalism. In regard to slavery, Lincoln believed that the Declaration of Independence was an ideal to be lived up to. The Founding Fathers, he felt, had not meant to say that all men were equal in all respects, but that they were equal in their right to life, liberty, and the pursuit of happiness. Thus he did not support full social and political equality for the Negro, but in the basic right of personal freedom he asserted that "no man is good enough to govern another man, *without that other's consent*." The proslavery argument was a return to despotism, and against Hammond's mud-sill theory, Lincoln championed the cause of free labor and, most importantly, its right to dominate the territories.[16]

Though the expansion of slavery in the territories was more a matter of principle than a geographic and economic reality to the South, Lincoln raised the specter of Negro slave labor spreading everywhere in the United States. In his Peoria speech, he declared:

> The whole nation is interested that the best use shall be made of these territories. We want them for the homes of free white people. This they cannot be, to any considerable extent, if slavery shall be planted within them. Slave states are places for poor white people to remove FROM; not to remove TO. New free states are the places for poor people to go to and better their condition. For this use, the nation needs these territories.

Compared with the popular sovereignty of the Democrats, which implied a kind of hands-off attitude in respect to the territories, Lincoln and the Republicans' emphasis upon no further expansion of slavery had strong appeal to both the North and the West. As Richard Hofstadter points out,

> Lincoln took the slavery question out of the realm of moral and legal dispute and, by dramatizing it in terms of free labor's self-interest, gave it a universal appeal. To please the abolitionists he kept saying that slavery was an evil thing; but for the material benefit of all Northern white men he opposed its further extension.[17]

By gaining the backing of the North, Lincoln and the Republicans were able to force the issue of the South's acceptance of the majority will in regard to the spread of slavery. With no hope of winning over the South, they proposed to disregard its minority rights and interests, however extreme the consequences. Lincoln's interpretation of the right of revolution included the view that any people, having the inclination and the power, might rise up and overthrow the existing government. This was also the principle of Southern extremists, but Lincoln added significantly: "More than this, a *majority* of any portion of such people may revolutionize, putting down a *minority*, intermingled with, or near about them, who may oppose their movement. Such a minority, was precisely the case, of the tories of our own revolution." Lincoln expected the majority will to prevail. He did not believe the Union would be dissolved or that it would continue a house divided. But, though he was confident that the future lay with the free labor system of the North, he also raised the cry that slavery might continue to grow and expand across the nation. Thus what Lincoln proposed was the ultimate necessity of the exclusion of slave labor and the acceptance only of free labor.[18]

(IV)

The dilemma of Northern democracy in regard to both the Negro and the Union was resolved when the Confederate batteries opened fire on Fort Sumter on the morning of April 12, 1861. The fact that, whether by accident or design on the part of North or South, the latter had fired the first shot helped Lincoln to maintain his thesis that the North was fighting to preserve the Union. The cause of the Union he, in turn, identified with democracy and the will of the majority, while the effort of the South to win its independence was dismissed as the work of a rebel minority. The victorious Republicans, though themselves a minority party in the election of 1860, had achieved majority status by virtue of the war. In his first Inaugural Address, Lincoln pointed out that, in the constitutional controversies facing the country, either the minority or the majority would have to yield or government would cease. To reject the majority principle by secession was to invite anarchy or despotism. Four months later, in his message to the special session of Congress, the President raised the question of whether there was some inherent fatal weakness in republics which made them either too strong for the liberties of their own people or too weak to maintain their existence. These doubts he resolved with his conclusion that "This is essentially a people's contest." On the side of the Union it was a war for democracy. "Our popular government," the President noted, "has often been called an experiment." But it still remained for the United States

> to demonstrate to the world that those who can fairly carry an election can also suppress a rebellion—that ballots are the rightful, and peaceful, successors of bullets; and that when ballots have fairly, and constitutionally, decided, there can be no successful appeal, . . . except to ballots themselves, at succeeding elections.[19]

To Lincoln, as the war took its terrible toll, the struggle seemed to achieve a kind of universality. "No one knew better than he," James G. Randall wrote, "the values at hazard. If the United States broke into pieces, it was a question whether any nation based upon popular rule could succeed. The issue was democracy at large. If America failed in its experiment of free government, if it fell apart from some inherent defect, the loss would be world wide."[20] It was to this theme that Lincoln recurred in the Address at Gettysburg:

> . . . a great civil war, testing whether that nation, or any nation so conceived and so dedicated, can long endure. . . . that we here highly resolve that these dead shall not have died in vain—that this nation, under God, shall have a new birth of freedom—and that government of the people, by the people, for the people, shall not perish from the earth.

Though he called the war "essentially a people's contest," Lincoln prosecuted it with an assumption of executive power and responsibility that came close to establishing a dictatorship. A civil war involved special problems regarding the citizen's loyalty to the government. In addition, the conflict of the North and the South was fought on such a vast scale that in many ways it became the first modern total war. Democracy in the sense of individual rights was weakened by policies of arbitrary arrest, military rule, conscription, and censorship. Yet elections continued to be held, Congress was not suppressed, and the President revealed few of the attributes of a modern dictator. Except in the exercise of his war powers, Lincoln adhered to the concept of Presidential restraint and did not interfere with the work of Congress and his Cabinet. He himself was on the whole generally modest and circumspect in his administration of the extraordinary controls he invoked during the war, but in a democracy even a benevolent and temporary dictatorship is open to question, and Lincoln accordingly was subjected to unceasing criticism for the government's violation of individual liberties and subordination of civil law to the rule of military necessity.

Neither Congress nor the Supreme Court was able to interpose any effective restraint on the military power during the war. At the very outset of the struggle Chief Justice Taney was rebuffed in his effort to permit civil trial of a prisoner held by the army on the authority of Lincoln's suspension of the writ of habeas corpus. Congress itself never approved this suspension until March 1863, and in all over 13,000 prisoners were held without trial in the course of the war. Though the peace group within the Democratic party was able to keep up the function of a political opposition, one of its leaders in the Middle West, Clement L. Vallandigham, was arrested by the army in 1863 and exiled to the South. Only after the war was over did the Supreme Court hand down its decision that "Martial rule can never exist where the courts are open and in the proper and unobstructed exercise of their jurisdiction."[21]

Lincoln's arbitrary conduct of the war occasioned much consternation abroad. Friends of American democracy were disheartened by news of the military arrests, coercion of the press, and suppression of dissent. Charges that Lincoln was establishing a military government were made by English newspapers, and the administration was compared to the despotic regimes of central Europe. Some fear was also expressed that, if American democracy degenerated into a military despotism, it might threaten world peace. In England conservatives, long annoyed by the liberals' constant invocation of the American example to push their plans for reform and greater democracy, now rather welcomed the Civil War. English liberals, in turn, were bothered not only by the disruption of American democracy but also by the fact that the South, after all, was fighting a war of self-determination to secure its liberty and independence.[22]

Political sentiment in the North was resentful of the English view that the Civil War endangered American democracy. Foreign opinion, it was felt, was taking advantage of the unfavorable circumstances in the United States. Northern editors argued that democracy would continue to prevail even though the Union divided. A New York newspaper which had supported Breckinridge in 1860 asserted that peaceful secession would prove the worth of American institutions. Secession, Republican journals declared, showed not the failure of democracy but its incompatibility with slavery. It was even pointed out that self-government had antedated the Union and would not cease with its dissolution. Thus it was felt that European monarchists were rejoicing prematurely over the demise of American democracy. "Let the politicians of other countries say what they please," the editor of a small western Democratic Douglas journal wrote,

> if they flatter themselves that a Republican government has proved a failure in America, time will show to them the contrary. Though the Union may be dissolved, and a southern nationality permanently established, still Liberty will survive, and Republican principles will ever be the basis, upon which the government will rest.[23]

In defending American democracy in the court of world opinion, it was the slavery question ultimately which furnished Lincoln and the North with a decisive diplomatic weapon to enlist English sympathies. When Richard Cobden complained to his friend Senator Charles Sumner that he would not have counseled a war for emancipation, the latter replied that the North could not surrender to slavery or accept the conditions imposed by the South for the restoration of the Union. In general English opinion over slavery was slow to form. Especially in the ruling aristocracy there was much indifference and pro-Southern feeling. The antislavery movement was regarded as bound up with the world-wide struggle for democracy; hence it was English liberal and radical opinion which was most concerned to see that American democratic principles were not placed in a false setting by the continuance of slavery. In spite of American eagerness to serve as an example of democracy, English liberals could not overlook the fact that by 1860 in all the civilized portions of the world, slavery existed only in the United States, Brazil, Cuba, and Puerto Rico.[24]

Yet, despite the liberal pressures from abroad and the continual prodding of the abolitionists at home, illustrated by Horace Greeley's famous "Prayer of Twenty Millions," in which he reproached the President for not striking boldly at slavery, Lincoln hesitated. The major purpose of the war, from which he never deviated, was the preservation of the Union. Within the Union slavery existed with full constitutional protection in the border states, and in the North there was much objection to fighting a war over slavery. Lincoln therefore agreed reluctantly to issue the Emanicipation Proclamation, which affected only the slaves of the South, and he continued at the same time to press for his own scheme of compensated emancipation in the loyal states. Lincoln's action was in harmony with his concept of the use of the war power to aid the cause of the Union. He was also motivated more by his desire to weaken the South economically and militarily than by any strong feelings of sympathy for the Negro.

The abolitionists, however, undoubtedly were correct in their view that the fate of slavery would inevitably become a part of the outcome of the war. As soon as Charles Sumner heard of the firing on Fort Sumter, he went to the White House to pledge his support "heart and soul" to the President. "I . . . told him," Sumner said, "that under the war power the right had come to emancipate the slaves."[25] Still Lincoln's conservatism concerning emancipation was not wholly undemocratic. In terms of his total responsibility his cautious policy in regard to slavery could easily be defended. Though the abolitionists stressed the moral issue of slavery, many of them overlooked the equally strong moral issue of peace and the part that they, along with Southern extremists, had played in helping to bring about the war.

In the conflict of loyalties that faced idealistic reformers, peace yielded to abolition as the war furnished the means of freeing the slaves and, at the same time, preserving the American Union. But neither Lincoln or his party, nor even many of the abolitionists, faced up to the matter of what place the former Negro slaves would take in American society. This was the dilemma which Frederick Grimké had posed in his work *Free Institutions.* How, he asked the advocates of freedom for the slaves, could the nation give the Negro his freedom and at the same time deny him his equal rights?

> How could we refuse to impart the benefit of those institutions, whose existence is the very thing which has suggested the change. And yet on the other hand, how could we consent to commit violence upon those institutions, by placing them in the power of a race who have no comprehension of their uses.[26]

The treatment of the free Negro on the eve of the Civil War in the North as well as the South augured ill for the hope of a democratic equality in the future. Universally discriminated against and regarded as inferior beings, free Negroes were allowed to vote only in Massachusetts, Maine, New Hampshire, Vermont, and

Rhode Island, while Illinois, Iowa, and Oregon forbade even their further entry. In the words of Allan Nevins, "Nothing better illustrated the impasse reached by the country than the harsh and increasingly harsher lot of the free Negro; a lot darkest in the South, but sad enough throughout the North."[27]

(V)

In the midst of the war it was convenient to gloss over problems that would inevitably recur once the fighting was stilled. The great civil struggle, despite its bloody carnage, encouraged an aura of romantic idealism. Surrounded by death, individuals often took on a new nobility and achieved a kind of abstract love of mankind in the mass. Thus the war stimulated democracy as well as nationalism and patriotism. Much of this spirit was celebrated in poetry and song. Emerson, Lowell, Whitman, and others caught the finer side of the conflict and helped perpetuate its memory in epic terms. Emerson, for example, became almost ecstatic in his naive belief in the mystic effects of the war. Hawthorne, more appreciative of American democracy since his experience as United States Consul at Liverpool, deplored the militarism which he found in Washington. But he also wrote that the atmosphere of the army camp and smoke of the battlefield were morally invigorating, causing the more enervating effects of civilization to vanish. Walt Whitman, in particular, saw the Civil War as a great surge of idealistic nationalism. Deeply concerned over the suffering of his fellow man in wartime, he was nevertheless confident that the fighting would be a step toward the achievement of a more thorough popular democracy.

In his feeling for democracy, as it was affected by slavery and the Civil War, Whitman ultimately came close to Lincoln's position. A loyal partisan of the Democratic party in the 1840's, Whitman's beliefs were fundamentally Jeffersonian. As editor of the party organ, the *Brooklyn Daily Eagle*, he supported a highly individualistic type of democracy, in which he avowed his opposition to "the doctrine of *force*, as applied in government. . . . Sensible men have long seen that the best government is that which governs least." Much of his criticism was directed at reformers who sought censorious legislation over individual morals and manners, but at the same time he favored reform in the Jacksonian sense of creating a greater equality of opportunity. Thus he supported such causes as women's rights, the abolition of capital punishment, better schools, and improved labor conditions. "It is only the novice in political economy," he wrote, "who thinks it the duty of government to *make* its citizens happy.– Government has no such office. To protect the weak and the minority from the impositions of the strong and the majority . . .–these are rather the proper duties of a government."[28]

Although Whitman abhorred slavery, he was not ready to follow the abolitionists in their demand that it be uprooted in the South. He believed that eventually it would be ended by the peaceful workings of the democratic spirit, but meanwhile he accepted the Constitution and the compromises agreed to by the North and South. Despite his individualism Whitman was a strong nationalist and expansionist–an apostle of manifest destiny. He approved of the War with Mexico and favored the annexation of as much territory in North America as the United States could secure, but like Lincoln and the Republicans he opposed the extension of slavery and claimed that he was the first editor in New York City to support the Wilmot Proviso. In the 1850's Whitman became increasingly disgusted with the concessions of the Democratic party to the Southern slave power, but he continued to go along with the party's aggressive and chauvinistic foreign policy. In the decade before the Civil War he was alternately depressed by the nation's materialism and mediocrity and exhilarated by increasing evidences of scientific progress, in which he saw greater benefits for the masses. Like Lincoln and the North his position in regard to slavery was dominated by his free soil and free labor convictions. When the constitution of the new state of Oregon included a clause prohibiting all Negroes, whether free or slave, from entering the state, Whitman saw such a stipulation as an example of a fundamental conflict between white and black labor. The Negro, he believed, should be colonized abroad, but, in any case, the economic barriers to the two races living together in the United States would spell the doom of slavery. "Once get the slavery question to be argued on, as a question of White Workingmen's Labor against the

Servile Labor of Blacks, and how many years would slavery stand in two-thirds of the present Slave-States?" Whitman asked.[29]

For Whitman, as for many Americans, the Civil War was a not unwelcome answer to the increasing contradictions of American society in the fifties. Although he was sincerely humane and peace-loving, his personality and philosophy also had facets to which the war made strong appeal. With all his odes to individualism and his strong desire for the greatest personal and physical freedom compatible with natural law, Whitman also had a democratic faith in the people and in the kind of unity and solidarity fostered by war.

> One's-self I sing, a simple separate person.
> Yet utter the word Democratic, the word En-Masse.

And, though he urged his readers to "Resist much, obey little," when he saw some regiments returning from the front, he wrote: "I never before so realized the majesty and reality of the American people *en masse*. It fell upon me like a great awe."[30]

The Civil War convinced Whitman of the need for a strong national government if democracy was to survive. His belief that politics was simply a practical way of getting things done, in which government was the machine and democracy the spirit, enabled him to accept the war as a means to a finer end. Although lifted up by the war and hopeful of its good effects, Whitman did not shirk its sad and shabby side. "Mother," he wrote home after Gettysburg,

> one's heart grows sick of war, after all, when you see what it really is; every once in a while I feel so horrified and disgusted—it seems to me like a great slaughterhouse and the men mutually butchering each other—then I feel how impossible it appears, again, to retire from this contest until we have carried our points (it is cruel to be so tossed from pillar to post in one's judgment).[31]

While a government clerk in Washington, he devoted much of his spare time to visiting the sick and wounded men who filled the city's hospitals. And his wartime poetry, despite its romantic yearnings, did not neglect to picture the horror of battle. Thus Whitman also tried to show the side of the fighting which he acknowledged could never really be told. Later, looking back upon these years after the struggle had ceased, he believed it demonstrated that

popular democracy, whatever its faults and danger, practically justifies itself beyond the proudest claims and wildest hopes of its enthusiasts. Probably no future age can know, but I well know, how the gist of this fiercest and most resolute of the world's war-like contentions resided exclusively in the unnamed, unknown rank and file; how the brunt of its labor of death, to all essential purposes, was volunteer'd. The People, of their own choice, fighting, dying for their own idea. . . .[32]

Whitman was both a critic and a prophet of democracy. "The final meaning of Democracy," he wrote as the war was drawing to its close,

is to press on through all ridicules, arguments, and ostensible failures to put in practice the idea of the sovereignty, license, sacredness of the individual. This idea isolates, for reasons, each separate man and woman in the world—while the idea of Love fuses and combines the whole. Out of the fusing of these twain, opposite as they are, I seek to make a homogeneous Song.[33]

To the two essential ingredients of his philosophy, the ideas of Love and Democracy, Whitman added a third—Religion. "For I say at the core of democracy, finally, is the religious element." After the war it was this mystic religious element which more and more gave Whitman hope for the future of democracy. In the midst of the sordid realities of the postwar reconstruction, he published his *Democratic Vistas*, devoted to the age-old dream that "ever seeks to bind, all nations, all men, of however various and distant lands, into a brotherhood, a family." Loyal still to his doctrine of a perfect individualism as the strength and character of the state, he now, however, also wrote of "adhesiveness or love, that fuses, ties and aggregates, making the races comrades, and fraternizing all." In the United States Whitman looked forward to a future embracing "a more universal ownership of property, general homesteads, general comfort—a vast intertwining reticulation of wealth." Thus Whitman's democracy was not merely political. "Did you, too, O friend," he asked,

suppose democracy was only for elections, for politics, and for a party name? I say democracy is only of use there that it may pass on and come to its flower and fruits in manners, in the highest forms of interaction between men and their beliefs—in religion, literature, colleges, and schools—democracy in all public and private life, and in the army and navy. . . . I submit therefore, that the fruition of democracy, on aught like a grand scale, resides altogether in the future.[34]

> Sail, sail thy best, ship of Democracy,
> Of Value is thy freight, 'tis not the Present only,
> The Past is also stored in thee.
> Thou holdest not the venture of thyself alone,
> not of the Western continent alone,
> Earth's *résumé* entire floats on thy keel O ship,
> is steadied by thy spars,
> With thee Time voyages in trust, the antecedent
> nations sink or swim with thee,
> With all their ancient struggles, martyrs, heroes,
> epics, wars, thou bear'st the other continents,
> Theirs, theirs as much as thine, the destination-
> port triumphant. . . .[35]

CHAPTER SEVEN

Reconstruction and Revolution

THE SURRENDER of the Southern armies in the spring of 1865, after four long years of Civil War, insured the preservation of the American Union. At the same time the destruction of the slave-owning aristocracy strengthened the forces of nationalism and popular democracy. In the Lost Cause of the South, weighted down by the heavy burden of slavery, the older doctrines of an individualist and states' rights democracy had met defeat. The Democratic party of Jefferson and Jackson stood discredited by its association with the late Confederacy, while the nationalistic tenets of the Whigs, which had never gained general support before the

Civil War, now won belated success under the Republican party's guidance.

In economic terms the period of the Civil War marked the transition from an agrarian to an industrial order. Whether the war itself should be considered the fundamental cause or mere catalyst in the reconstruction of the material foundations of American democracy is a matter of debate, but there is much to be said for the Beards' use of the term "A Second American Revolution" to describe the great civil conflict. The very magnitude and intensity of the struggle required the expansion and disciplining of the American democratic order. While the people of the North and South voluntarily contributed to their respective causes, the coercive power of government was fastened as never before upon the individual, commanding his person and property for the state. The enormous wartime needs for goods and services helped speed the shift from the individualist agrarian democracy of the ante-bellum years to the nationalistic mass democracy that was to mark the next century.

This change, of course, was more apparent in the North, "where the older and stabler trilogy of aristocracy, decentralization, and agriculture were sacrified to the newer and more experimental trilogy of democracy, nationalism, and industrialism. . . ."[1] In the manner of all victorious governments, the states above the Potomac assumed the right to speak for the whole people, interpreting American democracy in the light of their own ideas and interests. The North's first scholarly historian of the Civil War saw the future as full of hope. The Union's victory was a triumph of nationalism and progress which would make possible the extension of the area of freedom. "Centralization," he wrote, "is an inevitable issue in the life of nations. Power ever tends to concentration." Questioning much of traditional American democracy as, in fact, the rule of a minority, John William Draper asked:

> Why, then, should we view with despair or condemnation the retreat of power from the Individual or the Party. Why lament the loss of that which, if we will only open our eyes, we may see that we never possessed. Why not prepare to accept that which has been, and will ever be the lot of all nations—centralization? guiding ourselves in such a man-

ner that it may be a centralization resting on Intelligence, and not on brute force.[2]

Unlike Draper, Orestes Brownson, the former transcendentalist, feared the coming of a centralized government founded on majority rule. In his *American Republic*, published in the last year of the war, Brownson pointed out the danger that the world would interpret the North's victory as a triumph of social democracy along the lines of the revolutionary nationalism in Europe.

Brownson's and Draper's contrasting hopes and fears in regard to nationalistic democracy were repeated in the new theories of the nature of the American Union. Though secession and states' rights were still defended by Alexander H. Stephens, Vice President of the Confederacy, the Civil War, as President Jefferson Davis admitted, showed secession, at least, "to be impracticable."[3] As a threat to American nationalism, the states' rights argument proved almost as weak as secession until it became useful as a means of defending white supremacy in the South and of resisting federal civil-rights legislation. Meanwhile the North, with little dissent, followed Daniel Webster's and Lincoln's nationalistic interpretation of the Constitution and the Union. The Constitution was viewed as a perpetual contract derived from the people as a whole, while the Union in its origins was believed to go back to the common struggles of the American Revolution and as such to be older than the separate states.

To reinforce this classic nationalist concept of the American Union, political thinkers turned for support from John Locke and the theory of natural rights to Hegel and the German idealist philosophers. Following Hegel's organic theory, American scholars endowed the political state with the human characteristics of personality, conscience, and growth. As a moral organism the state was not a necessary evil but a means toward the realization of a more perfect freedom. It followed therefore that there were no absolute inalienable rights of the individual which existed independent of government. Thus the new political theory contributed to the ideology of a nationalistic mass democracy, while the older individualist values of the democratic tradition declined in relative importance. On the whole, as Draper observed complacently, it was not the liberal but the coercive side of democracy that was strengthened by the Civil War.

Although the Northern wartime elections of 1862 and 1864 had seemed to represent a victory for the moderate elements in the Republican and Democratic parties, radicalism triumphed after the war. The Lincoln-Johnson plans for the reconciliation and speedy reconstruction of the South were discarded in favor of the vindictive program of the Radical Republican Congressional leaders who were able to win majority support after 1866. Thus the North's initial disposition to be generous to its vanquished foe quickly gave way to a desire to enjoy some of the fruits of victory. Perhaps the war itself, like the circumstances of its coming, made impossible the realization of the kind of liberal democracy which encourages toleration and compromise between a majority and minority. Moreover, in the conflicting aspirations of the Southern whites and Negro freedmen, it was not easy for the federal government to work out a satisfactory democratic policy. The natural course, and the one which proved most popular in the North during the first decade of Reconstruction, was to make the South pay tribute to the rest of the nation. In forging a political and economic program congenial to the interests of the North and West, the minority rights of the South were substantially ignored. In fixed attitudes, reminiscent of those of the 1850's, the Northern majority pressed its new-found power upon a Southern minority determined to wage passive resistance. And yet, if the nation was ever to be reconstituted, compromise and reconciliation had to come.

(II)

At the center of the conflict over the reconstruction of American democracy after the Civil War stood the Negro freedman. As the Beards pointed out, nothing like emancipation "had ever happened in history, at least on such a scale." In Europe the liberation of the serfs had left them in possession as owners or tenants of the land they tilled. But in the South, though the planter class was ruined, the former slaves did not secure the "40 acres and a mule" which they thought they had been promised. Thus, Negro freedom "threw into the turbulent forces of democracy a strange and distracting element, . . . a large and anomalous class in the American social order—a mass of emancipated slaves long destined to wander in a hazy realm between bondage and freedom."[4]

Even before the adoption of the Thirteenth Amendment, there was no question that the Negro would receive his freedom if the North won the war. Far less certain, however, was prediction of the status that he might enjoy. In most of the Northern states Negroes did not possess political or social equality, and few Americans thought that they were ready to take their place in the political system as voters or officeholders. Yet it was clear that the American democratic tradition implied not only freedom of the individual but also his equality before the law. Democratic institutions and national stability might be threatened by the exclusion and relegation to second-class citizenship of some four million Negro freedmen. Political expediency as well as simple justice seemed to require granting the right of suffrage to the emancipated slaves. According to James Russell Lowell, the answer to the question, "What are we to do with the negro?" was short and simple. "Give him a fair chance," he wrote.

> We must get rid of the delusion that right is in any way dependent on the skin, and not on an inward virtue. Our war has been carried on for the principles of democracy, and a cardinal point of those principles is, that the only way in which to fit men for freedom is to make them free, the only way to teach them how to use political power is to give it to them.[5]

Wendell Phillips, the radical abolitionist, believed that land was the key to the Negroes' future welfare. "Every man knows that land dictates government. If you hold land, every man his own farm, it is a democracy; you need not curiously ask of the statute book." With land, in addition to education and the vote, the Negro would have his rights respected by the politicians. Only then would he enjoy "real freedom—not merely technical freedom."[6]

Lowell and Phillips were idealists also realistic enough to know that, unless made citizens, the Negroes, who would now be counted fully in figuring the Southern states' population quotas, would add to the power of the South while at the same time they increased their own political disadvantage. Thus there was a paradox, which the Radical Republicans were quick to perceive, that the defeated Southern states might come back into the Union with a greater representation than before the Civil War, when five slaves were counted the equal of three white men in determining Congressional quotas. Staunch abolitionists and democrats believed that the suffrage was a natural right and not just a privilege conferred by the state upon its citizens. Though certain qualifications of literacy or residence might be maintained, discrimination against the Negro's vote because of his race or color was incompatible with his emancipation or with democratic doctrine.

Unfortunately the simple logic of the natural-rights position never received sustained application in regard to the status of the Negro freedman. When the South refused to honor the intent of the Thirteenth Amendment, the North responded by setting the freedman apart as a special class to be protected as wards of the federal government. Though the Fourteenth Amendment asserted a broad national ideal of equality, its provisions were clearly aimed at the Negro. What were natural rights for most Americans had to be the subject of special legislation in the case of the freedmen. In this way the spirit of democracy was thwarted even though the nation tried by law to enforce its practice.

During the first years of Reconstruction, if democracy rather than political expediency had been the country's major concern, there was a possible means of compromise between the majority and minority interests of the North and the South. A waiting period with educational tests or qualifications might have been required before the Negro was allowed to vote. But such a stipulation would have had to be applied equally to all races and classes. And, once the Fourteenth Amendment was adopted, educational tests were no longer a practicable device. The stipulation in the amendment that, when the right to vote was denied by a state to any male citizen of the United States, the state's representation in Congress should be proportionately reduced, would have penalized any state in the Union with a considerable number of illiterates. Immigrants in the North, as well as poor whites in the South, would have been affected equally with the freedmen. The temporary exclusion of the Negro from his civil rights, until he met a minimum qualification, would not have been a denial of democracy. But, as one authority has well pointed out, "the North was unwilling to apply an educational test . . . either to the negro or to the illiterate immigrant, and the South to the 'poor white.' " Moreover, he concluded: "Educational tests run against all the selfish interests of practical politics and the stubborn belief in natural rights."[7]

The dilemma of the Radical Republicans was illustrated by Senator Charles Sumner of Massachusetts. Sumner, who believed that the Negro had a natural right to the suffrage, felt nevertheless that the Fifteenth Amendment had to be added to the Constitution.

> Without the colored vote the white Unionists would have been left in the hands of the rebels; loyal governments could not be organized. The colored vote was a necessity; this I saw at the beginning, and insisted pertinaciously that it should be secured. It was on this ground, rather than principle, that I relied most; but the argument of principle was like a reinforcement.[8]

Neither Sumner's principles nor Republican party necessity was sufficient to carry out the program of Negro suffrage in the South. Despite the Fourteenth and Fifteenth Amendments and the enabling legislation on civil rights passed by Congress, the freedman was not allowed to participate in the democratic process. Instead the South successfully resisted the will of the majority, and, when the last federal troops were withdrawn in 1877, Reconstruction came to a close. The Southern states were restored to self-government, which meant of course white supremacy and a democracy colored by caste lines. Democracy in the South therefore continued to be limited, as its benefits were transferred back to the white population.

But home rule for the South and the failure of the nation to extend democracy to the Negro did not mean a defeat for the nationalism that came out of the Civil War. Indeed the decision of 1877 demonstrated that nationalism was stronger than democracy in the United States. As Ralph Gabriel has pointed out, "The sentiment of nationalism was restored at the expense, as far as the colored race was concerned, of the doctrine of the free individual."[9] The Negro served as a scapegoat to help the South cooperate to recreate the

Union and strengthen American nationalism. Since the North as well as the South was party to the decision of 1877, democracy in the sense of the will of the majority was preserved, but only at the price of the Negroes' minority rights. The Negroes' place within the democratic tradition accordingly remained precarious—the continuing source of an unhappy dilemma for all the American people.

(*III*)

Restored to its position within the Union, ready to play a role in the reconstruction of American nationalism, the New South as a part of the bargain of 1877 was left free to control the Negro according to its own interpretation of the democratic tradition. Social equality, even during Radical Reconstruction, had been no more a characteristic of life in the South than in the North, as churches and schools enforced almost everywhere a pattern of racial segregation. But the complete separation of Negroes and whites and the drastic limitation of the civil rights and economic opportunities of the former developed more slowly. At first, conservative Southern white leaders, the so-called Bourbons or Redeemers, permitted the Negro to vote in limited numbers so long as his vote could be controlled. In South Carolina, for example, Wade Hampton, the first Democratic Governor after the state's "redemption" in 1877, openly supported Negro suffrage and used the Negroes' votes to help defeat his political rivals. Negroes for the most part were allowed to travel freely upon the railroads of the South, and for 20 years after 1865 no Southern state had segregation laws restricting such travel. But in the 1880's discriminatory practices in regard to the Negro began to mount. In October 1883, the Supreme Court declared the Civil Rights Act of 1875 unconstitutional. By taking the position that the Fourteenth Amendment prohibited only the states from discriminating against the Negro, the Court in effect legalized the practice of segregation by private individuals or organizations, including hotels, theaters, and railroads. Later Court decisions specifically upheld segregation in railroad accommodations and in the public schools.

The pattern of racial segregation in the South affected whites as well as Negroes. The great mass of the poverty-stricken "poor white" population was able to rationalize its inferior economic status only by accepting the Bourbon's arguments for white supremacy. Placing considerations of caste before the realities of their lower-class position, poor whites were reluctant to make common cause with the Negro in a concerted democratic movement. Any split within the ranks of the Democratic party was portrayed as a threat to white supremacy and the Solid South, and as an invitation to the Negro to attempt a return to politics. To avert the charge of fomenting this possibility, the democratic Populist movement of the 1890's gradually became anti-Negro. "Jim Crow" laws found their way into the statute books in increasing numbers, while the barriers of racial discrimination seemed to mount "in direct ratio with the tide of political democracy among whites."[10] Race relations deteriorated rapidly, and lynching, the most aggravated form of racism, reached its peak in the 1890's and early 1900's.

The Southern states now also began to incorporate in their constitutions the well-known barriers to Negro suffrage inaugurated by the Mississippi state constitution of 1890. Over the next two decades the South through property or literacy qualifications enormously reduced the amount of Negro voting. At the same time loopholes in the laws, clauses referring to persons of good character or whose grandfathers had voted, permitted propertyless and illiterate whites to exercise the suffrage. Finally, if Negroes somehow surmounted these restrictions, they were caught by the imposition of laws which reserved participation in the Democratic party primaries in the South to whites only. The effectiveness of the varied restrictions on the suffrage is illustrated in part by statistics in Louisiana which showed a drastic decline in the number of registered Negro voters: from 130,334 in 1896 to 1,342 in 1904. This and the similar decline in other Southern states also probably owed something to the growing political apathy of the section which followed the failure of the Populist revolt. Affecting whites as well as Negroes, this indifference continued well into the twentieth century.[11]

The Supreme Court, following its precedent in the civil rights and segregation cases, did not interfere with the South's complex plans to curtail Negro suffrage. The defeat of the Lodge "force bill" in the Senate in January 1891 marked the end of the post-Reconstruction efforts to enable the Negro to vote through passage of a federal law controlling elections. In the South the Republican party practically abandoned the Negro as a political ally. Accepting his disfranchisement as inevitable, the party turned to the building of the so-called "lily-white" factions as a nucleus for a two-party system in the South. "The fact is," wrote Ray Stannard Baker in 1908, "the Republican party, as now constituted in the South, is even a more restricted white oligarchy than the Democratic party. In nearly all parts of the South, indeed, it is a close corporation which controls or seeks to control all the federal offices."[12] Thus, by the turn of the century, little remained of the plans advanced at the end of the Civil War by the radical idealists who had hoped to see the Negro freedman gain his proper rights in a democracy. The American democracy of the Progressive era was to be for whites only.

Faced with the reality of the new national reconciliation of North and South, in which in considerable measure they continued to be the victims, Negroes accepted the compromise policy of acquiescence and adjustment suggested by their most influential leader, Booker T. Washington. In 1895, in a famous speech at the opening of the Atlanta Exposition, Washington, the president of the Negro industrial school at Tuskegee, Alabama, offered the framework of his theory of race relations. Yielding the militant approach of the first Negro leaders during Reconstruction, Washington pleased Southern whites by rejecting outside Northern intervention. At the same time he assured his audience that the Negro was more interested in securing industrial education and economic opportunity than political rights, and he agreed that property and educational qualifications for voting were desirable. The point of view for which Washington stood, and which he was able to enforce upon the great bulk of American Negroes before the First World War, was one of pragmatic compromise. Before he could achieve social and political equality, Washington believed that Negroes had to gain economic security. Whether the latter was possible without the former was open to question, but Washington's relegation of his race to a position as second-class citizens in the lower ranks of labor was popular with the American political and industrial figures with whom he associated on familiar terms. Following Washington's advice, the Negro found a place in American society—a place not in keeping with the equalitarian doctrines of the democratic faith, but one further down the social and political scale among the mudsills and bottom rails of the nationalized and industrialized economic order.

(IV)

The freeing of the slaves, followed almost immediately by the Negroes' exclusion from most of the promises of American democracy, was a part of the dilemma of the democratic tradition in the post-Civil War era of nationalism and industrialism. In 1865 the Republican party was simply a war machine which had accomplished its purpose and which was now in danger of breaking up as the Whigs and Federalists had done earlier in United States history. But the decline of the older agrarian democratic forces, which had been further weakened by the war, and the stigma of disunion affixed to the Democratic party provided new political opportunities. At the same time the rapid development of American industry and the centralization of power within the federal government made it possible for the Republicans to work out a political and economic program acceptable to the reconstituted nation. According to the sympathetic view of Herbert Croly there was no real problem.

> In its economic policy the Republican party was not merely giving positive effect to the economic theory underlying the Constitution, but it was entering upon a program of constructive democratic legislation, as democracy was then understood. Both its opposition to slavery and its stimulation of economic production were intended to enhance human values.

If the Constitution protected property, why, the Republicans seemed to ask, "should not the law be used to promote its acquisitions?"[13]

Against this proposition was ranged the fast-ebbing Jeffersonian democratic doctrine of the limited state, which the Civil War had pushed aside. "In the years following the war," Vernon L. Parrington observed in his classic description of America during the 1870's, "exploitation for the first time was provided with adequate resources and a competent technique." Parrington likened these postwar years to a great barbecue. "It was sound Gilded Age doctrine. To a frontier people what was more democratic than a barbecue, and to a paternalistic age what was more fitting than that the state should provide beeves for roasting." Loyal citizens had saved the government during the trying days of the Civil War, and it was only fair in return that the government should give some tangible reward to their patriotism. Thus the theory of Whiggery "asserts that it is a duty of the state to help its citizens make money, and it conceives of the political state as a useful instrument for effective exploitation. . . . But unhappily," as Parrington pointed out, "there is a fly in the Whiggish honey. In a competitive order, government is forced to make its choices. It cannot serve both Peter and Paul. If it gives with one hand it must take away with the other. And so the persuasive ideal of paternalism in the common interest degenerates in practice into legalized favoritism. Governmental gifts go to the largest investments."[14]

The rivalry of competing economic interests for federal preferment did not occasion any immediate crisis in American democracy. Although the South was crushed by defeat, the country as a whole enjoyed a postwar boom. Under the reigning Republican political philosophy it was believed that government should encourage expansion and lend assistance to every essential economic interest in the country. After all, had not Americans always associated the good life with productivity? Following the panic and depression of the mid-seventies prosperity revived, continuing in most of the nation until the 1890's. Spurred on by the opening of the vast reaches of the public domain in the trans-Mississippi West and by the tremendous industrial growth in the Northeast, the American economy seemed able to offer exceptional opportunities to almost everyone. If it had not been for the memories of the Civil War, another era of good feeling might have ensued.

In the generation after the Civil War, business received the richest endowments, while the needs of both farmers and factory workers were relegated to a subordinate place in the economic hierarchy. Loopholes in the Homestead Act of 1862 made it possible for speculative interests to acquire most of the Western lands. Meanwhile labor was disciplined, not only by the occasional armed intervention of the federal government to quell strikes, but, more importantly, by the open immigration policy of the United States, under which over 12 million aliens entered the country between 1865 and 1900. It is significant that in these years neither farmers nor labor were able to organize themselves as strong economic classes, in a position to compete on equal terms with the business and industrial community. Their lack of power was due in considerable measure to their large numbers. An easy land and immigration policy deprived both groups of the economic advantages of relative scarcity in the market place. Thus, while business with the aid of friendly court decisions was able to turn from competition to combination, the consolidation of farmers and labor into powerful economic and political pressure groups was postponed until the twentieth century.

In the industrial advance of the nation the South, once Radical Reconstruction was given up, became a junior partner of the North and West. Conservative Southern whites, descendants of the old antebellum Whigs, to whom C. Vann Woodward has given the expressive term "Redeemers," came to agreement with the nationalism and industrialism of the North. Welcoming Northern capital for its factories and actively seeking federal aid, the Redeemers of the New South were the counterparts of the Republican nationalists and business barons. While the South favored laissez faire as against Radical Reconstruction, it had no patience "with state rights and *laissez faire* if they implied abandonment of Federal subsidies, loans of credit, and internal improvements."[15] Of course the South did not entirely yield its traditions, but the Old South was interlaced with the New. In the perfervid words of her chief orator, Henry W. Grady, editor of the Atlanta *Constitution:*

> The Old South rested on slavery and agriculture, unconscious that these could neither give nor maintain healthy growth. The new South presents a perfect Democracy, the oligarchs leading in the popular movement—a social system compact and closely knitted, less splendid on the surface but stronger at the core, a hundred farms for every plantation, fifty homes for every palace, and a diversified industry that meets the complex needs of this complex age.[16]

Stripped of its sentimental rhetoric, the New South was far less democratic than Grady and many of its leading citizens implied. In the North the expansion of public education and its extension to the high schools and state universities kept pace with the intellectual needs of the new mass democracy. The immigrant, though forced to accept the least rewarding jobs, was not condemned to the inferior status of the Negro. But the South, poor despite the influx of Northern capital, was able to make little headway in providing the minimum necessities of a democratic culture. Public education declined after the brief period of expansion under the Reconstruction governments, and expenditures per pupil averaged only little more than one third of the national norm. The teaching of Negroes, especially necessary if they were to take their place in American democracy, was resented and neglected. Illiteracy in 1900 among Southern whites amounted to 12 per cent, while it was 50 per cent for the Negroes.[17]

In both North and South the drive toward national unity and industrial progress proved stronger than democratic doctrines. Economically the rising industrial and business order of the North was paralleled by that of the New South. Government contracts for military needs during the Civil War strengthened the alliance of government and business. Although business leaders subscribed in theory to the philosophy of laissez faire, in practice they learned to rely upon the benefits that were to be gained from the government. Minority groups, striving for a democratic equality, occupied an inferior place in the new nationalism. Though it was an age of competition, the various protagonists were not fairly matched. As combination and consolidation, concentration and monopoly, came to characterize the political and economic order, it became less easy to accept the view that the industrialists were the friends of democracy and foes of privilege. The extraordinary violence in the relations of capital and labor, culminating in the Haymarket bomb and in the Homestead and Pullman strikes of the 1890's, threatened all the essential elements of the democratic tradition.

The very fact that so many wealthy industrialists, like Andrew Carnegie and John D. Rockefeller, had risen from humble beginnings seemed to make them all the more ruthless in their climb to the top. Having achieved high eminence, the prosperous business leader was quick to rationalize his position in Darwinian terms of the survival of the fittest. Yet, at the same time, many businessmen felt a compulsion to contribute heavily to various worthy causes and to follow Carnegie in the assertion of a Gospel of Wealth. Carnegie believed that the acquisition of wealth as an end in itself was ignoble and that rich men, by disbursing their gains in philanthropic endeavors, helped to preserve individualism and avoid the growth of socialism. The steelmaster's *Triumphant Democracy*, published in 1886, was a statistical paen to the material progress of the United States since the Civil War. The explanation for the success of American democracy he found in the Anglo-Saxon race, the superior physical environment of North America, and the bestowal of equal citizenship upon the whole people.

Uniformly successful in their enterprises, Carnegie and Rockefeller were too outstanding as individuals to be in any way typical representatives of either the American plutocracy or democracy. In a cynical generation, in which government and business frankly exchanged favors and spoils, the more representative figure of the age was a small drab man who received from the electorate the highest award it was possible for the nation to bestow. Greatest of all the popular folk heroes created by the Civil War, Ulysses S. Grant was the perfect embodiment of the Gilded Age. While the image of the martyred Lincoln symbolized the idealism of the war, Grant came to personify the crasser realities that have a disturbing way of coming to the surface once the battle smoke has disappeared.

It may be accounted a misfortune for Grant and the country that he was twice elected to the Presidency, but there was no doubt of his victories, whether civil or military. A poor boy who had won little success before 1861, and a regular army officer who disliked war, Grant suddenly found himself in the topmost echelon of American civil and military life. With a simple naiveté, the victor at Appomattox presided serenely over his country, secure in the belief that exploitation was progress, that corruption and treason were confined to the South, and that the leaders of the Republican party and of big business could do no wrong. In these convictions President Grant was in no way unusual. Indeed his beliefs were as perfect an expression of the nationalism and democracy of the age as his own career had been. What better national leader was there than the General who had commanded the largest armies yet assembled in the world? And who was more democratic than a President whose every thought and action bordered on the commonplace?

Undistinguished in person or mind, and with no strong loyalties or ties except to his country, Grant was the living symbol of the new nationalistic mass democracy of his age. To Mark Twain, whose later books described the happier side of Grant's America, the General always remained a great man. As befitted a hero, he managed to stand above the battle, unbesmirched in the public mind by the dirt and corruption that Mark Twain himself depicted so caustically in his *The Gilded Age*.

(*V*)

In the quarter of a century following Grant's Presidency, his successors in the White House were hardly more capable and considerably less popular than he had been. A dull complacency settled over the country, disturbed only periodically by the outraged protests of farmer-labor parties and small groups of dedicated liberal reformers. As Henry Adams observed in retrospect, "No period so thoroughly ordinary had been known in American politics since Christopher Columbus first disturbed the balance of American society. . . ."[18] In this age of the spoilsmen, the public was mostly concerned with the business of exploiting the economic possibilities of the environment. So long as this business was not seriously interfered with, the average citizen regarded the activities of the politicians with good-natured contempt. Sections might become aroused over the tariff or free silver, but the people at large remained indifferent.

The most striking phenomenon of the times, the exaltation of national at the expense of state power, had little relation to the fortunes of party. It was due, rather, to a new sentiment of national unity which began to tide through American life as soon as Lee's surrender determined that the United States was to remain a geographic entity. Its force was increased by the notable growth of business and capital across state borders and the multiplying contacts resulting from improved means of travel and communication.[19]

Until the turn of the century neither of the two major parties felt impelled to cope with the problem of trying to reconcile the historic values of the American democratic tradition with the new revolutionary forces of a heightened nationalism and a growing industrialism. Real issues and principles were left to the third parties which hopelessly contested the state and national elections. Once the question of Reconstruction was resolved, Republicans and Democrats competed chiefly for the spoils of office. Although the Republicans attempted to keep sectional feeling alive by waving "the bloody shirt" of the late Civil War, the only thing that mattered was to win. And the main reason for winning was to control the civil service and the patronage. Since tenure in virtually all government positions depended on the party in power, the stakes in any election ran high. Despite the passage of reform legislation, especially the Pendleton Act of 1883, at the turn of the century appointment to more than half of the federal civil service, some 100,000 positions, was still not subject to examination or merit. A decade earlier President Harrison in his first year in office made over 35,000 removals—15,000 more than in the previous Cleveland administration.[20]

Extensive corruption in government was fairly new in American politics. Despite scandals from time to time, as in the New York Customs House under the Jacksonians, the government played too minor a part in the economy of the country before the Civil War for political patronage to become a serious threat to democracy. After 1865 it was not so much that individuals became suddenly greedier as that the role of the government grew larger and its relations with business more complex. War contributed to a breakdown of general ethics and morality, while lavish grants and subsidies required heavier taxation and an enlarged civil service.

> The combination of a great war and a rapid expansion of business after 1861 greatly extended the activities of political government and multiplied political officeholders. New excises entailed a host of new tax collectors. High tariffs made the customhouses hum with unwonted activity. Army and navy contracts opened employment to purchasing agents, inspectors, bookkeepers, clerks. Government munition factories gave work to thousands; homesteads and railroad grants occupied surveyors, recorders, clerical assistants; new internal revenue taxes, the growing budget, the expanding population, the constantly increasing immigration once the war was over, created new jobs in the Treasury, the post office, and the ports. The phenomenal growth of American cities . . . added thousands more to public pay rolls.[21]

Concluding this graphic description, the authors of *The Age of Enterprise* declare that "In the decades after the Civil War politics thus became one of the great businesses of the nation, steadily employing thousands of workers, seeking profits like any other enterprise in a competitive society." In return for political favors to business interests, politicians expected suitable rewards. As long as the party received its share of the spoils in the form of graft and offices, it could control votes and win elections. Thus the corruption of American politics grew. The "carpetbag" governments in the South, the Tweed Ring in New York City, and scandals in the executive departments during Grant's Presidency were only the better-known cases which attracted widespread protest.

The postwar degradation of American politics encouraged a growing impatience with the principles as well as the practice of democracy. Liberals together with conservatives shared some of the misgivings that Henry Adams voiced in the novel which he published anonymously in 1880 under the title *Democracy*. Francis Parkman complained of "The Failure of Universal Suffrage." Democracy, the new king in America, he wrote, was being ruined by the influx of the hordes of immigrants who filled the nation's factories and cities. The solution, he believed, was to reform city government by taking it out of the hands of the masses and entrusting it to the leadership of the so-called better class.[22] In discussing the "Character of Democracy in the United States," Woodrow Wilson called for a more effective political leadership. Democracy required a certain popular consensus and homogeneity which was being threatened by European immigration. Since the masses could not govern themselves properly in the complex modern society of the 1880's, Wilson believed that "This vast and miscellaneous democracy of ours must be led; its giant faculties must be schooled and directed. Leadership cannot belong to the multitude; masses of men cannot be self-directed, neither can groups of communities."[23] Unlike Parkman and Adams, Wilson was able eventually to realize a lifelong desire to enter politics. In this he followed the example of his later rivals, Theodore Roosevelt and Henry Cabot Lodge, who had already plunged into political life as reformers.

Among a number of intellectuals and advocates of civil-service reform, who did not themselves run for elective office, the idea of creating a governing class or elite group of career officials took hold as the answer to the problem of political corruption. Without going this far, Edwin Lawrence Godkin, founder and editor of the *Nation* magazine, became a leader in the crusade for political reform. Godkin did not entirely dismiss American fears that civil-service reform might create a bureaucracy similar to those of the European powers. No objection to a merit system was more serious, he admitted, but in a democracy like the United States he was confident that the danger of abuse was slight. Godkin and his fellow reformers maintained that the United States, in contrast to Europe, enjoyed the protection of its federal system and separation of powers, while governmental controls over the citizen, though growing, were still relatively weak.

The real problems of democracy, Godkin suggested, came from the failure to analyze it broadly enough, taking into account the whole society and not just political externals. Godkin was one of a number of observers after the Civil War who saw in the movement of population to the West the source both of certain strengths and weaknesses in American democracy. Many of the changes in American life for which conservatives were quick to blame democratic principles might actually be better ascribed, he felt, to "the frontier life." "The great fault of new countries is their newness," he wrote, "and for this the great remedy is time." The American electorate, he believed, though not able to judge technical and scientific arguments, had a pragmatic common sense and a willingness to change its opinions in the light of the evidence. The solution which Godkin offered to the growth of political corruption was a return to Jeffersonian principles of limited government. In an editorial analyzing the Credit Mobilier scandal, he wrote:

> The remedy is simple. The Government must get out of the "protective" business and the "subsidy" business and the "improvement" and the "development" business. It must let trade, commerce, and manufacturers, and steamboats, and railroads, and telegraphs alone. It cannot touch them without breeding corruption.[24]

Godkin's editorials in the *Nation* served as a conscience to the raw democracy of America in the era from the seventies to the nineties. Like his English Victorian friends, he feared the illiberal tendencies of the mass democracy of the nineteenth century. The conduct of Radical Reconstruction by the carpetbag regimes in the South and the revival of Northern prejudices against the Negro led him to accept the qualification which white supremacy placed upon American democracy. But until the Spanish-American War and imperialism clouded the scene, he continued to be moderately hopeful of the future of American democracy.

(*VI*)

Godkin and his fellow liberals in the East were the staunch foes of paternalism and corruption in government. They opposed tariffs and subsidies and turned away from Radical Reconstruction to civil-service reform. The democracy they favored had an individualistic and even aristocratic flavor, and the radical ideas and fiscal theories of Western farmers and Eastern workingmen were little to their taste. In its popular sense therefore, the democratic tradition in the eighties and nineties was advanced more notably by Henry George and his followers and by the Western farmers who banded together in the Populist movement. The theories of George and the political and economic changes advocated by the Populists went far beyond the mere purification of democracy desired by the civil-service reformers.

In the manner of Jefferson and of other early American liberals, Henry George united a strong faith in democratic ideals with a healthy skepticism of centralized power. Also, like Godkin, he perceived the dangers of a paternalistic democracy which offered its favors to the highest bidder. "Railroad subsidies," he complained in 1870, "are condemned by the political principle that government should be reduced to its minimum—that it becomes more corrupt and more tyrannical, and less under the control of the people, with every extension of its powers and duties."[25] But for George the fundamental problem of American democracy in the last third of the nineteenth century was an economic one—the existence of want or poverty in the midst of plenty or so-called progress. This was the thesis of his famous work *Progress and Poverty*, which was first published in 1879. Though George's solution—the single tax on the unearned increment or profit derived from the ownership of unimproved land—seemed to lack reality in an age of increasing industrialization, his broader ideas continued to have an unusual influence upon the American democratic tradition, while George himself stirred the thought and feelings of the plain people in both England and America.

The single-tax panacea had little appeal among American farmers, who were, after all, for the most part owners of the land they tilled. But by the late eighties and early nineties, hard times and low prices were making radicals of many Americans in the agricultural West and South. Using the power which they had found earlier in the Granger and Alliance movements, the embattled and embittered farmers turned in the 1890's to the organization of the People's, or Populist, party. At Omaha, Nebraska, in the summer of 1892, the delegates of the new party adopted a platform which marked a sharp break with the conventional democracy of the older parties. Ignoring such issues as the tariff and the civil service, the Populists placed their stress instead on economic reform and upon a frank expansion of the powers of the government. Along with their demand for the free coinage of silver and gold at the ratio of 16 to 1, the Populists called for a graduated income tax, postal savings banks, government ownership and operation of the railroad and telegraph and telephone lines, plus shorter hours for labor and restrictions on immigration. Though some of their economic program was clearly socialist, the Populists maintained their essential belief in private property and protested that they sought merely to regulate the few in order to free the many and restore competition. To insure that the government, whose powers they proposed to augment, would remain in the hands of the people, the Populists advocated a more direct form of democracy through such techniques as the secret ballot, popular election of United States Senators, and the initiative and referendum in the states.

In the Presidential election of 1892 the Populists became the first new party to carry a state since the Republican campaign in 1856. Winning over a million votes that year, and almost half a million more two years later, the Populists then lost their identity as a party by joning with William Jennings Bryan and the Democrats in 1896. Despite the intense excitement of the campaign and

Bryan's strong popular backing in the South and West, "the Great Commoner" was defeated by William McKinley and the Republicans. Fundamentally agrarian and rural in outlook, the democracy of the Populists and Bryan Democrats failed to win over the workingmen and urbanized middle class in the East. With the return of prosperity and the advent of the Spanish-American War, radical democracy was temporarily eclipsed. According to Tom Watson, the Populist candidate for Vice President, the war doomed all hopes of reform. "The blare of the bugle drowned the voice of the Reformer," he complained bitterly.[26]

Although the war helped make the reconstruction of the American national union an accomplished political fact, the tremendous industrial progress of the country had created new problems of class conflict, social distress, and open violence between capital and labor. While democracy was coming to have greater mass significance than ever before in American history, its benefits and responsibilities were also being shared in unequal fashion, and the Negro minority especially was compelled to accept an inferior status. But, despite the grim forebodings of Watson and the Populists, protests against special privilege and demands for political and economic reform won renewed popularity in the Progressive era of the early 1900's. Though the People's party had been swallowed by the Democrats, its principles had a liberalizing effect upon the older organization, and many of the best features of its program were accepted by the two major parties and gradually enacted into law.

CHAPTER EIGHT

The Triumph of Nationalism and Reform

BY THE CLOSE of the century, a generation after the crisis of the Civil War, the American democratic tradition again had reached a critical turning point. The bitter class conflict of the 1890's forcibly suggested that large numbers of Americans were dissatisfied with the status quo. Although, as yet, there were few who questioned the worth of democracy as a political system, many thoughtful observers believed that democratic values were seriously threatened by the great concentrations of wealth and power being built up as a result of America's industrial growth. Under the joint ministrations of an advancing technology and helpful federal legislation, the United States had become the leading manufacturing nation of the world, but at the same time the dilemma which Henry George posed in *Progress and Poverty* was still unresolved. More than ever before in American history there seemed to be much truth in Jefferson's prediction that democracy would be endangered when the bulk of the population lived clustered together in large cities, earning their bread in factory labor. The question, stated very simply, was whether democracy was compatible with bigness. In the midst of the nationalizing of business, of labor, and of government, the major problem was somehow to reconcile the older, more traditional concepts of democracy with these new revolutionary developments.

According to the ominous announcement of the Census Bureau in 1893, there was no longer a frontier in the sense of large areas of Western lands available for easy economic exploitation. Even if science and technology were able to provide "new frontiers" in the future, it seemed clear that, as Frederick Jackson Turner pointed out in his famous essay "The Significance of the Frontier in American History," one of the important influences in support of American democracy was gone.

The changes in American life accented by the passing of the frontier had already attracted the attention of the celebrated English observer James Bryce. In a concluding chapter of his *American Commonwealth* (1888) forecasting the future of political institutions in the United States, Bryce took an economic interpretation of American history similar to Turner's. In a generation or half century, he predicted, "the chronic evils and problems of old societies, such as we see them today in Europe, will have reappeared on this new soil." The underlying differences of America and Europe by then would have disappeared, and America might no longer enjoy such advantages as "an absence of class distinctions and class hatreds, a diffusion of wealth among an immense number of small proprietors all interested in the defense of property, an exemption from chronic pauperism and economical distress. . . ." The last advantage especially, but in a sense all three, Bryce believed, was due to the demand for labor in the United States and to "the outlet which the West now provides for the overflow of the great cities." But, with the close of the frontier and rise of large corporations, these favorable conditions would diminish.[1] Bryce's analysis implied the need of positive effort and possible government intervention to restore a frontier-type of opportunity, and the *American Commonwealth*, with its implications for the nationalistic reform of American democracy, continued to be revised and read throughout the Progressive era.

More pessimistic than Bryce or Turner, Brooks Adams, the lineal descendant of two Presidents of the United States, discounted the still fashionable belief of the industrial plutocracy that its supremacy was guaranteed by evolution and the survival of the fittest. In his book *The Law of Civilization and Decay*, Adams depicted history as a series of cycles. The progress of civilization indicated further centralization and consolidation, with a resulting loss of freedom and elasticity, until finally distintegration and decay set in. Theodore Roosevelt, who wrote a generally favorable review of Adams' volume, dissented nevertheless from the author's pessimistic conclusion that capitalism could not escape his "law." "I do not think his diagnosis of the disease is in all respects accurate," Roosevelt wrote in 1897. "I believe there is an immense amount of healthy tissue as to the existence of which he is blind; but there is disease, and it is serious enough to warrant very careful examination."[2]

(*II*)

In a few short years, by one of the quirks of fate which enliven and complicate history, Roosevelt was President of the United States, thrust into the very center of the conflicting forces described by Brooks Adams. The rising Progressive movement, in which Theodore Roosevelt was to emerge as the popular and dramatic leader, was characterized by nothing so much as its nationalistic interpretation of democracy and reform. Unlike agrarian-dominated Populism, the reform of Progressivism, as Eric Goldman points out, was to be "a product of the cities as much as of the farms, an amalgam of the Best People's liberalism and the nobody's Populism, a middle doctrine for a nation rapidly committing itself to middle-class ways of thinking. Progressivism accepted business America, even was enthusiastic about it, and aimed merely to correct abuses. . . .

The restoration of opportunity by giving stronger powers to more democratized governments, a businesslike restoration with no disreputable caterwauling, . . . was a sweepingly appealing program, the most national one since the Republican platform that rode Lincoln into the White House. . . .[3]

It should be noted that many of the political and economic problems which the Progressives faced were historically of the people's own making. For example, the Fourteenth Amendment, ostensibly designed to protect the civil rights of the Negro freedmen, in practice went far beyond this intention. Under the interpretation of the Supreme Court, which decided that the amendment's due process clause protected corporations as well as individuals, the states were deprived of their normal regulatory and police powers. In its contests with the states the Court also used the federal power over interstate commerce to protect large nation-wide corporations. By this line of judicial reasoning, not only was monopoly encouraged, but the potential authority of the federal government as against that of the states was also strengthened. At the same time, although both the Interstate Commerce Act and the Sherman Antitrust Act proved ineffective instruments of federal regulation, they tended toward the centralization of economic power in the national government. Thus Henry Steele Commager correctly asserts:

> From the Interstate Commerce Act of 1887 and the Antitrust Act of 1890 we can conveniently date the beginnings of federal centralization; from Fuller's appointment to the Chief Justiceship in 1888, that revolutionary shift in the interpretation of the Fourteenth Amendment which did so much to nullify state action in the economic and social area. . . .[4]

In its faith in a nationalistic type of political and economic reformation, American Progressivism was part of a general European movement toward state socialism. Although the extent to which Progressivism in the United States was influenced by European ideas has usually been overlooked, one authority on the growth of the administrative state has observed that a "perusal of the literature of reform and Progressivism creates a strong impression that the stimulation of European example has been tremendous."[5]

By the late nineteenth century the large numbers of American students who traditionally went abroad for graduate study were coming into firsthand contact with the social reform programs in England and the Continent. German-trained Ph.D.'s, in particular, returned to the United States to take up positions in the various branches of American government and in leading universities. While their educational experience gave these Americans a deep respect for the specialized scholarship and intellectual freedom of Germany, it also impressed upon them the importance of institutions and the role of the state as an agency of reform. As early as the 1880's, Germany under Bismarck adopted its well-known social security laws designed to blunt the force of labor and radical opposition to the state and to heighten national loyalty and patriotism. England followed suit, and in the 1900's Lloyd George's social legislation offered a parallel with the Progressive reforms in the United States.

The social justice movement in England especially served as an example for Americans. Settlement houses, slum clearance, the Salvation Army, and Christian social reform were all soon duplicated in the United States. English leaders, like the reformers John Ruskin and William Morris and the prominent Fabians Sidney and Beatrice Webb, were important personal influences. Jane Addams worked at Toynbee Hall in the slum section of London before she established Hull House in Chicago. The young historian Charles Beard, who had been at Hull House before he went to England for graduate study, associated himself with the British labor movement and helped found Ruskin College. Beard also had some contact with Fabian Socialism, and he saw the future significance of the whole social reform movement for United States history. Later, in his text *Contemporary American History*, which he published at the height of Progressivism in the United States, Beard observed in retrospect:

> Eminent economists turned aside from free trade and *laissez faire* to consider some of the grievances of the working class and many abandoned the time-honored discussion of "economic theories," in favor of legislative programs embracing the principles of state socialism, to which countries like Germany and Great Britain were already committed.
>
> Charity workers whose function had been hitherto to gather up the wrecks of civilization and smooth their dying days began to talk of "a war for the prevention of poverty," and an examination of their concrete legislative proposals revealed the acceptance of some of the principles of state socialism.[6]

Summing things up, Herbert Croly, perhaps the leading theoretician among American Progressives, wrote in his biography of Mark Hanna that by the 1900's the "United States had become more like a European country than like the United States of 1830."[7] If Croly and Beard exaggerated European influences, it was not from any lack of sympathy with the general course of Progressive reform in either Europe or America. Rather they welcomed the example of the Old World reforms as a stimulus to guide the United States in its slower development along these same lines.

(III)

An important facet of the new reform philosophy was an ideology of social change derived from the Darwinian theory of evolution and the economic interpretation of history. Darwinism, as set forth in the voluminous writings of Herbert Spencer, applied organic biological evolution to all the various aspects of social and political life. Spencer's philosophy stressed the adjustment of the individual and society to the gradual evolution of the environment and to the natural laws of the universe. Professor William Graham Sumner of Yale, the chief academic disciple of Spencer in the United States, in his famous *Folkways* demonstrated that individuals were governed by the folkways or mores, which in turn were a result of adaptation to the environment. Though Sumner himself fought actively for a number of worthy reform causes, the cultural determinism of his *Folkways* denied the free will and faith in progress which were so much a part of the American democratic tradition.

In its hostility to radical reform or drastic change, in comparison with a gradual evolution, the Spencer-Sumner philosophy proved particularly congenial to American educators and business leaders in the late nineteenth century. Many Americans, however, came to take a more hopeful view of evolution, regarding its doctrines as scientific justification for their belief in progress and improvement. Evolution, according to the advocates of social reform, was not primarily a story of individuals in a "dog-eat-dog" competition with each other, but it indicated rather the success of men in a struggle with their environment. The lesson it taught was not laissez faire but social control. Instead of individuals being forced to adapt themselves to their environment, governments and reform agencies, the Progressives believed, could reshape the environment to meet the needs of society.

Evolutionary precepts were specially useful in revamping American ideas of government and jurisprudence. Political institutions and ideals no longer were regarded as fixed creations. Progress in government was believed to result from the struggles of organized pressure groups and political parties to break down older conservative customs. Democracy, accordingly, seemed less a matter of traditional individual rights than of pragmatic social cooperation and reform. In his book *Constitutional Government*, published in 1908, Woodrow Wilson wrote that government was not static but dynamic and living. Its future was dependent upon men's "quick cooperation, their ready response to the commands of instinct or intelligence, their amicable community of purpose. Government is not a body of blind forces; it is a body of men. . . . Living political constitutions must be Darwinian in structure and in practice."[8] Legal thinking, too, was affected by Darwinian evolution, and Justice Holmes became a pioneer of the new jurisprudence of the Progressive era in his view that the law itself was empirical and changing. Although Holmes did not consider himself a Progressive, his criticism of the moralism and excessive deference to precedence which characterized the courts helped prepare the way for a more sympathetic judicial interpretation of Progressive legislation.

Also put to new use was the economic interpretation of history. Formerly the doctrine of conservatives who accepted it as an argument for government protection of property interests, economic determinism was now called upon to justify government regulation of big business in the interests of the state and the people. The economic motive was invoked to explain the rapacity of the plutocracy, and the thesis was advanced that reform could be accomplished only by opposing interest to interest. Thus the national economic interest was deemed superior to that of the individual or group self-interest, and reform efforts were directed to furthering what was considered the welfare of the nation as a whole. While economists and sociologists called for the abolition of laissez faire and the institution of planned social reform, political scientists and historians united to show how the Constitution and the courts had long supported laissez faire and conservative property interests in violation of popular democracy. J. Allen Smith's *Spirit of American Government*, a pioneer work in the economic interpretation of the Constitution, later much reinforced and documented by Charles Beard's famous volume, influenced among other Progressives both Theodore Roosevelt and Robert M. La Follette. The book strengthened Progressives' demand for constitutional changes and weakened the case for conservatives' devotion to the sanctity of the Constitution. Beard's *An Economic Interpretation of the Constitution* was also important as a reform document utilized by the Progressive movement, although Beard did not necessarily have such a purpose in mind.

Both the economic interpretation of history and the theory of evolution were important as weapons of social criticism. The contention that all ideas represented economic interests offered a medium through which abstract ideas, hitherto conceived as absolutes, could be tied to the motives of a single class, group, or individual. At the same time the evolutionary hypothesis posited a world in a state of constant change or development, in which ideas too were changing, and in which the truths of one generation might become the falsehoods of the next. "The eternal verities become, first, relative truths, then half-truths, or less than half-truths, even deliberate falsehoods. . . . Truth, in short, is a plan of action which is operationally successful." Such arguments, pointing to the relativist nature of truth and to its continual evolution under the impact of economic forces, were summed up in the philosophy of pragmatism and popularized in the writings and teachings of William James and John Dewey. Although the pragmatists were much concerned with the individual, they emphasized the importance of society and the environment in effecting their goal of individual improvement. Inevitably, too, they stressed social and political reform and looked to the national state as a means of attaining their goals.[9]

(IV)

The revolution in American social thought at the turn of the century was paralleled by a growing spirit of criticism in American literature. In the generation following the Civil War, the major novelists who concerned themselves with the subject gave a generally unfavorable picture of a business civilization. In *The Gilded Age* (1871) Mark Twain satirized political corruption, while the novels of his friend William Dean Howells depicted American businessmen as crude and uneducated and as lacking in culture and refinement. In 1887 Edward Bellamy set a model for Utopian novels of social criticism with his futuristic romance *Looking Backward*. This immensely popular book inspired the founding of a number of Nationalist clubs and a magazine, all devoted to hastening the advent of Bellamy's ideal collectivist society. Although Howells in his less successful Utopian volume, *A Traveller from Altruria* (1894), complained that the millionaire had come to dominate the American scene, big business was far from popular with American writers.

Some of the younger novelists of the period—Stephen Crane, Frank Norris, and Hamlin Garland—were pessimistic over the fate of the individual in his struggle against the uglier aspects of an industrial civilization. Garland, for example, in his stories of the Middle West, portrayed the blighting effects of monopoly upon the lives of the farmers. But most American members of the European Naturalist school were not convinced or consistent Naturalists. They did not believe that men were completely the victims of their environment or of natural laws. Thus, with all their doubts and despite themselves, they continued to hope and work for a better society. For many of these writers the bitterness of the 1890's was transformed in the next decade into "The Years of Hope" or "The Age of Confidence." As the muckraking article or novel succeeded the critical or Utopian volumes of the nineties, literature became an increasingly important adjunct of concrete and positive reform. Indicative of popular dissatisfaction, the muckraking literature also helped provide public encouragement for practical reforms.

Muckraking as a term was somewhat unfairly applied to all the popular reform literature of the 1900's after President Roosevelt likened its more extreme writers to the character in *Pilgrim's Progress* "who could look no way but downward with the muckrake in his hands." In itself the practice of the sensational literary exposure of corruption and evil was not a novel phenomenon. Henry

Demarest Lloyd's *Wealth Against Commonwealth*, published in 1894, and Benjamin O. Flower's *Arena* magazine anticipated many of the techniques, but not the great popular success, of the muckrakers. What was new and significant for American democracy in the muckraking literature of the Progressive era was its achievement of a mass circulation and nation-wide appeal.

Muckraking was also a most dramatic illustration of the important changes taking place in American journalism at the turn of the century. In both newspaper and magazine publishing, technological improvements, involving new special features and higher costs, added immensely to the problems of owners and editors. Significantly as the burden of financing a newspaper or magazine increased, the volume of advertising and number of readers became more important than the quality of the editorials. The day had passed when a major newspaper could be purchased for a few thousand dollars, and instead the nineties saw the beginnings of the great journalistic empires of Hearst, Pulitzer, and Munsey. In the continuous search for ever-larger circulation, newspapers outdid each other in sensationalism. In 1898 Hearst and Pulitzer were even willing to help stir up a war over Cuba as a by-product of their competitive struggle for more sales in New York City. But some publishers also used the great influence of their papers to support various worthwhile Progressive reforms.

The particular vogue of the muckraking article began with the publication in *McClure's* in the fall of 1902 of Ida Tarbell's and Lincoln Steffens' famous series dealing with the Standard Oil monopoly and the corruption of American city government. Although the articles seem not to have been the result of any set policy, the ensuing increase in circulation from 200,000 to 700,000 indicated the extent of public interest, and other magazines soon followed *McClure's* lead. Of the hundreds of articles and books of the muckraking sort, some merely trivial or only seeking to shock, a good proportion, however, dealt with important problems and contributed to the public education. As Louis Filler has shown, "Muckraking was, first of all, constructive and democratic." But despite the quality and popularity of a number of the muckraking articles, business hostility and public apathy were not easy to overcome. If the results therefore often seemed slight, it was perhaps partly because later generations did not understand how hard many of the writers had had to work to arouse the public to support even modest reforms.[10]

Many of the muckraking journalists, coming from comfortable middle-class backgrounds, had something of the old liberal philosophy of the civil-service reformers, and they also shared the growing popular distrust of big business. At the same time a number of the writers saw Progressivism as a last demonstration of what Alfred Kazin calls the gusto of American life. Roosevelt, feeling fit as a Bull Moose, was a prime example of this gusto, but the muckrakers and the novelists like Frank Norris, Jack London, and Upton Sinclair had much of the same enthusiasm. If there was a paradox in the Progressives' attack on the trusts and wealth and their admiration of strength and vigor, it was perhaps because Theodore Roosevelt, the Nietzschean Superman, and the writers' muckrake were twin symbols, expressing the elements of nationalism and reform in Progressive democracy.[11]

(*V*)

In his vigorous assertion of Presidential power, Roosevelt was probably closer to Andrew Jackson than to any of his other predecessors. Although Lincoln was apotheosized by martyrdom, Theodore Roosevelt was the first President since Jackson to enter the White House as a popular reform hero. Better than any of his contemporaries—better than Bryan, La Follette, or Wilson—he seemed to express the mass sentiments of his generation. Just as the Jacksonians had modified Jeffersonian individualism and liberalism with a strong infusion of a romantic nationalism and mass democracy, so Roosevelt and the Progressive reformers proposed to go beyond the individualist liberalism of a Godkin and a Henry George, or the agrarian democracy of the Populists. Frankly accepting as a fact the concentration of economic power that resulted from industrialization, the Progressives hoped to control it by an equal centralization of political power in the federal government, and more particularly in the executive branch of the government. Under Theodore Roosevelt and Woodrow Wilson the office of the President acquired increasing scope and importance, while the Square Deal and the New Freedom became Republican and Democratic versions of the new nationalistic democracy of the twentieth century.

As President, Roosevelt pursued what was essentially a compromise position in regard to the problem of monopoly and the trusts. He believed that only those combinations which engaged in an unfair restraint of trade or competition should be subject to prosecution. Later he came to accept the point of view which favored government regulation and publicity, rather than dissolution of the trusts. But several successful antitrust cases early in his administration—notably the breaking up of the Northern Securities Corporation, a railroad combine put together by E. H. Harriman, James J. Hill, and J. P. Morgan—won Roosevelt a reputation as a trustbuster and staunch Progressive.

While the Northern Securities trial was being fought out in the courts, Roosevelt had occasion to intervene dramatically in an important labor dispute. In contrast to some of his predecessors who had not hesitated to sanction the use of federal troops to quell strikes, Roosevelt proposed to make the government an impartial arbitrator. He was not unaware that the growth of big business heightened labor demands for the right to join trade unions and bargain collectively, but in 1900 only about 4 per cent of the working force was organized. In the summer of 1902, anthracite coal miners under the leadership of John Mitchell struck for an eight-hour day, wage increases, and union recognition. The owners of the mines aroused the ire of the public and the President by their refusal to accept arbitration, but Roosevelt was finally able to put enough pressure on the operators to secure a compromise settlement.

In dealing with organized capital and labor, Roosevelt held to the position that the government's power must be greater than that of either of the protagonists. At the same time the government had a responsibility to be impartial and neutral. It must not be anti-business or anti-labor. This policy, illustrated in the coal strike and in the antitrust cases, was popular with the middle classes, who feared both big business and a militantly radical labor movement. It also typified the Progressives' concept of a democracy that was nationalistic as well as reform-minded. During most of his term in office Roosevelt enjoyed the advantages of economic prosperity and comparative labor peace. Although he failed to prosecute many trusts—fewer than Taft, for example—his reputation as a trustbuster contributed to a popular psychology congenial to the passage of other reforms, including railroad rate regulation, the Pure Food and Drug Act, and the conservation of natural resources. If the consolidation of big business was hardly interrupted, the growth of the large corporations was matched by that of organized labor. The American Federation of Labor's membership, for example, increased from 278,000 in 1898 to 1,676,000 in 1905. By modifying the older nineteenth-century Republican attitudes regarding big business and labor, the Progressives helped to restore popular confidence in democracy. At the same time, however, they also weakened the traditional American hostility to a dominant national state. Thus democracy, in the process of its redemption from the post-Civil War plutocracy, was also being revamped along the lines of an all-powerful nationalism.

(*VI*)

In the midst of this concentration of economic and political power in Washington, Progressive reforms of considerable democratic significance were also receiving local application. There were still Progressives who believed that "It is in our state and municipal governments that democracy is likely to win its first victories." Drastic changes in American local governments were in fact long overdue. The corruption and misrule of the Tweed Ring and its successors in New York and other large cities was an American scandal, which Lord Bryce in his *American Commonwealth* pointed to as "the one conspicuous failure of the United States."[12] Although reformers rose periodically in agonized protest, little was done to overhaul the machinery of city government or to get at some of the real causes of municipal corruption. Perhaps the main difficulty stemmed from the fact that the cities had borne the brunt of the revolutionary changes in American life after the Civil War. Despite the attention to the settlement of the frontier, most of the increasing American population and European immigration found its way to large urban centers. American industrial growth was also concentrated in the cities, and factories and slums accordingly developed together.

To meet the needs of the growing cities a great variety of expensive municipal services was required. Lucrative construction contracts and monopolistic franchises created opportunities for special privilege and graft, contributing to the corruption of businessmen and politicians alike. According to the humorist Finley Peter Dunne, "Mr. Dooley," "th' on'y thing to do is to keep pollyticians and business men apart. They seem to have a bad infloonce on each other. Whiniver I see an aldherman an' a banker walkin' down th' sthreet together I know th' Recordin' Angel will have to ordher another bottle iv ink."[13]

While the expansion of the city frequently invited bribery and graft in its government, it also resulted in a decline in the older American standards of civic virtue that had characterized small-town life. Faced with large numbers of poltically ignorant immigrants, the native population abdicated its civic responsibilities to the party machine and city bosses, who worked out a system for managing the vote. In the states, where the immigrant could not be so easily blamed, corruption took the more complicated form of jobbery in lands, in railroad taxes, and in natural resources. State bosses dominated governors, legislatures, and judges, as well as political parties. But, as Lincoln Steffens discovered in his tour of American cities and states, it was often the best people who were most involved in the sorry story of corruption and bribery. Frederic C. Howe, an assistant to Tom Johnson, the reform mayor of Cleveland, declared: "It is privilege, not wealth; franchises, not business; the few, not the many, that have overthrown our cities within the past few years." "The greatest movement in the world today," Johnson himself wrote in 1911, "may be characterized as the struggle of the people against Privilege."[14]

By the late 1890's the notorious defects of American city and state government resulted in the beginnings of a reform movement. Municipal leagues and clubs provided a nucleus for non-partisan reform-minded efforts. Better people were attracted to government work. Business principles were introduced into the cities by the commission or city-manager type of administration. Some cities turned to municipal ownership or to socialist administrations. In a number of cities, particularly in the Middle West, exceptionally able mayors were chosen on reform tickets. Toledo in 1897 elected "Golden Rule" Samuel M. Jones, who invited the wrath of all the respectable elements when he attempted to run the city on Christian principles. In Cleveland Tom Johnson, a disciple of Henry George and a believer in decentralized government close to the people, won Steffens' praise for being the "best mayor of the best governed city in the United States."[15]

If the American city was really to be what Howe called the hope of democracy, more than honesty and efficiency was required. The argument that democracy operated best at local levels, where people were familiar with their needs and where public opinion could be effective, had hardly been supported by the past history of American cities. Charters voted by rural state legislatures did not provide adequately for democratic self-government or home rule. Moreover, when the voter had to choose among a bewildering number of minor officials, it seemed that democracy might be better served if only the most important and responsible offices were made elective. Lord Bryce, for example, though he found much to praise in American Presidential elections, complained that in local matters the "elective offices are so numerous that ordinary citizens cannot watch them, and cease to care who gets them."[16] The shorter ballot and, at the same time, a secret ballot not printed by the political parties, and an honest count–all became important technical reforms in Progressive democracy. By the 1900's both the Australian, or secret, ballot and also voting machines were being adopted in many of the states.

In the states Progressivism was often an outgrowth of the reform movement in the cities, as figures like Hiram Johnson in California and Joseph W. Folk in Missouri moved on to the governor's chair. Governors Robert M. La Follette in Wisconsin and Charles Evans Hughes in New York provided outstanding reform administrations, and both states pioneered in the establishment of direct primaries and in setting up regulatory commissions to control the railroads and public utilities. A number of the state constitutions were also amended in a Progressive direction during the early 1900's. In general, these changes gave added powers to the governors, centralized administrations, and increased popular control. At the same time the functions of the legislatures, singled out by Progressives as the most corrupt branch of state government, were reduced. Thus representative government seemed to be yielding to a combination of direct democracy and an administrative state.[17]

(*VII*)

Of all the democratic innovations in the Progressive era, the initiative, referendum, and recall, the direct primary, women's suffrage, and the popular election of United States Senators stand out as the most significant nationally. Oregon in 1902 was the first state to attract general attention by adoption of the initiative and referendum, permitting the people to force the legislature either to take up or to submit back to them measures in which there was a genuine reform interest. The recall of officials as a device of direct government was more popular in the cities than in the states, and in the latter it was bitterly opposed by conservatives, especially when it was proposed to extend it to include the recall of judges. Wisconsin in 1903 was the first state to enact a direct primary law, and as other states adopted this device, pressure mounted for the popular election of United States Senators. Finally, in 1913, this was accomplished by the Seventeenth Amendment. Although the adoption of a constitutional amendment for national women's suffrage was deferred until after the First World War, a number of the states followed the example of Wyoming, Colorado, Idaho, and Utah in providing partial or equal suffrage during the 1900's. The advocates of women's suffrage felt that with this right secured, other undemocratic restrictions upon their sex could soon be voted away.

As governmental authority was expanded at all levels in the Progressive era, there was reason to fear that democracy might only be exchanging masters—substituting the tyranny of big government for that of big business. Direct democracy therefore seemed to provide a device for keeping government close to the people and for preserving popular control of policy and administration. The techniques of direct democracy also offered exceptional opportunities for interested and enlightened reformers to arouse the public mind. To win the support of a majority of a state legislature, which perhaps knew little or nothing about a particular reform, deals and compromises inevitable became necessary, but by the use of such methods as the initiative and referendum, a simpler and swifter way to popular approval might be found.

"Nearly all the proposals designed to checkmate legislative abuses," Charles Beard pointed out, "have been based upon the assumption that the hope for better government lay in more democracy rather than less." However, he added: "If, in real practice, we should demand the deliberate and carefully informed will of a majority of all the voters of a commonwealth or their representatives on every important measure, progressive and enlightened legislation would be difficult indeed to secure. All that we can ask of a law in a democracy . . . ," Beard concluded, "is that it shall be reasonably acceptable to that vague thing which we call public opinion."[18] To accomplish this, A. Lawrence Lowell, the well-known political scientist and later president of Harvard University, argued that in the long run popular government would be preserved better through those traditional institutions which reflected a real consensus of the people. An easily aroused public opinion, he feared, could degenerate into a tyranny of the majority. "In order that it may be public," he declared, "a majority is not enough, and unanimity is not required, but the opinion must be such that while the minority may not share it, they will feel bound, by conviction not by fear, to accept it; and if democracy is complete the submission of the minority must be given ungrudgingly."[19]

The general lines of Lowell's criticism of direct democracy were shared by many conservatives, including two distinguished members of Roosevelt's Cabinet. In accepting his election as United States Senator from the New York state legislature in January 1909, former Secretary of War and State Elihu Root took the opportunity to reprimand those who talked of states' rights but who were also "the most willing and the most desirous to have the national Government step in and usurp the functions of a state when there is an appropriation carried with the usurpation." Fearful of excessive national centralization and dubious also that democracy could stand the strain imposed upon it by complex modern conditions, Root, however, saw no solution in such innovations as the direct election of senators. In the last analysis democracy depended on the voter, he declared. "If the people of any state are not satisfied to trust their legislature to discharge the constitutional duty of electing senators, let them cure their own faults and elect a legislature that they can trust."[20]

Another Roosevelt Cabinet member, William Howard Taft, continued his election controversy with his old Chief after both had been defeated in the Presidential campaign of 1912. Taft vigorously questioned the wisdom of Roosevelt's enthusiasm for direct democracy and stronger Presidential powers. While people made a fetish of democracy, it remained true, he felt, that there could be no truly popular government in the sense of all the people participating as the electorate. The Progressives' goal of a more honest government could be achieved better under representative institutions. If the people did not choose their legislators and Congressmen wisely, Taft asked, how could they decide intelligently the varied legislation presented for their consideration under the initiative and referendum?[21]

One solution to the question which Taft posed was the establishment of independent boards of experts to administer the complicated details of modern government. If the government was to assume a broader range of regulatory functions and deal with the complex problems of an industrial civilization, its effectiveness might depend on the development of an impartial corps of public administrators—a bureaucracy of experts and intellectuals removed alike from the corrupting influences of business and politics. This was the view of Herbert Croly, one of the most nationalistic of the Progressives. Croly feared that direct popular government might damage democracy by decreasing its efficiency. It also would tend to break down majority rule by encouraging the rise of organized minority interests and groups.[22]

Croly's feelings were illustrative of those of many of the Progressives who had, as a recent student of government regulatory commissions has pointed out, "an abiding faith in regulation, expertness, and the capacity of the American government to make rational decisions provided experts in the administrative agencies could remain free from partisan political considerations. They consistently believed that regulation would overcome privilege, restore decency, and save industry from its own avarice and self-destruction."[23] The difficulty, of course, was that the regulatory commissions and boards, which often wielded great powers, had no direct responsibility to the people. In New York state, where there were nearly 100 such boards, a student of the problem observed:

> The boards are practically irresponsible bodies. They are beyond the control of the people, or of any one who is responsible to the people for their actions. Appointed as they are for a definite term of office, they cannot be removed during that term except after an investigation, which amounts to an impeachment. The governor who appoints them in many cases can only appoint a single member, the terms of the others extending beyond his own, so that he can neither mould the policy of the board nor can he be held responsible for it.[24]

According to Seth Low, the reform mayor of New York City, "State commissions for any other purpose than for inquiry are the most dangerous bodies, because they exercise authority without responsibility. Power without responsibility is always dangerous, but power with responsibility to a constituency, which can readily call it to account is not dangerous."[25]

In by-passing the traditional methods of representative government in favor of a more direct popular democracy, and in expanding the powers of administrative bodies at the expense of those of the state legislatures and of Congress, the Progressive reformers were evolving a new concept of the function of public opinion in a democracy. Leadership in forming public opinion was now no longer confined to elective officials headed by the President. As Croly pointed out, the new government administrator had to be not only an expert but also a promoter and propagandist.[26] As such he tried to educate the public which, in turn, sought to enforce its will directly upon the candidates for elective office. It was on this theory that Gifford Pinchot acted in gaining popular and governmental support for his conservation program.

Like Roosevelt, but in advance of most public officials of his day, Pinchot saw clearly the close relationship between propaganda, control of public opinion, political lobbies, law-making, and appropriations. To mobilize public opinion behind the cause of conservation he used the Bureau of Forests to conduct an extensive publicity service. The Bureau provided technical information, lantern slides, and other materials for schools and associations, and for lecturers, teachers, and writers, while Pinchot and his subordinates did much writing and speaking and issued frequent news releases. In his correspondence Pinchot pointed to the value of good public relations. "Nothing permanent," he said in 1903, "can be accomplished in this country unless it is backed by a sound public sentiment. The greater part of our work, therefore, has consisted in arousing a general interest in practical forestry throughout the country and in gradually changing public sentiment toward a more conservative treatment of forest lands."[27]

(*VIII*)

Although some of the Progressives regarded direct democracy and administrative efficiency as ends in themselves, more often these changes were considered as means to further reforms. Much of Progressivism had as its long-range goal the more equal distribution of wealth through a comprehensive program of social and economic legislation. In entertaining this goal the Progressive movement came into conflict with the more traditional view which limited democracy to political rights and processes. To conservatives social and economic equality, as distinct from individual liberty, was the badge of a false democracy, but to the Progressives it was true democracy and also the logical continuation of their political reforms. In contrast to the theory of laissez faire or to the doctrine of a government paternalism in the interests of the propertied classes, Progressivism proposed a new nationalistic democratic philosophy of more or less equal benefits for all, subject to the corollary of government regulation and control. "The finest and largest meaning of democracy," wrote James H. Tufts of the University of Chicago, "is that all people should share as largely as possible in the best life. This is a view not so much about government itself as about what government is for."[28]

In the circle of persuasive Progressive thinkers, no one excelled Herbert Croly either in the enthusiasm of his vision or in the details of his blueprint for a stronger national state. His best-known work, *The Promise of American Life*, which he published in 1909, was noteworthy not only for its influence on Roosevelt and other Progressives but even more for the way in which it forecast much of the future course of American government. In repudiating the whole Jeffersonian tradition of individualism, natural rights, and laissez faire, Croly expressed his dissent from the idea that opposition to national consolidation was the true mark of a democrat. "The plain fact is," he wrote, "that the individual in freely and energetically pursuing his own private purposes has not been the inevitable public benefactor assumed by the traditional American interpretation of democracy." Calling upon democracy to exercise "constructive discrimination," he pointed out that:

> Whatever the national interest may be, it is not to be asserted by the political practice of non-interference. The hope of automatic democratic fulfillment must be abandoned. The national government must step in and discriminate; but it must discriminate, not on behalf of liberty and the special individual, but on behalf of equality and the average man.
>
> Thus the Jeffersonian principle of national irresponsibility can no longer be maintained by those Democrats who sincerely believe that the inequalities of power generated in the American economic and political system are dangerous to the integrity of the democratic state.[29]

For reform to be effective, Croly believed it had to be national in scope, with a corresponding abandonment of the Jeffersonian doctrine of non-interference. Roosevelt accordingly won his highest praise as a political leader who identified the national principle with the ideal of reform. "He has, indeed, been even more of a nationalist than he has a reformer." Roosevelt, in Croly's eyes, was a Hamiltonian, with the difference that he accepted democracy but emancipated it from its Jeffersonian heritage.[30]

As the Progressive movement unfolded, Croly was disturbed to see among Republican insurgents in the West a revival of Jeffersonian concepts rather than an attempt to recast the party along Rooseveltian lines. In his *Progressive Democracy*, a valuable appendage to his *Promise*, Croly warned that many of the liberal Jeffersonians were not rigorously consistent in their version of democracy.

> If a localized economic system wishes to hold its own against a centralized economic system, it must take care to strip the agencies of big

business of every shred of governmental favor. Nay, considering the favors which those agencies have enjoyed in the past, and the grip which they have obtained upon the vitals of the American economic system, they must be discriminated against and reduced to impotence.

Because such a strict laissez faire was difficult, if not impossible, Croly believed that the "Republican rule of special privilege for all is less contradictory and promises much more useful results; but in so far as it implies that privileges can be distributed equally as well as generally, it rests on a baleful illusion." Progressives, he felt, should grant privileges in such a way that those previously discriminated against might receive special attention. Already, he noted that legal traditions, in the sense of the ideal of individual justice, were being supplanted by the ideal of social justice. American Progressivism was receiving the kind of assurance that came only with faith—almost a religious faith. But the faith of Progressive democracy did not stem from individual ideals; it came only from social ideals. "Progressivism means a relation between political and social democracy which is both mutually dependent and mutually supplementary," Croly concluded.[31]

Behind the Progressives' quest for social and economic justice was a popular support marshaled by an extraordinary number of national organizations, many of which were newly formed in the 1900's. Child labor committees, housing associations, organizations for the colored people, consumer's leagues, charities aid societies, neighborhood settlement houses in slum areas, women's clubs, and church organizations added their influence to the cause of social reform. The Social Gospel movement led to special church committees and funds in behalf of labor and industrial reform legislation. Religious denominations also gave their backing to prohibition, feeling that the liquor traffic contributed prominently to prostitution, disease, poverty, and other social ills.

The prohibition movement, which for the first time became a nation-wide crusade in the Progressive era, was an extreme example of the tendency of democratic government to interfere with private habits and morality out of its concern for the general welfare. Often, however, the standards of morals legislation were much higher than the means of enforcement, with a resulting demoralization of both personal and community ideals. "Living under free institutions," one critic of such legislation complained, "we submit to public regulation in ways which would appear inconceivable to the spirit of oriental despotism. . . ."[32]

Probably the most striking immediate achievement of the Progressive movement in terms of social and economic democracy was the labor legislation passed by many states in the decade before the First World War. In New York alone Governor Hughes signed over 50 model labor laws between 1903 and 1907. Early child labor legislation, applying only to factory work, was widened to include most children employed outside the home or farm. In 1908 the United States Supreme Court gave judicial sanction to state laws limiting women's hours, but the Court refused to uphold a federal child labor law or state minimum wage legislation. Other state legislation of the period dealt with workingmen's compensation, public health, and factory and tenement house construction. On a national level an event of the utmost significance was the adoption of the Sixteenth Amendment, making possible the levy of a federal income tax. In the judgment of a recent student of the period, "It is almost impossible to see how most of the social legislation passed since 1912 could have been financed without the income tax. Lack of the tax must also have meant the almost complete frustration of any government seeking to redistribute income in an orderly fashion. The modern democratic social service state, in fact, probably rests more upon the income tax than upon any other single legislative act."[33]

Frequently the most in need of help, and yet the most ignored, were the immigrants and the Negroes in the United States. While the Negroes faced continued social and economic discrimination in the rural South, the immigrants were crowded into the urban slums of cities like New York. There they endured the kind of living conditions graphically described by the popular journalist and Danish immigrant Jacob Riis in his books *How the Other Half Lives* and *The Battle with the Slum.* With the return of prosperity after the 1890's, hostility to the immigrant temporarily diminished, while their numbers reached an all-time peak of approximately one million arrivals per year. But racist feeling, fear of radicalism, and the pressure of organized labor all contributed to the growing demand that Congress adopt a literacy test as a means of restriction.

In the case of the Negro, although a few militant leaders, notably W. E. B. DuBois, called for full social and political equality with an end to all discrimination, most Progressives continued to accept the gradualistic policy of vocational education and hard work prescribed by Booker T. Washington. The Progressive era accordingly brought little change in the Southern pattern of discrimination and segregation, and the years 1900 and 1901 were characterized by a holocaust of lynchings and race riots. In 1900 the last of the Southern Negro Republicans from Reconstruction days was defeated, and a Negro was not elected again to Congress until 1928. Yet the beginning of the twentieth century also witnessed indications of the Negroes' advancement. The number of skilled laborers, operating farmers, and home owners all increased at a greater rate than the population. Lynchings gradually declined, although no year before World War I had fewer than 49 such crimes. Especially promising was a drop in the proportion of illiterates from 50 per cent in 1900 to 30 per cent in 1910. In that year the National Association for the Advancement of Colored People was founded by a distinguished group of reformers. DuBois became an officer of the association, while Oswald Garrison Villard, the grandson of William Lloyd Garrison, wrote the first appeal for its support in which he said: "We call upon all believers in democracy to join in a National conference for the discussion of present evils, the voicing of protests, and the revival of the struggle for civil and political liberty."[34]

(IX)

If race prejudice, social distress, and poverty still remained as flaws in American democracy, Progressive democrats were confident that it was the function of the state to effect a cure. As Herbert Croly observed, "Plans of social legislation which formerly would have been considered culpably 'paternal,' and, if passed at the solicitation of the labor unions, would have been declared unconstitutional by the courts, are now considered to be a normal and necessary exercise of the police power."[35] Many conservatives as well as Progressives shared Roosevelt's feeling that social reform was necessary now in the United States, as in Europe, to ward off more radical doctrines. President Charles W. Eliot of Harvard University, for example, saw an American collectivism as a result of population growth. In contrast to confiscatory socialism this American collectivism would merely be a continuation of the old New-England type of community cooperation. "The development," he declared, "has been constructive, not destructive, inevitable in consequence of other profound social and industrial changes, beneficial in the present, and hopeful for the future." Untroubled by the fine semantic distinctions of Harvard's president, Herbert Croly, in defending the nationalistic program of his *Promise of American Life*, wrote that "if any critic likes to fasten the stigma of socialism upon the foregoing conception of democracy, I am not concerned with dodging the odium of the word."[36]

Although the Socialist party was organized in 1901 as militantly anti-capitalist, it soon became less radical, winning the respect and sympathy of non-socialist middle-class reformers. In the process of its conversion American socialism seemed to ignore the warnings of some of its more independent thinkers. For example, Henry Demarest Lloyd, an old Populist, noted that the "least democratic countries in the world have state coal mines and state railroads, but they have no ownership by the people. The socialism of a kingly state is kingly still; of a plutocratic state, plutocratic." And W. J. Ghent, who saw the American capitalism of the reformers as a kind of "benevolent feudalism," concluded: "The State becomes stronger in its relation to the propertyless citizen, weaker in its relation to the man of capital."[37]

In contrast to Ghent and Lloyd, most socialists, like most Progressives, pictured society as moving toward a more equal social democracy and a truer individualism. "We shall *grow* into democracy," wrote Progressive Walter Weyl in his *New Democracy*.[38] Socialist William English Walling in *Progressivism—and After* expressed his enthusiasm for the Progressive type of reforms as a means to the end of socialism. According to Walling, the United States was moving through the stages of State Capitalism and State Socialism to an eventual nationalist and then internationalist socialism of the working class. To Benjamin P. DeWitt, the contemporary historian of the Populist and Progressive movements, there was little distinction between radical Progressives and conservative socialists. "In its relation to the Progressive movement at the present time, socialism may be said to be the goal toward which the movement is tending. It is an ideal which the movement hopes some day to see realized. . . . As time goes on these parties will undoubtedly grow even closer together."[39] Under the leadership of Eugene Debs the American Socialist party espoused a moderate program not unlike that of the British Labour party. Foregoing a good deal of its doctrinaire Marxism, the Socialist party became an Americanized or Yankee version of socialism, or a left-wing Progressivism.

If the socialists were becoming good middle-class Yankee Progressives, this was only what seemed to be true of almost all Americans by the summer of 1912. The Presidential campaign that year marked the climax of Progressivism. Although there were differences among the candidates and parties—the Socialist Debs on the left, Republican Taft on the right, with the Progressive Roosevelt and Democratic Wilson somewhere in between—the differences were less important than the broad similarities. To the voters it seemed that all contenders were committed to various versions of a Progressive democracy that was nationalistic and reformist in its major intents and purposes. Even Taft was not the conservative creature of big business depicted by his enemies, but he did fear an all-powerful central government, and he disliked the Progressives' ideas of direct democracy. Old-fashioned Midwestern Progressives, who would have preferred La Follette as a candidate, and liberal Jeffersonian democrats in Wilson's party also were hostile to the Roosevelt-Croly version of nationalist democracy. To Roosevelt, however, La Follette's Progressivism was "a kind of rural Toryism," while Wilson, according to Theodore Roosevelt, was a good man, "But he is not a Nationalist. . ."[40]

In the course of the campaign the most direct clash of issues and personalities was between Wilson and Roosevelt. The New Freedom, as outlined by the former Princeton professor and such advisers as Louis D. Brandeis, revealed considerable nostalgia for the ways of Jeffersonian democracy. Wilson argued that it was possible to enforce competition through government regulation, while Brandeis decried the bigness and monopoly which Roosevelt and his conservative business supporters had come to accept as inevitable.

During the Congressional campaign in 1910, Roosevelt had already presented the outlines of his New Nationalism in a famous address at Osawatomie, Kansas. The political philosophy was similar to that of Croly's *Promise of American Life*, but the address was suffused with Theodore Roosevelt's own peculiar mixture of nationalism and moralistic reform. Equality of opportunity, he told his listeners, while essential to give every man a fair chance in life, also meant that "the commonwealth will get from every citizen the highest service of which he is capable. No man who carries the burden of the special privileges of another can give to the commonwealth that service to which it is fairly entitled."[41] Restating Roosevelt's own emphasis, a California Progressive politician neatly summed up the program of the New Nationalism. "Progressivism," he said, "believes in nationalism, in individual citizenship, and in the whole people, not in any class as a unit of government. It opposes class government by either the business, the laboring or any other class, and resists the formation of class parties. It is, in other words, the twentieth-century evolution of democracy."[42]

To many of the enthusiastic reformers who supported Roosevelt's New Nationalism, the Progressive party heralded the deliverance of American democracy from the corrupting influence of the older political organizations. It seemed the answer to the plea of Ostrogorski's influential work, *Democracy and the Organization of Political Parties*, which had called for a new party divorced from machine politics and representing a voluntary association of citizens united on specific issues. To Jane Addams and other active social reformers, the Progressive party was a crusade for a greater democracy. But to such conservative supporters as George W. Perkins of J. P. Morgan and Company, and Frank Munsey, the publisher, it was the paternalistic nationalism and statism advocated by Roosevelt, rather than the hope of reform, which made the party acceptable.

Although the Progressive party was broader in its base than the Populists had been, there is evidence that Roosevelt's nationalism was lacking in grass-roots appeal and that it repelled many old-line liberals and agrarians. At the same time much of the party's program was too demagogic and too shallow intellectually to carry weight with many liberals and reformers, who turned instead to Wilson. As expected, Roosevelt and the Progressives met defeat, but their emphasis upon nationalistic reforms pointed the way to the future course of American democracy. By the close of Wilson's first administration, the Democratic Congressional majority had enacted almost every important plank in the Progressive platform of 1912. Wilson had not come into office to carry out a program of positive social reform, but the weakening of the administration's original antitrust program, the growing concessions to business, and the flood of labor legislation in 1916 completed the surrender of the 1912 New Freedom dictum of "special privileges to none."

As the New Freedom was transformed into the New Nationalism, the attentions of President Wilson and the country were increasingly taken up by the great war in Europe. The Progressive era, which had its beginnings after the war with Spain, was foreclosed as the United States found itself involved in the First World War. Buoyed up by the concept of an American mission to make the world safe for democracy, the nation was made ready to recross the oceans.

CHAPTER NINE

American Mission Under Arms

THE YEARS at the turn of the century embraced a period that was vastly significant for the American democratic tradition. In foreign as well as domestic policy it was an era of change, as the Spanish-American War, imperialism, and World War I combined to reshape the course of American democracy. Whether the Constitution followed the flag across the Pacific to the Philippines, or whether democracy could be preserved at home in its new imperial setting were novel questions for the American people to have to decide. It is true that the United States had been a great nation long before 1898, but the war with Spain underscored with dramatic emphasis the increasing disposition of the country to enter actively into world politics. "Until near the end of the nineteenth century," Charles and Mary Beard wrote, "few if any persons in the United States ever dreamed that any responsible official high in public life would call upon them to use the armed power of the country for the purpose of imposing civilization on other peoples in distant parts of the earth or underwriting civilization throughout the world."[1]

The United States, to be sure, had never sealed itself off from other areas of the globe. The long-standing popular notion that democracy was destined to spread throughout the world encouraged many Americans to sympathize with revolutionary movements abroad. Foreign trade and such naval expeditions as the Perry voyage to Japan also took Yankee merchants and sailors to far-off places. But neither the American interest in expanding its overseas commerce or in advancing the cause of world democracy was sufficient to involve the nation in foreign alliances or war. The most widely accepted statements of American foreign policy—Washington's Farewell Address and the Monroe Doctrine—rather set forth the idea that there was a distinct set of differences between the Old World and the New, which it was in the interests of each to preserve.

Until the closing decades of the nineteenth century, American expansionist tendencies had been largely satisfied by the westward movement across the North American continent. This so-called agricultural imperialism had led to almost continual difficulties with the Indian tribes, to various diplomatic wrangles with England and Spain, and finally to full-scale war with Mexico. But, on the whole, Americans believed that their manifest destiny portended not foreign war but the peaceful penetration of a contiguous, and almost virgin, territory. They pictured their mission "as building at home, on the ever-expanding continental domain a civilization of plain folk secure in the enjoyment of political freedom and economic opportunity."[2] The best possible advertisement for American democracy, it was thought, would be the example of a free and prosperous people living in peace and contentment in their New World environment.

The reasons that finally impelled the United States to abandon this relative isolation in favor of an imperialist course are not hard to discover. As a century of continental expansion drew to a close,

American business and political leaders naturally tended to look outward and to take a more active interest in affairs overseas. At the same time the depression and labor troubles of the nineties suggested that American industry might require new markets for its products. The United States, it was argued, had to keep up with the European powers in their mad scramble for colonies and trade. In a famous statement of justification for imperial expansion, Senator Albert J. Beveridge of Indiana declared:

> American factories are making more than the American people can use; American soil is producing more than they can consume. Fate has written our policy for us; the trade of the world must and shall be ours. . . . Our institutions will follow our flag on the wings of our commerce. And American law, American order, American civilization, and the American flag will plant themselves on shores hitherto bloody and benighted, but by those agencies of God henceforth to be made beautiful and bright.[3]

Beveridge's patriotic eloquence pointed not only to the economic foundations of the new foreign policy but also to its powerful ideological base. For many Americans imperialism was the twentieth-century version of the older concepts of mission and manifest destiny. Nationalism and patriotism also found support in the racist doctrines of Anglo-Saxon superiority. Despite the glaring failure to share its democracy with the Indians and Negroes at home, the United States by the close of the century was ready to take up the white man's burden in the Caribbean and the Pacific. The vague idea that American progress was due to the predominantly Anglo-Saxon character of its civilization and people became an increasingly popular concept after the 1880's. Partly a reflection of Darwinian notions of the survival of the most fit races of mankind, as well as of hostility to the newer types of immigrants, this belief provided a most useful rationale with which to justify America's imperial adventure.

Both English and American scholars advanced the view that it was the duty of the Anglo-Saxon nations to carry their political institutions to the rest of the world. According to the historical philosopher John Fiske, the American federal system offered an opportunity to incorporate the principles of peace and democracy in an imperial union of many diverse states. In 1885, the same year in which Fiske's popular lecture on "Manifest Destiny" was published in *Harper's Magazine*, the Reverend Josiah Strong's influential book *Our Country* made its first appearance. Strong's work, which was intended as a plea for support of the home missionary movement, enjoyed sensational sales in the hundreds of thousands of copies in England and America. Disturbed by domestic social problems, which he associated with industrialism and "the exhaustion of the public lands," Strong nevertheless turned his attentions abroad. It would be the future destiny of the United States, he predicted, to save the world through the spread of Anglo-Saxon institutions and Christian principles.

A coming *pax Americana*, enforced with the help of the British navy, was also a prominent feature in the philosophy of such navalists and imperialists as Alfred Thayer Mahan. Mahan, whose theories took on added importance after his friend Theodore Roosevelt entered the White House, believed that an enlarged and powerful naval force would be the most important adjunct of American commerce and civilization. Critics of the new navalism, however, pointed out that it would go far to reverse the long-standing anti-militarist traditions of the Republic. In vast armies and navies they saw the death of civil liberties and of American democracy. Much of this feeling was summed up by James Bryce, author of *The American Commonwealth*, who stated that in his opinion the "policy of creating great armaments and of annexing territory beyond the seas would be an un-American policy, and a complete departure from the maxims—approved by long experience—of the illustrious founders of the Republic."[4]

(II)

In the midst of the strong material and ideological forces that were encouraging the American people to reconsider their national destiny along the lines of an imperial democracy, the warnings of Bryce and others went unheeded. The Spanish-American War, long brewing, finally came to a boil in the spring of 1898. In Washington a small but influential group of expansionists, including Theodore Roosevelt, John Hay, Henry Cabot Lodge, Elihu Root, Beveridge, and Mahan, were ready with plans to carry forward the so-called larger policy of overseas imperialism. Less interested in freeing Cuba than in taking over the moribund Spanish-Empire, Roosevelt and his friends made sure that the American navy was primed for its celebrated dash from Hong Kong to the Philippines. The ensuing destruction of the Spanish fleet at Manila Bay confronted the American people with a problem which, in contrast to Roosevelt and his associates, they had hardly envisaged before Admiral Dewey fired the famous "shot heard around the world."

Along with other territories gained at this time, the Philippines, and beyond them the lure of trade with China and the Far East, made imperialism a substantial reality. The Hawaiian Islands, annexed in the summer of 1898 in the middle of the war with Spain, had long been an object of American interest and agitation. In the peace treaty with Spain, Puerto Rico and Guam were ceded to the United States, while Cuba was liberated under conditions which made it a virtual American protectorate. None of these islands, however, was in the same category as the Philippines. Hawaii had a large American population and, like Alaska, was quickly given territorial status and the hope of eventual statehood. Guam was sought mainly as a naval base in the Pacific, while Puerto Rico and Cuba fell within the traditional orbit of American interest in the Caribbean. But acquisition of the Philippines was susceptible of no such easy rationale. As in Cuba a strong native revolutionary movement was seeking independence for the islands. Thus there was the disturbing and incongruous fact that a war fought for the liberation of Cuba had become the means of suppressing freedom in the Philippines. In any case President McKinley's fateful decision, insisting on the cession of the islands, stirred up more controversy in the United States than had the war with Spain. While swelling annexationist sentiment opposed any notions of hauling down the American flag and abandoning the Philippines to either independence or possible European aggrandizement, opponents of the treaty protested no less vigorously the threat of imperialism to American democracy.

The anti-imperialist movement, though never well-organized outside Boston and a few other large cities, included some of the most distinguished statesmen and men of letters in America. William Dean Howells, Mark Twain, William Vaughn Moody, and Thomas Bailey Aldrich all opposed colonial expansion, while Samuel Bowles,

E. L. Godkin, and Finley Peter Dunne were important journalistic critics. In the Democratic party eight members of Cleveland's Cabinet, including the former President and his Secretary of State Richard Olney, were ranged against imperialism. Among Republicans it was mostly the liberal reform element of elder statesmen carrying on the old antislavery traditions who protested McKinley's annexationist policies.[5] Typical of this group was Carl Schurz, who had long been an opponent of the type of aggressive militarism and navalism that he now publicly linked to Theodore Roosevelt. In the press and on the platform Schurz repeatedly denounced the new imperial policy. Replying to an open letter of anxious inquiry from the Swedish pacifist Björnstjerne Björnson, Schurz declared:

> I believe that this Republic, in that sense, can endure so long as it remains true to the principles upon which it was founded, but that it will morally decay if it abandons them. I believe that this democracy, the government of, by, and for the people, is not fitted for a colonial policy, which means conquest by force, or, as President McKinley called it, "criminal aggression" and arbitrary rule over subject populations. I believe that, if it attempts such a policy on a large scale, its inevitable degeneracy will hurt the progress of civilization more than it can possibly further that progress by planting its flag upon foreign soil on which its fundamental principles of government cannot live.

In answer to the imperialist argument that the United States also had a mission to serve those outside its own boundaries, Schurz replied that, although the United States was naturally concerned to advance the progress of civilization, it could not assume a universal responsibility for every place and people in the world, or American democracy itself would break down.[6]

According to William Graham Sumner's address and essay, *The Conquest of the United States by Spain*, the decay of American democracy had already set in. All nations talked of their civilizing mission, but the United States still had lands at home to people, while the American doctrine of equality formed a constitutional barrier to the acquisition of overseas territories filled with uncongenial populations. At the same time their attitude toward the Negro hardly qualified the American people to assume the white man's burden over Asiatics, unless they too were to be kept in an inferior position. The imperalists, Sumner noted, now were engaged in repudiating the very American traditions he had been accused of flouting, and he predicted that through imperialism the United States would eventually lose its freedom and democracy. "The answer is: war, debt, taxation, diplomacy, a grand governmental system, pomp, glory, a big army and navy, lavish expenditures, political jobbery—in a word, imperialism." Like Sumner, President David Starr Jordan of Stanford University believed that imperialism was not suited to democracy. It entailed an active aggressive foreign policy leading to militarism and war. And "As militarism grows democracy must die," he warned.[7]

Although there was little explicit opposition to imperialism on the part of labor leaders or businessmen, Andrew Carnegie was a staunch critic and Samuel Gompers showed some interest. In a sense William Jennings Bryan, who campaigned on the issue in 1900, spoke for many of the plain people who may have doubted the wisdom of an expansionist policy. Bryan was also typical of those politicians, especially among the Populists and radical Democrats, who had used the Cuban issue to embarrass the Cleveland and McKinley administrations. Enthusiastic over the war so long as it was to free Cuba, Bryan and many of his supporters, however, disavowed the ensuing imperialism. Willing to back the war as a humanitarian crusade, they opposed it when it became an imperialist adventure. Because he feared continuation of the war and wanted to give the American people a chance to vote on the whole issue, Bryan refused to use his influence to prevent ratification of the peace treaty with Spain. Despite these strange tactics, Bryan maintained his stand against imperialism, and the Democratic platform in 1900 reflected his views. The war waged against the Filipino insurrectionists was condemned as unnecessary and unjust, and McKinley's policies were censured for placing the United States, "previously known and applauded throughout the world as the champion of freedom, in the false and un-American position of crushing with military force the efforts of our former allies to achieve liberty and self-government."[8]

On the whole the anti-imperialist movement was based more on abstract political and ideological principles than on economic, religious, constitutional, or humanitarian considerations. Imperialism was opposed as contrary to the traditions of American democratic government as stated in the Declaration of Independence, Washington's Farewell Address, and Lincoln's Gettysburg Oration. The abandonment of these principles in favor of imitating the ways of the Old World, the anti-imperialists believed, would destroy the Republic. At first the anti-imperialists paid little attention to the Filipinos' own demands for self-government, but after their failure to prevent annexation they turned to support of the Filipino independence movement under Aguinaldo.

(III)

Although the anti-imperialists made their strongest appeal to the American democratic tradition, imperialists also called upon democracy in order to bolster their view of American foreign policy. Democracy, the imperialists maintained, could be extended only to a people fitted to receive it. Self-government depended on a nation's capacity for political action, and if a people were not ready for independence, they must undergo a period of political tutelage and protection. Thus the imperialists joined the American conception of manifest destiny with Rudyard Kipling's call to the Anglo-Saxon nations to take up the white man's burden. In the curious reasoning of an official United States commission to the Philippines, "American sovereignty was only another name for the liberty of the Filipinos."[9] Before the National Education Association, in an address entitled "An Educational Policy for Our New Possessions," William T. Harris, United States Commissioner of Education, sketched out a program which American teachers in the Philippines were soon engaged in applying. According to Harris,

> If we cannot come into contact with lower civilizations without bringing extermination to their people, we are still far from the goal. It must be our great object to improve our institutions until we can bring blessings to lower peoples and set them on a road to rapid progress. We must take in hand their education. We must emancipate them from tribal forms and usages, and train them into productive industry and the individual ownership of land. We must take them out of the form of civilization that rests on tradition and mere external authority, and substitute for it a civilization of the printed page which governs by public opinion and by insight rather than by mere authority. Such a civilization we have a right to enforce on this earth.[10]

Imperialist books helped to acquaint the American people with their new responsibilities. The Reverend Strong, in his *Expansion*, rejoiced that his earlier visions had come true, while Brooks Adams, in stressing the economic arguments for imperialism, urged the country to emancipate itself from its older traditions. There was little democracy in Adams' conclusion that "If the New Empire should develop, it must be an enormous complex mass, to be administered only by means of a cheap, elastic, and simple machinery. . . . If these deductions are sound, there is but one great boon which the passing generation can confer upon its successors; it can aid them to ameliorate that servitude to tradition which has so often retarded submission to the inevitable until too late."[11] More hopeful than Adams, Franklin H. Giddings, professor of sociology at Columbia University, took issue with Sumner's thesis that democracy and imperialism were incompatible. The future progress of world civilization, Giddings wrote in his *Democracy and Empire*, would be determined by the extension of American ideals of liberty and equality. Drawing upon the theory of biological evolution, Giddings decided that political progress depended on the absorption of smaller states and colonies into large democratic empires.

Much of the imperialist argument fitted in well with the Progressives' conception of democracy. Roosevelt himself was a romantic nationalist, one of the chief architects of American imperialism as well as its principal executive officer. Progressives in Congress supported not only his domestic program of nationalistic reforms but also the naval and military measures needed to back up his imperialistic foreign policy. Imperialism, like Progressivism, was in opposition to many of the values of a traditional liberal and individualistic democracy. "The spirit of imperialism was an exaltation of duty above rights, of collective welfare above individual self-interest, the heroic values as opposed to materialism, action instead of logic, the natural impulse rather than the pallid intellect." In his book *Democracy and Reaction*, the English critic L. T. Hobhouse maintained that by the close of the nineteenth century "a positive theory of the State in domestic affairs was matched by a positive theory of Empire, and the way was made straight for Imperialism. . . ."[12] "Most important," as William E. Leuchtenburg has pointed out, "imperialism and progressivism flourished together because they were both expressions of the same philosophy of government, a tendency to judge any action not by the means employed but by the results achieved, a worship of definitive action for action's sake . . . and an almost religious faith in the democratic mission of America."[13]

Although imperialism in the more active sense of the acquisition of overseas dependencies waned, there was no slackening of American economic and political interests abroad. Dollar diplomacy, military intervention in Latin America and the Far East, and Theodore Roosevelt's own attempts at global peacemaking were examples of continued American involvement overseas. At the same time the growing peace movement and the increasing criticism in Congress of militarism and navalism were indications that the new departure in American foreign policy continued more from inertia than from enthusiastic public backing. Even Roosevelt had some misgivings in regard to the policies he had helped to engineer, and he talked of giving up the Philippines as the Achilles heel of the United States. Like the anti-imperialists, Roosevelt was troubled by the question of whether an imperial power could preserve democracy at home and at the same time rule its colonies abroad. "The problem of the control of thickly peopled tropical regions by self-governing northern democracies is very intricate," he wrote in 1908. "A legislative body, most of the members of which are selected by constituencies that in the nature of things can know nothing whatever of the totally different conditions of India, or the Philippines, or Egypt, or Cuba, does not offer the best material for making a success of such government."[14]

Once the United States had assumed the task of bringing democracy to colonial peoples, it was less difficult to take the next step and embark upon a world crusade for democracy. If this expanded version of the idea of the American mission seemed in curious conflict with older democratic ideals of individualism and self-government, it must be remembered that the democratic tradition in these years was being transformed by the Progressive forces of nationalism and reform. Active participation in international affairs, like Progressivism, meant the disciplining of American democracy. Just as the Progressives' program in the 1900's increased the significance of a mass democracy, so imperialism and foreign war placed a premium on patriotic unity and popular conformity. Throughout much of the nineteenth century the citizen and his government had demanded little of each other. Individualism ruled political and economic life. But such a conception of democracy came to have less reality in the America of the twentieth century. Compared to the relatively simple needs of an age of agriculture and small business, the appetite of an industrial society was enormous. If the military conscription, mass indoctrination, and heavy taxation required to support larger armies and navies and an expanding federal bureaucracy were ill-suited to an individualistic conception of democracy, they were not basically at odds with the new nationalistic and paternalistic version of democracy current in the twentieth century. And the interests of a mass democracy in social reforms through the agency of the state could easily be broadened to encourage world reformation through a league of nations.

Looking back on these early years of the new century, the political scientist Charles E. Merriam observed:

> The acquisition of overseas dependencies floated the nation gently into the swift current which was certain to lead to the mingling of international waters. Doctrines of international duty and mission were developed and widely, although not universally accepted. America slowly awakened to international consciousness. . . . Whether as imperialist or pacifist in tendency; whether to bring to the world peace or a sword; whether inspired by selfish motives of gain or altruistic sentiments of humanity was not so significant in the general growth of American thought as the fundamental fact that the international instinct and interest awoke, and that internationalism won its way against the historic traditions of "splendid isolation."[15]

(IV)

The transformation of the American democratic mission, initiated in the imperialism of the war with Spain, was substantially completed by intervention in the First World War. In the external facets of his personality Woodrow Wilson, the war President, was much less militant and aggressive than Theodore Roosevelt. Yet the notion of a crusade came naturally to this scholarly son of a Presbyterian minister, imbued with a stern Calvinist sense of determinism and devotion to duty. His study of government and history convinced him of the need for strong leadership, both of the President in relation to Congress and of the United States in relationship to the rest of the world. Wilson felt confident that isolation was outmoded and that the United States must assume its proper place in international affairs. Though a man of peace, he did not shrink from using force to back what he felt was the American mission to extend democracy abroad. Believing an expansion of foreign trade vital, not only to the interests of the United States but also to world peace, the Wilson administration aggressively encouraged American commerce with Latin America and the Far East. It is revealing that, although the language of dollar diplomacy and imperialism was repudiated under Wilson, the Democratic President was as ready as Taft or Roosevelt to play the role of apologist for the white man's burden and to intervene abroad.

In the European war, once the Allied struggle against Germany was joined, Wilson accepted wholeheartedly the doctrine that it was a holy crusade for peace and democracy. But, like the rest of the country, the President found it difficult to take the last portentous steps along the road to war. At first he shared the widespread disposition of Americans to see the conflict in Europe as the almost inevitable result of the preceding militarism and imperialism of the great powers. Anxious to preserve American neutrality, he opposed the demand for a rearmament program in the United States. The American democratic tradition, he noted in 1914 in his first annual wartime message to Congress, was one of peace and hostility to standing armies. Yet within a year the President yielded to the pressure of the preparedness advocates. In his December 1915 message to Congress urging a stronger army and navy, he discussed the place of war in a democracy:

> Great democracies are not belligerent. They do not seek or desire war. . . .
>
> But just because we demand unmolested development and the undisturbed government of our own lives upon our own principles of right and liberty, we resent, from whatever quarter it may come, the aggression we ourselves will not practice. We insist upon security in prosecuting our self-chosen lines of national development. We do more than that. We demand it also for others.[16]

Thus Wilson turned from neutrality to the idea of an American mission to preserve democracy. Meanwhile the firm stand of the United States against Germany's submarine warfare deprived Wilsonian diplomacy of the flexibility and neutral point of view necessary to keep America at peace. The decision for war, though difficult, was rendered easier by the preceding years of preparation for world involvement and by the President's increasing disposition to see in the war a great moral struggle between right and wrong. With the overthrow of the autocratic Czarist government and the establishment of what promised to be a democratic and constitutional order in Russia, Americans were more easily convinced that justice and democracy were on the Allied side. Hopeful that the war might still be brought to a close in Europe, Wilson continued to call for a democratic peace—"a peace without victory" based on the equality of nations. "No peace can last, or ought to last, which does not recognize and accept the principle that governments derive all their just powers from the consent of the governed, and that no right anywhere exists to hand peoples about from sovereignty to sovereignty as if they were property."[17]

The initiative, however, had passed from the United States, and Germany's resumption of the unrestricted use of its submarines on February 1, 1917, decided Wilson. "The present German submarine warfare against commerce is a warfare against mankind. It is a war against all nations. . . . The challenge is to all mankind." In contrast to the policies of the German government, the American President told Congress it was the intention of the United States to fight "for the ultimate peace of the world and for the liberation of its peoples. . . . The world must be made safe for democracy." Continuing to hold to this lofty conception of the American mission under arms, the President concluded his War Message: "It is a fearful thing," he said, "to lead this great peaceful people into war, into the most terrible and disastrous of all wars. . . . But the right is more precious than peace, and we shall fight for the things which we have always carried nearest our hearts,—for democracy. . . ."[18] Echoing the President, his political foe Senator Henry Cabot Lodge, in concluding his speech in favor of the war resolution, asserted: "What we want most of all by this victory which we shall help to win is to secure the world's peace, broad-based on freedom and democracy. . . ."[19]

Wilson's call for an American crusade for world peace and democracy was not convincing to all members of Congress. A small minority—50 in the House and 6 in the Senate—cast their votes against the declaration of war. Expressing views typical of many of the Progressives, even those who voted with Wilson, Senator George Norris declared: "We are going into war upon the command of gold, . . . and all because we want to preserve the commercial right of American citizens to deliver munitions of war to belligerent nations." A persistent theme among the opposition was the undemocratic nature of Wilson's sudden appeal to arms after he had won re-election as a man of peace. "We criticize European monarchies for forcing their subjects into war against their will," complained Asle J. Gronna, Senator from North Dakota, "but we refuse to entertain by a referendum vote of the American people whether they desire peace or war." In the longest of the anti-war addresses, a grim and bitter Senator La Follette sought to refute, point by point, the contentions of the President's War Message. The Senator questioned both the popularity of going to war and the rightness of the American case against Germany. What was democratic, he asked, about British policy toward Ireland, India, or Egypt, or in Wilson's announced determination to impose democracy upon a defeated Germany?

> Is it not a remarkable democracy which leagues itself with allies already far overmatching in strength the German nation and holds out to such beleaguered nation the hope of peace only at the price of giving up their Government? . . .
>
> Are the people of this country being so well represented in this war movement that we need to go abroad to give other people control of their governments? Will the President and the supporters of this war bill submit it to a vote of the people before the declaration of war goes into effect?[20]

(V)

The President himself had no illusions that war, even a war for democracy, could be fought by democratic means. Toleration and constitutional rights, he predicted, would give way to popular hysteria and governmental controls. "If there should be disloyalty, it will be dealt with with a firm hand of stern repression. . . ." In Wilson's mind it was now a "People's War" in which there could be no dissent "except from a lawless and malignant few."[21] This sensitivity concerning his interpretation of the war, coupled with his own curious misgivings over its prosecution, exemplified the problem of a great democracy under arms. As the President knew from history, dissident individuals and minority groups were bound to suffer from the solidarity of sentiment and singleness of purpose enforced in wartime. Lofty abstractions had to be transformed into popular propaganda, even if this meant that the war for peace and democracy should become a fight against the Hun or a drive to kill the Kaiser. In response to the urgings of the President, Congress a few weeks after the declaration of war approved legislation for military conscription, the establishment of an official propaganda agency, and an espionage law. All these measures were justified by the administration as vital to winning the war, and liberals' protests were brushed aside.

Of the wartime legislation adopted hastily in the spring of 1917, military conscription—or Selective Service, as it was called to soften the blow—was the most obivously war-related. It was also the supreme example of the conflict between the demands of an individualistic and a mass democracy. While proponents of the draft saw universal military service as a realization of the equalitarian ideals of democracy, the opposition denounced the degree of compulsion which it placed upon the individual. Henry Adams, for example, was amazed at the general conformity which characterized the country once war was declared. "As far as I know," he wrote, "we have obeyed like lambs and have done everything we were told to do. Never could I have conceived that in a short three months we could have gone into a great war and adopted a conscription not unworthy of Germany, at the bidding of a President who was elected only a few months ago on the express ground that he had kept us at peace." Henry's younger brother Brooks, however, enthusiastically described universal military service as "The American Democratic Ideal." Harking back to the day when every man shouldered a rifle, the draft seemed to realize the concept of the citizen soldier. "The free man and the soldier," Harvard philosopher Ralph Barton Perry declared, were not incompatible.[22]

Yet the true citizen soldier had fought only infrequently and then for purposes of home defense. He was neither a highly trained professional, nor a mercenary soldier of fortune expected to serve for long periods overseas. Throughout most of their history the American people had respected Tocqueville's dictum that "a large army in the midst of a democratic people will always be a source of great danger." The body of unorganized militia from which volunteers sprang to arms in wartime was as close to an actual citizen army as the United States was willing to come. Such a force, however, was unsuited to modern war, and some form of universal service accordingly became the military pattern for those twentieth-century nations that took war seriously. In the United States, Selective Service continued the trend begun in the early 1900's when Secretary of War Elihu Root, following European practice, secured legislation for a general staff and a federalized militia.

Conscription, whatever wartime needs, seemed to violate all the tenets of an individualistic liberal democracy. As Frederick Palmer, the biographer of Secretary of War Newton D. Baker, later wrote: "America for the first time had regimentation on the European system, naively unaware of its effects." Although Palmer saw the workings of Selective Service as "an exhibition of democracy triumphant," he also noted that it was "our first great standardization of human material in mass production." In decrying such a view, a Western Senator told his colleagues that he was not able to change his lifelong opinions and accept conscription as democratic. "Call it anything else," he said, "and I may make no protest. You say it is based upon equality. But democracy does not mean equality and that alone. The terms are not interchangeable. . . . If the reasoning in favor of this bill be sound, Germany is the most democratic of nations. And Austria also."[23]

In terms of the great ideological struggle in which President Wilson and his followers conceived of the war, the moulding of popular opinion was of utmost importance. The Committee on Public Information, created by executive order of the President less than two weeks after the declaration of war, became, in the words of its unofficial historians, "America's propaganda ministry . . . charged with encouraging and then consolidating the revolution of opinion which changed the United States from anti-militaristic democracy to an organized war machine. . . . It was a gargantuan advertising agency the like of which the country had never known, and the breathtaking scope of its activities was not to be equalled until the rise of totalitarian dictatorships after the war."[24] To discourage dissenting views as well as real disloyalty, Congress in June passed the administration's Espionage Act. This measure, with the later amendments of the Sedition Act, became the basis for the wartime modifications and suppression of the right of free speech as enjoyed under the First Amendment. Together the two laws made possible the prosecution of socialists, radicals, and pacifists, as well as those guilty of incautious or injudicious remarks reflecting upon the government's conduct of the war.

The most famous of the free speech cases involved Eugene Debs, the socialist leader, who in a talk before a group of workers at Canton, Ohio, defended the role of minority groups in American history and praised the young men who had the courage to go to jail for their anti-war convictions. Debs, who pled no defense except the right of free speech "in war as in peace," was sentenced to 10 years in prison, a decision that was upheld on appeal to the Supreme Court in an opinion written by Justice Holmes. But even if the government was justified in its prosecution of the radicals and pacifists who opposed the majority will in wartime, there was danger still in the suppression of all hostile criticism. In a democracy, how was the justice of a war, the wisdom of the way it was fought, or the advisability of its continuance to be determined if all unorthodox views were deemed subversive? As one historian of the war years pointed out, American democracy deprived of the challenge of an effective minority soon approached a state of mobbism.[25]

(VI)

To the President and his more pragmatic supporters, this suppression of dissent was a part of the process of winning the war and accomplishing the American mission. Convinced that substantial democratic unanimity was necessary for an American victory, Wilson refused to modify his war policies by individualistic humanitarian considerations. "In the last years of his administration," writes Daniel Aaron, "he tried to blend national unity and private profits, service and salesmanship, manifest destiny and dollar diplomacy without any awareness, apparently, that such ingredients would not mix. He saw no paradox, once he had embarked upon his course of war leadership, in conducting a fight against autocracy and militarism abroad and giving the superpatriots a free hand at home. For Wilson, democracy had simply become a battle cry."[26]

Although many of those liberals who clung to their faith in an idealistic crusade for democracy, at home as well as abroad, gradually became disillusioned, others accepted John Dewey's initial disposition to believe that the war would strengthen American democracy. Before the United States entered the war, Dewey had criticized the pacifists for their unwillingness to countenance the use of force. Historically he did not feel that war could be disassociated from the functions of the political state or the ends it sought to achieve. What was objectionable was the unwise use of force and the narrowing of preparedness solely to military measures. Believing that noble ends in war could not be separated from the means of its prosecution, Dewey opposed the creation of a patriotic hysteria. Thus he warned against the growing "conscription of thought" in America, urging instead a practical intelligence to complement Wilson's note of "an underlying national idealism." Although he decried the excesses of war and nationalism, Dewey did not have any solution as to how the good elements were to be kept away from the bad or as to how the emotional and irrational aspects of war were to be avoided.[27]

According to Randolph Bourne, Dewey's former disciple and most important wartime critic, illiberalism was a part of the very nature of war. "It is only 'liberal' naivete that is shocked at arbitrary coercion and suppression. Willing war means willing all the evils that are organically bound up with it." To another radical young intellectual, the historian William E. Dodd, "What Wilson played for was a united country," and the German government helped by its inept decisions. "But for a democracy to go to war is to take its life in its hands." Perhaps by the end of the war, Dodd speculated, "the United States will become a democracy in fact as well as name."[28]

"The War and the Intellectuals" was Bourne's answer to the liberals' pragmatic case for the war. "To those of us who still retain an irreconcilable animus against war," he wrote, "it has been a bitter experience to see the unanimity with which American intellectuals have thrown their support to the use of war-technique in the crisis in which America found herself." Not content with merely confirming the fact of war, the intellectuals "are now complacently asserting that it was they who effectively willed it . . . against the hesitation and dim perceptions of the American democratic masses. A war made deliberately by the intellectuals! A calm moral verdict, arrived at after a penetrating study of inexorable facts! . . . A war free from any taint of self-seeking, a war that will secure the triumph of democracy and internationalize the world!"[29]

While the intellectuals identified themselves with the least democratic elements in the United States, Bourne lamented: "No one is left to point out the undemocratic nature of this war-liberalism. In a time of faith skepticism is the most intolerable of all insults." In his unfinished book on the state, published in 1919, a year after his death, Bourne demonstrated how war, in its cultivation of the herd instinct, made minority opinion a crime and unswerving loyalty the sole test of citizenship. "The slack is taken up, the cross-currents fade out, and the nation moves lumberingly and slowly, but with ever-accelerated speed and integration, towards the great end, towards that 'peacefulness of being at war. . . .' "[30]

If the World War stifled the side of democracy that is identified with civil rights and liberal reform, it also showed the capacity of democracy to achieve a singleness of purpose in a time of crisis. The emphasis on solidarity of thought and opinion which led to the persecution of minorities also stimulated a great outpouring of mass effort. Unfortunately for the more idealistic aspects of the American mission, popular enthusiasm in the war tended to be limited largely to material things—more men for the armies, a greater industrial productivity, and in general anything that enhanced the efficiency of the American war-making machine. Altogether over 24 million men were registered for possible military duty under the Selective Service laws. Only 3.5 million, however, were actually drafted, of which number two million were sent overseas in the American Expeditionary Forces, and one million saw action on the battlefield. The navy, which did not use the draft, had as its major responsibility the convoying of shipping to the war zones, and by the close of the war America rivaled England in the size and power of its battle fleet. Compared to the other belligerents, United States losses were small—115,000 dead and over 200,000 wounded—but the American contribution in lives as well as material was decisive in the final stages of the Great War.

Mobilization of American manpower was paralleled by the almost equally thorough regimentation of the entire American economy on the home front. Under the over-all supervision of the War Industries Board, American manufacturing was regulated and standardized in the effort to increase its productive capacity. At the same time the government assumed operation of the railroads and merchant marine. New sources of labor took up the slack left by the withdrawal of several million young men into the armed forces and by the cessation of immigration in wartime. Women assumed a variety of jobs formerly held by men, and Negroes from the South migrated to swell the labor force in many industrial plants in the Middle West. Wages rose, especially in war-related industries, while collective bargaining was strengthened by government support. In turn most organized labor adhered to an informal no-strike pledge. Food and raw materials were in short supply, in large part because of transportation difficulties, but with the stimulus of new high prices, American farmers were able to meet most of the demands of both Europe and the United States. In all, some $32 billion were spent on the war, either directly or in the form of loans to the Allies. Of this amount, approximately one third was raised through taxes, chiefly the various excise taxes, but with some help from the new income tax. The rest of the money came from the sale of Liberty Bonds to the people.

(VII)

Despite the great achievements of the nation and the considerable prosperity enjoyed by many Americans, the war also created dissatisfactions. Shortages of civilian goods, symbolized by meatless days, lack of coal and gasoline, and a lowered standard of living for those with fixed incomes, made many Americans critical of the administration. With the war almost over in the fall of 1918, President Wilson appealed to the people to elect a Democratic Congress to aid him in his peace-making. Already, in the program exemplified in his Fourteen Points address to Congress, he had outlined a postwar settlement based on the "principle of justice to all peoples and nationalities, and their right to live on equal terms of liberty and safety with one another, whether they be strong or weak." Crucial to Wilson's conception of a lasting peace was his Fourteenth Point, in which he called for "a general association of nations . . . for the purpose of affording mutual guarantees of political independence and territorial integrity to great and small states alike." To the vindication of the principle of international justice, Wilson hopefully declared, the people of the United States were "ready to devote their lives, their honor, and everything that they possess."[31]

Unfortunately for Wilson's aspirations, his request for support in the 1918 midterm elections met with popular disapproval, and the Democrats lost control of both houses of Congress. While Americans accepted readily enough the concept of a war to make the world safe for democracy and to end all war, they were disillusioned with the process of the war itself. In contrast to the Civil War, World War I, over 3,000 miles away, never became a reality to the American people. When Randolph Bourne pleaded, "There is work to be done to prevent this war of ours from passing into popular mythology as a holy crusade," his words had more meaning for the future than for his own generation. Nevertheless the generality of American opinion at first accepted the end of the Great War as a victory for democracy. Frank Cobb, editor of the New York *World*, summed up the popular belief that Germany's defeat exposed the fallacy of militarism. "The disciplined forces of militarism yield at every point to the hurriedly assembled hosts of democracy," he wrote two days before the Armistice. "A peace of peoples," from which "militarism is stripped bare," concluded the *World* on the morning after the Armistice was signed.[32]

In Europe, on his triumphal tour before the Paris Peace Conference, Wilson was greeted with tumultuous popular enthusiasm.

But this public frenzy also supported the conflicting nationalistic aspirations of the victor powers at the peace table. And these same nationalistic forces of mass democracy endangered the prospects of a liberal democratic peace along the lines of Wilson's Fourteen Points. Intoxicated by their governments' wartime propaganda, people lost sight of all other objects in their single-minded desire for military victory. Back home in the United States, the illiberal policies with which the administration sealed itself off from hostile criticism also deprived the President of the kind of realistic discussion of war aims which might have made possible a better peace settlement. The pent-up feelings suppressed during the war broke out after 1918 in an angry tide of postwar antagonisms and disillusionment. Wilson's liberal backing, formerly so unquestioning, was now predicated on a challenge which the skeptical and critical *Nation* magazine put before the President while he was bound for Paris. "We are told that this was a war for democracy: very well, by its fruits we shall know it."[33]

Although a variety of motives entered into the United States rejection of the Treaty of Versailles, a primary basis for discontent was the Treaty's inconsistency with Wilson's own earlier idealistic peace proposals. In the Senate, it was true that many opponents of the League of Nations were isolationist Republicans in whom partisan politics played a decisive role. But at least some of the "irreconcilables" who fought the League—Senators Norris, La Follette, and Borah, for example—were among the staunchest advocates of an international understanding based on disarmament and mutual cooperation.

In his speeches across the nation in behalf of the Treaty of Versailles and the League of Nations, Wilson pictured the new mission of American democracy in terms of world leadership and international peace. "America," he said, "is the only Nation which can sympathetically lead the world in organizing peace." Until the United States entered the late war, it had been a commercial and industrial struggle of Germany and the Allies. If the United States now stood apart from the rest of the world in the peace settlement, it would have to be prepared to compete with other nations in the same kind of rivalry that had originally caused the European war. "We may say what we please of the German Government that has been destroyed, my fellow citizens," Wilson declared at St. Louis, "but it was the only sort of a government that could handle an armed nation. You cannot handle an armed nation if it is democratic, because democracies do not go to war that way." Predicting another world war if the nations of the world did not concert a way to prevent it, Wilson added: "When I think of the homes upon which dull despair would settle if this great hope is disappointed, I should wish for my part never to have had America play any part whatever in this attempt to emancipate the world."[34]

Broken by illness and shorn of much of his political power, Wilson lost his fight for the League of Nations. In the struggle with the Senate over ratification of the Treaty, he refused all compromise, and in his final annual message to Congress in 1920 he again identified American destiny in war and peace with the eternal principles of right and justice.

> This is the mission upon which democracy came into the world. Democracy is an assertion of the right of the individual to live and to be treated justly as against any attempt on the part of any combination of individuals to make laws which will overburden him. . . . The old world is just now suffering from a wanton rejection of the principle of democracy. . . . This is the time of all others when democracy should prove its purity and its spiritual power to prevail. It is surely the manifest destiny of the United States to lead in the attempt to make this spirit prevail. . . .
>
> The United States is of necessity the sample democracy of the world, and the triumph of democracy depends upon its success.[35]

CHAPTER TEN

Disillusionment and Prosperity

THE GREAT CRUSADE for peace and democracy came to a close in an atmosphere of increasing disillusionment. A year after the Armistice, a young American intellectual was writing:

> The plain truth of our war to make the world safe for democracy is that today there is less freedom of speech and right of assemblage, less tolerance, more governmental control over political and economic opinion, less liberty for teachers and college professors, more reaction and militarism than was the case the day we declared war on Germany.[1]

Never had the spirit of victory seemed to turn so quickly into an aura of defeatism. In emphatic rejection of the doctrine of an American world mission, the United States refused to join the League of Nations. Not only did the country turn its back on Europe, but it also repudiated the whole ideal of internationalism. In the new post-war era America's historic faith in the superiority of its institutions often degenerated into an intolerant nationalism and super-patriotism. The late war now was regarded simply as a horrible mistake.

Judged by the peace terms at Versailles and by the economic and political chaos in Europe, the end of the World War was not going to bring any immediate realization of the high aims which President Wilson had held up to the peoples of the world. The editors of the *New Republic*, who had given strong backing to Wilson's concept of the war, had also voiced the sentiments of the country in hailing the Armistice as a great victory for peace and democracy. Yet, before the month of November was up, the magazine's confidence was wavering. With Bolshevism spreading and national rivalries rampant, it seemed unlikely that any league of nations could overcome the realities of postwar power politics. "The outcome of this war is less the triumph of democracy than the downfall of autocracy. . . . Democratic nations have had to compromise some of the most precious ingredients of their democracy in order to win such a prolonged and exhausting war." Seeing no real peace or democracy in the world of 1918, the *New Republic* concluded: "Democracy, if it is to thrive, must be thoroughgoing."[2]

By linking together the process of the war and the cause of democracy, Wilson helped to forge a base for the postwar criticism of democratic government. Thus the idea of a lost peace and of a failure of democracy became intertwined. "The phrase 'to make the world safe for democracy,'" wrote one of the expert advisers to the American delegation at Paris, "had become a by-word for cynics; and for this the optimists are to blame. They failed to appreciate the dimension of the task."[3]

(II)

The collapse of wartime visions of international democracy was paralleled by the postwar defeat of democracy at home. During the war most Americans had accepted the Wilson administration's restraints on individual freedom, while the sense of common effort seemed to strengthen democracy. With the return of peace, however, the need for this social cooperation diminished. But there was no similar post-Armistice slackening in the vigor of the wartime campaign to stamp out all radical or dissenting views. While the demobilization of the armed forces and of American industry was quickly accomplished, there was little accompanying demobilization in the realm of thought and opinion. In this continued disregard for individual and minority rights, American democracy after the war became synonymous with a witchhunt. Aroused by the specter of a communist world revolution, the American people succumbed to the Red Scare of 1919. The number of avowed communists or anarchists in the United States was small, but a series of bombings in 1919 and 1920, presumably by radical terrorists, provided an excuse for the continuance of wartime patterns of suppression and censorship.

The President's dedication to the cause of world democracy was paralleled by the indifference of his second administration to the spirit of democracy at home. Ideals of future peace contrasted oddly with Wilson's use of the threat of American armed power as a lever at the Paris Conference. Although administration plans for peacetime military conscription were defeated, the policy of building up the American navy to a position second to none was continued. Pacifist and radical opponents of the war were refused amnesty, and Eugene Debs was kept in federal prison even though he was nominated to the Presidency by the Socialist party in 1920. Radical aliens were rounded up in mass raids and deported after cursory hearings to countries where they had not lived in years. "Gone was the age-long welcome to the distressed and discontented laborers of Europe. Instead, a nationwide outcry arose for wholesale deportations."[4] In the absence of a peacetime sedition law, American citizens could not be treated in such arbitrary fashion, but the excitement of the deportations and Red Scare aroused the country's feelings against all vestiges of liberalism. Organized labor, identified in the public mind with radical and foreign "isms," also felt the full force of both popular and official condemnation. A series of postwar strikes from Seattle to Boston, and in such key industries as steel and coal, contributed to conservative fears of revolution and added to the pressures of intolerance and reaction.

Aggravated instances of the violation of the democratic process occurred in the refusals of Congress and the New York state legislature to seat duly elected members. In November 1918, Victor Berger, a prominent anti-war Socialist, was sent to Congress from Milwaukee while under trial for violating the Espionage Act on the grounds of certain wartime editorials in his newspaper, the *Milwaukee Leader*. Although his conviction was later reversed by the United States Supreme Court, Congress denied Berger the seat in the House of Representatives to which he was re-elected by his constituents. In New York in 1919, the legislature established a joint committee of six under the chairmanship of Senator Clayton R. Lusk to investigate seditious activities. In its search for materials the Lusk Committee staged a series of spectacular raids upon radical organizations. On the basis of its charges, five Socialist Assemblymen, duly elected by the people to represent their districts in the state legislature, were denied their seats and expelled from the Assembly chamber. The Lusk Committee was also responsible for two new school laws providing for the licensing of private schools and the expulsion of any teachers deemed guilty of advocating "a form of government other than the government of the United States or of this state." In approving the subsequent retraction of these laws, Governor Alfred E. Smith declared that they were repugnant to American democracy and a violation of freedom of opinion and freedom of speech for teachers and schools. In signing the repeal measure, the Governor asserted: "I firmly believe that I am vindicating the principle that, within the limits of the penal law, every citizen may speak and teach what he believes."[5]

By the end of 1920 the Red Scare was over. In Europe the communist wave was turned back. In the United States anti-radical hysteria subsided in part because it had so largely accomplished its intent. The organizations capable of providing leadership for any sort of mass radical or labor movement had been broken up or hopelessly weakened. Thus the IWW, the Nonpartisan League, and the various Socialist and Communist parties were all depleted in membership and influence. At the same time the success of Harding's campaign for "normalcy" indicated a general desire for release from all evidences of the late war. People wanted an opportunity to enjoy peace without internal strife. The spirit of the twenties, accordingly, despite its chauvinism and conservatism, was hostile to the feverish temper of the Red Scare. It was to be an era of popular complacency. Yet, as William Leuchtenburg points out, "the Red Scare left a bitter heritage of suspicion of aliens, distrust of organized labor, hostility to reformers, and insistence on political conformity."[6] At least one unpleasant product of postwar hysteria that lingered on into the 1920's to become a *cause célèbre* was the Sacco-Vanzetti case. Nicola Sacco and Bartolomeo Vanzetti were two Italian aliens and admitted anarchists who were accused of a payroll robbery and murder at South Braintree, Massachusetts, in April 1920. Brought to trial in the midst of the anti-alien and anti-radical atmosphere of the twenties, the anarchist philosophy of the defendants seemed to many liberals an important factor in their conviction. This highly controversial case, which touched off demonstrations of protest abroad, continued to trouble the American conscience long after the defendants themselves had been executed in 1927.

The year of the Red Scare also witnessed an intense reaction against American Negroes. Talk of democracy during the war had raised hopes among many Negroes that its full realization might be achieved in the foreseeable future. Instead, by 1919, racial friction was worse than at any time since Reconstruction. From June to the end of the year, approximately 25 race riots disgraced American cities in the North as well as in the South. In Chicago alone in 13 days of rioting, 15 whites and 23 Negroes were killed and over 500 persons were injured. Meanwhile lynchings increased, and the Ku Klux Klan was revived as an instrument of hate and intolerance.

(*III*)

Although the anti-radical movement of the first postwar years lost its popular appeal, economic and political conservatism continued to dominate the twenties. In place of the widespread faith in reform that had characterized the Progressive era, the postwar decade was distinguished by its smug satisfaction with American institutions. Nowhere was this more evident than in national politics. The three Republican Presidents, Harding, Coolidge, and Hoover, were elected by tremendous majorities, and all accepted the desirability of a return to "normalcy." Harding himself captured 61 per cent of the popular vote in 1920, carrying 37 states located in every section of the country except the Solid South. No other President, not even Franklin Roosevelt in 1936, was able to gain the White House with a greater popular mandate.

Electoral victories of landslide proportions, however, were not always a measure of general voter interest. Since the Bryan-McKinley campaign of 1896, Americans had been staying away from the polls in relatively increasing numbers. The right to vote for which the propertyless workingman, Negro freedman, and suffragettes had struggled seemed to be little valued by many citizens. And political democracy, now that it had been substantially achieved for the first time in American history, was weakened by this public indifference.

Seemingly the availability of the democratic process exceeded its actual use. Not only could most adults now qualify for the suffrage, but as a result of the reforms of the Progressive era, government was in theory more responsive to their will. The Seventeenth Amendment, ratified in 1913, provided for the popular election of United States Senators, and by the close of the war direct primaries were in operation in all but four of the states, while the initiative and the referendum were sanctioned by a large proportion of states and cities. As a climax to the movement for greater democracy, the women's suffrage, or Nineteenth Amendment, was ratified in June 1919, in time for the Presidential elections the next year. With the adoption of this amendment, a much larger number of American citizens could vote than ever before in the history of the country, but the results, as Eric Goldman suggests, "in no way justified the hopes and the claims of the progressives. The most conspicuous result was the lack of any result. The initiative, referendum, and recall were invoked sparingly, and to a lessening extent."[7]

Women at first were especially slow to use the ballots they had been so long in winning, and their votes also had little effect in accomplishing any sudden reformation in American politics. Gradually, however, and especially in local elections, they came to assume a larger role in political life. If women were sometimes guilty of political apathy and indifference, they could point to the example of American males. In state and local elections it was well known that only a fraction of those qualified to vote ever bothered to go to the polls except when some dramatic issue stirred their self-interest. Political lassitude on the part of the American electorate probably helped to encourage the usual postwar outbreak of scandals and corruption in the government. These, in turn, weakened popular confidence in democracy. The difficulties of Harding's administration, like those of Grant's after the Civil War, were the most notorious, but on all levels of American government eternal vigilance continued to be the price of freedom from corruption and tyranny.

While some Americans were indifferent to the exercise of their democratic rights and privileges, others were deprived of these advantages. In a number of states the voter was hampered by restrictive registration and election laws. In virtually every state, urban as compared to rural voters were relatively disfranchised by unequal or gerrymandered election districts. Ostensibly designed to eliminate fraud and corruption in elections, poll taxes and long residence requirements also made it more difficult to vote. In the South the discriminatory devices to curtail Negro voting continued unchecked, and in many areas a combination of indifference and suppression prevented the Negro from exercising his constitutional rights and privileges in regard to the suffrage. Finally, as a product of the anti-radical feeling which followed the war, a number of states passed laws which made it difficult for third parties to have their candidates included on the ballot. Thus the citizen qualified to vote and willing to go to the polls might well find his effective choice narrowed to the candidates of the two major parties.[8]

Despite the evident organizational problem faced by third parties, especially on a local level, the remnants of the 1912 Progressives, with the help of other reform groups, again made the effort after the war to win over the American public. Early in 1922 a Conference for Progressive Political Action was launched at a meeting attended by the delegates of farm groups, the Nonpartisan League, the railway brotherhoods, the Socialist party, and various religious welfare organizations. Their hopes kindled by the successful campaigns of the British Labour party and National Progressive party in

Canada, the Conference at a later meeting in St. Louis in February 1924 declared its intention to nominate and elect candidates for national and local offices "who are pledged to the interests of the producing classes and to the principles of genuine democracy in agriculture, industry, and government." On July 4, at Cleveland, the CPPA nominated Senators Robert M. La Follette and Burton K. Wheeler for President and Vice President. The Progressives' platform stressed the economic plight of the farmers and labor and called for government ownership of the railroads and of water power resources. The party also advocated the popular election of judges and a Congressional veto over Supreme Court decisions. Although these plans for a more direct democracy and a modified socialism had some appeal among reform elements, the bulk of the farm and labor vote appeared to remain with the Republicans.[9]

Despite the scandals of the Harding regime, neither the Democrats nor the Progressives were able to garner enough ballots to prevent Coolidge from winning a clear majority of the popular total. With fewer than five million votes, the Progressives ran third in a campaign in which only half the number of eligible voters went to the polls. Meanwhile the idea of founding a new third party died hard, as the notion continued to interest small groups of progressive reformers and intellectuals. In some states, particularly Minnesota, Wisconsin, and New York after the onset of the depression, third parties once more exercised an important political influence, but nationally none of the parties was able to do more than serve as a pressure group or stimulus to the Republicans and Democrats. The Socialists, the most permanent of the minor parties, never again attained the percentage of the total popular vote that Debs' near-million ballots won for them in 1912.

(*IV*)

The political conservatism of the twenties reflected more than a disillusionment with the late war. It was also a result of the economic prosperity which returned after the depression of 1920 and 1921. Under the spur of rising production and wage rates, a business and middle-class point of view dominated the thinking of the majority of Americans. Though the prosperity of the twenties has been questioned, chiefly on the grounds that its benefits were not widely or equally shared, there was no doubt that it was a decade of tremendous economic expansion. And for a majority of Americans the boom, although not ever-lasting, was real enough for seven years. Reaping the fruits of the industrial progress of the nineteenth century, the United States by the mid-twenties enjoyed a total wealth just under that of Europe and amounting to perhaps as much as two fifths of the entire world. Per capita national income, which had jumped from $339 in 1914 to $700 in 1920, again reached this figure in 1929 after recovering from a decline in the 1921 depression. Corrected to overcome the postwar inflation and changing monetary values of the 1920's, real income for those gainfully occupied increased gradually throughout the decade. While wages went up, especially for skilled workers, the working day was cut to eight hours, and for some also a five-day week was begun. The output and efficency of American manufacturing was increased largely through the use of machinery and new techniques of mass production. At the same time there was a surge of business concentration and consolidation, along with the development of giant new industries, particularly in electricity, synthetics, and chemicals. On the other hand, the real income of the farmer declined, and some industries such as coal mining and the railroads were far from prosperous. Child labor, especially in the textile mills of the South, and unemployment also continued to pervade the industrial scene.[10]

Most important of the amazing new things that the average American consumer could buy to raise his material standard of living was the automobile. The cheap motor car, pioneered by Henry Ford, opened up new vistas to the average American family, while Ford himself

personified the farmboy-mechanic who in a single lifetime reached the top. He fulfilled the dream of an acquisitive society committed to a belief in individual advancement. He brought the automobile to the masses of the world; he was the magical tinkerer who revolutionized human life. He was the high priest of mass production, which people the world over saw as more important than any ideological doctrine as a solution to the curse of poverty. His firm was family-owned; he was hostile to Wall Street; he founded, so it was believed, the doctrine of high wages and low prices, of sharing the benefits of his genius with the world—he was, in short, the Good Businessman. He resolved the moral dilemma of a Puritan-capitalist society. He achieved material success without losing his primal innocence.[11]

Thus, in William Leuchtenburg's graphic description, Henry Ford, perhaps the richest man in the world, became an important symbol, one of the major folk heroes of American democracy, a rugged individualist in an increasingly complex industrialized society.

Throughout the period of the twenties, most American business enjoyed the helpful backing of the federal government. President Harding believed that what the country wanted was "a period in America with less government in Business and more Business in government." President Coolidge contributed the famous remark, "The business of America is business," while President Hoover, in turn, declared that Alexander Hamilton "well comprehended the necessities of Federal Government activity in support of commerce and industry." Accordingly the task of the regulatory agencies developed during the Progressive era was now diverted to the encouragement and protection of business. Hoover, as Secretary of Commerce, encouraged business to organize itself into trade associations and to develop its own codes of fair competition and self-regulation. "We are passing," he said, "from a period of extremely individualistic action into a period of associational activities."[12] So long as prosperity continued, there were few who questioned the Republicans' paternalistic policies. Although the renewed growth of big business and monopoly seemed to pose some of the same problems for American democracy that it had at the turn of the century, the day of reckoning was postponed till the crash of 1929.

Business leaders, with their great prestige, meanwhile spoke not only as the representatives of their own interests, but also often for the great body of the public. There was danger therefore that, in the golden glow of the twenties, business would be able to eliminate all other groups as the interpreter of the American democratic tradition. The business thinking of the period accepted democracy and the virtue of the people only so long as neither was misled by radical leaders or doctrines. It was confident that under the philosophy of individualism the best reached the top, with the top measured chiefly by an accumulation of wealth. "I verily believe," said the president of the National Association of Manufacturers in his annual address in 1924, "that the essentially sound and more dependable elements of American citizenship, who are always in the majority when not divided by political shibboleths and narrow prejudices, are getting tired of chasing the will-o'-wisps of radicalism in government, in religion, in art, and in social life, and are about ready to return to the God, the Bible, and the fundamental principles of their forefathers."[13]

Convinced, however, that men were fundamentally selfish and egotistic, business leaders feared the corrupting influence of too much leisure time for their employees. Opposed to government regulation, except for disciplining labor and protecting property, the president of the NAM, for example, also complained that, "in the names of Democracy and Progress, all sorts of legislative crimes are being attempted, the idea prevailing among many of the people that democracy means unrestrained and unrestricted liberty of thought and action. . . ." "Dare To Be a Babbitt!" was the advice that *Nation's Business* gave to its readers.[14]

(V)

The country's economic prosperity, political conservatism, and general disillusionment over the late war resulted in a remarkable intensification of American nationalism. Democracy and Americanism no longer were regarded as values to be shared as widely as possible. Instead of a gospel to all nations, they became a national secret confined to those who met the tests of race, creed, color, and political and economic orthodoxy. In an effort to seal off the United States from foreign competition, Congress raised tariff rates and took steps to stop the tide of immigrants waiting to enter the United States after the war. In a series of measures culminating in the National Origins Act of 1924, it reversed the historic liberal immigration policy of more than a century. Selectively higher tariffs and immigration restriction had some economic justification, and both had strong backing in Progressive and labor as well as in business and conservative circles. For example, not a single Progressive opposed the immigration-restriction bill when it passed the Senate in 1924. And an historian of the rights of man in America has recently pointed out that American feelings of superiority to the immigrant "broke the logic of an equalitarian society and accustomed Americans to think in class terms. . . . Unrestricted immigration to America was always a powerful force for class consciousness and class exploitation. . . . The immigration restriction laws of the 1920's brought an end to three centuries of commerce in human lives which always had worked to sap the vitality of the democratic spirit."[15]

A substantial part of the appeal of the new immigration legislation rested on the fact that it made possible drastic cuts in the numbers of those arriving from Southern and Eastern Europe or from Italy and the Slavic countries. Thus, in addition to the understandable American desire to prevent, for economic reasons, the continued large-scale immigration of the poverty-stricken masses of war-torn Europe, the new legislation also had a racialist base. United with old fears of radicalism or labor competition from the immigrant was a strong prejudice against many of the foreigners on the grounds of their national origins. To a student of American immigration policies, it seemed that the "old belief in America as a promised land for all who yearn for freedom had lost its operative significance. And the new equation between national loyalty and a large measure of political and social conformity would long outlive the generation that established it."[16]

The long-standing tradition of America as a melting pot of all races and creeds was now being surrendered. The theory of democracy as a mixture of cultures and the quiet assurance that the immigrant's Old World ways would gradually be modified by contact with American free institutions yielded to strident demands for an enforced assimilation of all newcomers into a 100-per-cent Americanism. In self-defense therefore, the immigrant, along with various racial and religious groups, turned for solace to exclusive organizations of his own making. Catholic and Protestant societies and clubs were matched by the efforts of Jews and Negroes, the two domestic groups hit hardest by the intolerance of the twenties, to found militant nationalist movements. Among Jews Zionism took on a new popular appeal, while Negroes by the thousands supported the "Back to Africa" crusade of Marcus A. Garvey, an adventurer and promoter who attempted to appeal to Negro racial pride.

The most extreme example of postwar hostility toward foreigners and other minority groups was the Ku Klux Klan. Though there was no direct connection with the original organization that had flourished in the South after the Civil War, the revived Klan copied many of the methods of its predecessor and also borrowed much of the nativist philosophy of the mid-nineteenth century Know-Nothing movement. The Klan united in its program all the most intolerant and illiberal features of the cult of postwar nationalism. Its slogan of "native, white, Protestant" supremacy was directed almost as much against the Catholic, Jew, and alien white immigrant as against the Negro. In the Democratic party the Klan fought the nomination of Alfred E. Smith for President because of his Catholicism. Conservative and ultranationalistic, the Klan fostered hate and intolerance. In addition it regarded itself as a private law enforcement agency to support Prohibition and censor private morals.

Prohibition, despite its backing by the Klan and its popularity in rural regions and among fundamentalist religious groups, was a curious anomaly in the twenties. As a local and state measure, it had a long history in the United States, but its more direct origins were rooted in the Progressive movement and in the First World War, when it was imposed as a conservation measure. Prohibition was thus an interesting example both of wartime controls over the citizen and of the Progressive reformers' belief that the state knows what is best for the individual. It also illustrated the ability of organized minorities to enforce their will upon a majority and keep on the statute books laws which were no longer popular nor readily enforceable. Lobbying by church, temperance, and women's organizations intimidated politicians who personally had little sympathy with the Eighteenth Amendment. Moreover, because of the temptation to break the law, Prohibition resulted in a nation-wide wave of bootlegging and racketeering which bred contempt for democratic government.

Other efforts of the federal government to enforce moral standards, such as the Mann Act, or White Slave Traffic Act, and the Harrison Narcotic Drug Act, were accorded greater general acceptance in the twenties, but some observers were inclined to view the growing interference of the government with personal habits by means of social and morals legislation as an example of the Puritanism of democracy. With the rise of modern democracy they saw a tendency for government to become more aggressive in the passage of such legislation, while the mass of the people came to cherish the reputed middle-class virtues of chastity, temperance, and thrift. The theory that the average citizen must be protected by his government from the temptations of vice was also invoked as justification for the growing number of state and local statutes authorizing the censorship of books and motion pictures. Control or censorship, particularly over school textbooks and history teaching, was attempted by private organizations such as the American Legion, which often reinforced the chauvinistic nationalism of the Klan.

In revolt over Prohibition and other restraints on the individual, the younger generation read Sinclair Lewis and the disillusioned writers who satirized the late war and the values of America's business civilization. In *Main Street* and his other popular novels of the twenties, Lewis defended the noncomformist individual in his struggle with a commonplace and prejudiced society. Through the pages of the *American Mercury* magazine H. L. Mencken also directed caustic criticisms at the mass of his fellow citizens, while he aired his own increasing doubts over democracy and social reform. In his *Notes on Democracy*, published in 1926, Mencken contended that fear and envy were the two main characteristics of democracy and "its twin, Puritanism." Evidence of fear he saw in the American bent to chase monsters from the time of the British Redcoats in the American Revolution to the Bolshevists in the Red Scare of 1919. In a democracy driven by such hysteria, "The statesman becomes, in the last analysis, a mere witch-hunter, a glorified smeller and snooper. . . ." The Department of Justice he attacked as misnamed and as the chief violator of the Bill of Rights it was supposed to protect. Nine-tenths of American Presidents, he pointed out, had reached office by making promises that were basically immoral. Yet, after their election, they were criticized not for making the promises but for failing to keep them. "No man," he wrote, "would want to be President of the United States in strict accordance with the Constitution. There is no sense of power in merely executing the laws; it comes from evading or augmenting them."[17]

(VI)

The censorious invasion of intellectual and personal life and the intolerant racist concepts popular in the twenties were at odds with the traditional democratic faith in individual freedom and equality. At the same time the political and economic conservatism of the era undermined the confidence of old-line Progressives in the efficacy of the state as an agency of social reform. The dilemma of the liberal democrat and reformer in an age of reaction and conformity was documented in the writings of J. Allen Smith and Vernon L. Parrington. Close friends and colleagues at the University of Washington, both men were scholars who also exercised a wide popular influence. Smith first attracted the attention of Progressives when he anticipated some of Charles Beard's emphasis on the economic origins of the Constitution. In a later book, *The Growth and Decadence of Constitutional Government*, which he wrote during the twenties, Smith became more pessimistic over the prospects of democracy and reform. The war, with its encouragement of centralized power, demonstrated to Smith the undemocratic and illiberal side of government. There was a wide discrepancy between the theory and practice of democracy, and the growth of the suffrage and of majority rule was no guarantee of individual liberty. The achievement of political democracy, by removing the main ground for the people's distrust of governmental authority, concealed the steady rise of governmental supremacy over the citizen under the guise of popular sovereignty. Centralization, accompanied by militarism and imperialism, he believed, was a direct threat to popular rule. "Democracy, in any true sense of the term," he concluded, "is possible only when there is the largest practicable measure of local self-government."[18]

Parrington's work, *Main Currents in American Thought*, developed Smith's general point of view with a vast amount of rich historical detail. And in a letter to a friend, written a few months before his death in 1929, Parrington summed up the essential problem of American democracy, which neither he nor Smith was able to resolve.

Wherever power is lodged a great struggle for control and use of that power follows. When one controls the political state, whatever one wants can be done under cover of the law and with the sanction of the courts. Have you been able to convince yourself that the corporate wealth of America will permit the centralized political state to pass out of its control and become an agent to regulate or thwart its plans? . . .

You see the dilemma in which I find myself. We must have a political state powerful enough to deal with corporate wealth, but how are we going to keep that state with its augmenting power from being captured by the force we want it to control?[19]

The unhappiness of the liberal in the twenties was illustrated in the career of Frederic C. Howe. A long-time reformer with his roots in Progressivism, Howe had attempted as Wilson's Commissioner of Immigration to resist the alien deportations. Embittered by the collapse of idealism in the war and postwar hysteria, he wrote: "Democracy had not failed; it had never been tried. We had created confusion and called it democracy."[20] The political state, with its discriminatory taxation and paternalistic subsidies, was an instrument of economic exploitation. In his *Revolution and Democracy*, published in 1921, Howe became one of the first of the prewar Progressive reformers to turn expectantly to the example of social change in Soviet Russia. Lincoln Steffens, the leading muckraker, whose *Autobiography* stimulated a generation of college students after the war, was another reformer whose faltering hopes for democracy were buoyed up by the Soviet Union.

Especially after the onset of the depression, a number of disillusioned Progressives came under the influence of Marxist concepts. But in the twenties, faith in institutional reform of whatever sort usually remained at a discount. Liberal and radical elements, which before the war had worked for Progressive social ideals, now felt it necessary to defend the individual personality against the growing demands of a conservative business civilization for social and political conformity. Much of the intellectual rebellion of the twenties, therefore, was in the direction of individual nonconformity, rather than of social reform. As majoritarian democracy became identified with conservative middle-class business and political views, it was attacked by those who believed that the natural rights of the individual were being endangered. Democracy, complained Ralph Borsodi, author of *This Ugly Civilization*, "makes conformity the greatest good in the

World."[21] In the general disillusionment of the decade, there was a prevalent assumption on the part of an aristocratic minority that democracy could never rise above the level of mob rule. Thus popular intolerance was paralleled by the disbelief of an influential intellectual elite in the wisdom and virtue of the people. Whether in terms of the will of the majority or of the rights of a minority, a shadow was being cast over the American democratic tradition.

Faith in the advantages of an aristocratic society was often based on the assumed existence of a superior race or elite group of exceptional individuals. The crude prejudices of organizations like the Ku Klux Klan received quasi-scientific support from the racist theories of American scholars who feared the impact of a mass migration from other parts of the world. The postwar resurgence of the old emphasis upon the superiority of the Anglo-Saxon or Nordic races was illustrated by the popularity of such works as Madison Grant's *The Passing of the Great Race* and Lothrop Stoddard's *The Rising Tide of Color Against White World-Supremacy*. It was now argued that democracy, which had worked fairly well when America enjoyed a relatively homogeneous population drawn from the British Isles and Northern European countries, could not survive the accelerating decline of racial purity. Democracy, Grant declared, tended to the "transfer of power from the higher to the lower races, from the intellectual to the plebeian class."

> Democratic ideals among an homogeneous population of Nordic blood, as in England and America, is one thing, but it is quite another for the white man to share his blood with, or intrust his ideals to, brown, yellow, black, or red men.
>
> This is suicide pure and simple, and the first victim of this amazing folly will be the white man himself.[22]

If American democracy was menaced by racial mixture, it also seemed threatened by its disregard of the natural and biological differences among men. Through the study of eugenics or the improvement of the race, a number of anthropologists, biologists, sociologists, and psychologists emphasized anew the importance of heredity as against environment. In his book *Is America Safe for Democracy?*, William McDougall, professor of psychology at Harvard University, posed the problem of whether modern progressive civilization was impairing the human qualities and abilities of its population to the obvious detriment of democracy. Pessimism over the quality of the population appeared to be supported by the widely publicized results of certain mental tests given to draftees during the war. The seeming low-level intelligence of the average American youth could hardly be regarded as compatible with the realization of democratic ideals of self-government. Moreover, since most eugenicists believed that the portion of the population with the least intelligence tended to bear the greatest number of children, there was additional reason to fear a deterioration in the quality of democratic government. According to its more implacable critics, modern democracy was either impossible or undesirable, or both. Despite differences in the biological and intellectual capacities of races and individuals, the modern state tended to enforce a democratic equality upon its citizens. In the mind of a wide variety of observers, therefore, the probable coming of an era of mass rule through the power of public opinion would result either in the collapse or corruption of American government.[23]

Even among its friends, the war and postwar experience, in enforcing a popular consensus, raised certain doubts about democracy. The use of propaganda to influence public opinion and to create artificial unity was disturbing to the belief that democracy rested on the free and rational consent of the governed. In an age of mass communication, popular majorities that could be created and sustained by official indoctrination represented a threat to the idea of a free and responsible electorate. Over a year before America entered the First World War, a report of the Committee on Academic Freedom of the American Association of University Professors pointed out "the dangers connected with the existence in a democracy of an overwhelming and concentrated public opinion. The tendency of modern democracy," the Committee declared,

> is for men to think alike, to feel alike, and to speak alike. Any departure from the conventional standards is apt to be regarded with suspicion. Public opinion is at once the chief safeguard of a democracy, and the chief menace to the real liberty of the individual. It almost seems as if the danger of despotism cannot be wholly averted under any form of government. In a political autocracy there is no effective public opinion, and all are subject to the tyranny of the ruler; in a democracy there is political freedom, but there is likely to be a tyranny of public opinion.[24]

In his postwar analysis of public opinion, Walter Lippmann observed in retrospect how the Wilson administration through the Creel Committee on Public Information tried and, while the war continued, very largely succeeded "in creating something that might almost be called one public opinion all over America." Lippmann believed that for public opinion to function well in a democracy, for it to be spontaneous and well-informed, there had to be an ideal environment in which the society itself remained relatively simple, intelligible, and easily managed. But in the complex modern world, peoples and nations mistook images for realities, accepted the public facade thrown up before them, and spoke in generalities and stereotypes. "It is idle under such circumstances," he wrote, "to talk about democracy, or about the refinement of public opinion. With such monstrous complications the public can do little more than at intervals to align itself heavily for or against the regime in power. . . ." As Lippmann made clear, the proponents of democracy could no longer assume that the truth would prevail if only it were given an opportunity to be heard. The problem of public opinion now transcended such relatively simple issues of civil liberties as free speech or a free press. Under the propaganda of governments and of highly organized and well-financed pressure groups, minorities could sway and control majority opinion.[25]

The very success of democracy in expanding the sphere of both the economic and political rights of man added to the problem of decision-making and contributed to a certain inevitable disillusionment. In his lectures in the United States on *The Essentials of Democracy*, the English political scientist A. D. Lindsay asked whether democracy was mainly an effort to secure popular consent or to carry out the people's mandate. The generality of the population, hardly ever wanting anything definitely or unanimously, "can only consent," he declared, "to what government or some other organized group of people proposes to do." If unanimity was desired, then mass propaganda was the instrument to achieve the kind of conformity illustrated, he suggested, in both Puritan New England and Fascist Italy. However, Lindsay concluded, democracy rested on more than the consent of the governed. What mattered was not that everyone agreed but that everyone should have made some contribution to the decision, even if only as a loyal opposition. Thus will, not force, was the basis of the state in the sense that most people mostly must wish to obey its dictates.[26]

(*VII*)

In the midst of the misgivings of its detractors, defenders of the democratic tradition attempted to redefine its significance and purpose in American life. Accepting as a fact the insufficiency of a mere political reformation, proponents of democracy called for further improvement along social and economic lines. Confident that intelligent social action offered a solution, educators urged that the schools and local communities become laboratories of democracy. During the war a heightened preparedness and patriotism had stimulated a concern with the educational promotion of democracy. And after the war many educators, in seeking some form of federal aid for schools, insisted that education was a matter of national interest which required national planning and support. They re-emphasized the traditional American belief that democratic ideals could be realized only through more and better education.

While stressing the need for a greater attention to education if President Wilson's democratic ideals were to be achieved, educators also showed an awareness of the undemocratic character of their schools. In 1916 John Dewey, who more than anyone was responsible for applying the pragmatic philosophy of Progressivism to the school system, published his influential *Democracy and Education.* As a criterion of democracy, Dewey and his followers emphasized the importance of social experience and shared actions. "A democracy," he wrote, "is more than a form of government; it is primarily a mode of associated living, of conjoint communicated experience." At the same time, however, Dewey warned that a "progressive society counts individual variations as precious, since it finds in them the means of its own growth. Hence a democratic society must, in consistency with its ideal, allow for intellectual freedom and the play of diverse gifts and interests in its educational measures." Democracy in education should include, Dewey believed, both realist and idealist theories.[27]

The conflict between democratic ideals and democratic realities involved more than the extent to which theory might be realized in practice. Under the impact of the war and the Progressive reforms of the 1900's, an increasing number of educators and scholars held that the democracy of the future should involve positive efforts at social control. Professor Charles A. Ellwood of the University of Missouri called modern democracy "a form of social control which attempts to reconcile the freedom of the individual with the needs of objective social life." Equality and equality of opportunity were important to democracy, but they were relative in his opinion to democracy as a means of social control. Thus a democratic solution to the problem of the Negro in the United States, Ellwood argued, required "the meeting together of both races upon a fraternal basis," rather than an absolute liberty and equality of the individuals concerned. Democracy was to the group what self-realization and self-determination were to the individual. While democracy inculcated liberty and equality, both were relative to the more fundamental principle which Ellwood called fraternity.[28]

Like Ellwood, the distinguished biologist Edwin Grant Conklin believed that democracy was moving toward greater social control. Democratic government, which depended upon the intelligence of its citizens, had been benefited, he felt, by the way in which World War I broke down older class distinctions and opened the way for individual advancement through intelligence instead of social rank. Despite the view of the eugenicists that intelligence was declining, Conklin was confident that the long view of human history continued to offer a basis for hope. Seeking to discover what were the teachings of biology in regard to democracy, he asked: "How can we develop social organization in spite of hereditary inequality, universal fraternity in spite of national and class antagonisms?" With the growth of the modern complex society, he asserted, "Personal freedom must be subordinated more and more to social freedom. . . ." The further evolution of society must lie in the direction of a greater cooperation of man.

> The liberty we worship is not, or at least should not be, that of the individual, but rather that of society as a whole—the freedom of nations and races rather than that of individuals, the self-determination of peoples rather than of persons. This is the biological ideal of freedom, and it should also be the democratic ideal.[29]

During the twenties the most systematic development of the concept of social democracy was contained in the writings of John Dewey. In *The Public and Its Problems* and his *Individualism Old and New,* Dewey attempted a reformulation of democracy in terms of the changes taking place in American society. More than just the product of political forces, democracy to Dewey represented "the convergence of a great number of social movements, no one of which owed either its origins or its impetus to inspiration of democratic ideals or to planning for the eventual outcome." The praise or condemnation of democracy, based on conceptual interpretations, whether true or false, good or bad, was irrelevant because they were "reflections of facts in thought, not their causal authors." Thus, despite the institution of political democracy, a democratic society had not yet been achieved. "The democratic public is still largely inchoate and unorganized," but Dewey also felt that "Perhaps the apathy of the electorate is due to the irrelevant artificiality of the issues with which it is attempted to work up factitious excitement."[30]

To Dewey the major question was when the Great Society, fashioned in the last century by the discoveries and uses of steam and electricity and by technology in general, would become the Great Community. The traditional individuality of Western European civilization, which now was threatened by American mass culture, had been a very limited boon in which the peasantry and proletariat had hardly participated. In America many of the attributes of rural community life, which had formerly given focus and direction to personality, were being lost, and as a consequence, the individual found himself bewildered. Thus insecurity with unemployment was often a feature of modern industrial civilization. But it was also true, Dewey wrote, that "Evils which are uncritically laid at the door of industrialism and democracy might, with greater intelligence, be referred to the dislocation and unsettlement of local communities." American democracy, which had developed out of small community life and been taken over from English political institutions, now was in the process of evolving into a public or democratic socialism. Yet, Dewey also believed that "Democracy must begin at home, and its home is the neighborly community." The problem therefore was somehow to preserve the individualistic values of the older community and transmit them into the newer social or collective democracy that Dewey called "corporateness."[31]

Unfortunately, Dewey felt, the kind of knowledge and insight that was a prime condition of a democratically organized public did not as yet exist. It was not enough that men were politically and intellectually free. "Removal of formal limitations," he wrote, "is but a negative condition; positive freedom is not a state but an act which involves methods and instrumentalities for control of conditions." Dewey complained that, in the existing stage of public opinion, "We seem to be approaching a state of government by hired promoters of opinion called publicity agents. But the more serious enemy is deeply concealed in hidden entrenchments." What was needed was the application of the experimental method used in physical and technical matters to human concerns. Science and education therefore offered the best hope for the achievement of true democracy.[32]

Democracy, though probably subject to more criticism after the First World War than ever before in American history, was not without strong defenders. John Dewey and his followers sought through a new conception of the role of education to find a way of adjusting the democratic tradition to the demands of the twentieth century. Believing that the old individualism and liberalism were outmoded, they hoped nevertheless to see some of their values preserved in the new social setting of an increasingly interdependent and collectivized world. It was this faith in social democracy that resulted paradoxically in a gradual resurgence of confidence in the thirties despite economic collapse and rise of totalitarianism abroad. For many Americans fascism and the depression provided the kind of challenge to democracy that had been lacking in the decade of postwar disillusionment and prosperity.

CHAPTER ELEVEN

Challenge and Response

NEITHER DEPRESSION nor war was unprecedented in the history of the American democratic tradition. Democracy in the United States had, after all, survived the massive impact of the Civil War and the hard times of the seventies and nineties. Even disillusionment over the First World War had not been able to destroy popular belief, as democracy became associated again with nationalist and isolationist ideals. After the war, despite the illiberal pressures which encouraged mass conformity with the standards of a business civilization, a minority of individualists managed to keep alive the democratic tradition of dissent. But the inner conflicts in

American democracy that had been heightened by the First World War were still unresolved when the stock market crash of 1929 struck the United States. Prosperity and contentment, which had merely been jostled by the disillusionment and criticism of the twenties, now succumbed to the most profound depression and pessimism. Not until the advent of the New Deal did a measure of optimism return. In the sense of common purpose gained in fighting financial disaster and in the effort to resist the example of totalitarian dictatorship as practiced abroad, the American people gradually recovered their faith in democratic processes of government. In the words of Charles and Mary Beard, "It took the great economic depression, the domestic conflict, the rise of Hitler, and the consolidation of fascist forces abroad, to arouse what appeared to be a fierce affection for democracy and to produce a tumult of praise for the idea and its institutional embodiments."[1]

The financial crisis and ensuing depression helped to substantiate the views of those who had been critical of the reigning business and political philosophy of the twenties. Industrial technocracy no longer won plaudits for its vaunted efficiency or productive capacities. Instead, enthusiasm developed for agrarian democracy and a back-to-the-land movement. Even science, with its growing relativism and uncertainty, was now subject to attack, while religion, its traditional adversary, was also unable to provide either spiritual or material sustenance to the army of the unemployed. In Europe the despair and passivity of the masses, as much as their revolt, led to new totalitarian governments. In America a growing demand for radical action threatened to overturn normal democratic procedures and methods. In this rise of totalitarian mass movements many observers discerned an imminent threat to traditional concepts of an individualistic American democracy. The lesson of a century, James Truslow Adams, author of the best-selling *Epic of America*, wrote in 1932, was that "in every crisis democracy has had to give way to autocracy or a dictatorship."[2]

Uncertain of the fate of both democracy and capitalism, leading American thinkers turned hopefully to some form of economic collectivism and scientific planning. The question whether centralized planning was possible in a democratic society which allowed its citizens a large measure of freedom of choice in their private economic decisions was almost ignored because of the depression. In urging that the older American individualism of the frontier be supplanted by modern scientific planning, Dean Guy Stanton Ford of the University of Minnesota asked: "If our democratic craft is waterlogged with the individualism, localism, and laissez faire suitable to that bygone day will it reach port in safety?" Herbert Agar, in his popular study of American Presidents, announced that there were only two ways democracy could be made to work in the United States—through Jefferson's agrarian ideal or by John Quincy Adams' concept of positive governmental action. In practice neither had been adopted, and American democracy, he believed, had degenerated into a plutocracy supported by the massed city-dwellers. Fearing that some kind of tyrant-state was presently impending, Agar called regretfully for planning as a more practicable twentieth-century solution than Jefferson's agrarianism.[3]

(II)

In Washington the Hoover administration, which had been launched on the high tide of prosperity, foundered completely on the shoals of the depression. Neither Hoover's rugged individualism, nor the new business philosophy he had espoused as Secretary of Commerce, was suited to the all-prevailing hard times. Deterred by individualist leanings from calling for stronger government action, and suspected in what measures he did recommend of favoring big business, Hoover was doomed to failure.

In the mid-term Congressional elections of 1930, the Democrats made large gains—over 50 seats in the House and 16 in the Senate—which presaged victory in 1932. At the same time, in New York, Franklin D. Roosevelt won re-election by an unprecedented popular plurality of over 700,000 votes to become a favored prospect for the Democratic nomination, and probable election, as President two years hence. As governor he made an impressive, if not brilliant, record, following after Alfred E. Smith's eight years in Albany. His willingness to push the state into new economic and social activities foretold the reform policies he would pursue as President. Yet, during most of these early depression years, Roosevelt did not differ materially from Hoover in his concept of the role the national government should play. Both men believed in economy and opposed direct relief spending by the federal government; both favored keeping the main reliance on state and private welfare agencies. But Roosevelt, unlike Hoover, was able to give to the public the dynamic image of a man of action. Roosevelt, moreover, seemed to have the common touch; like his distant relative Theodore he had great popular appeal. With some justification in the campaign of 1928, he had contrasted his own and Al Smith's belief in the people with what he charged was Hoover's conviction of "the incapacity of the mass of average citizens either to think or to build."[4]

In the election of 1932 probably nothing Hoover could have said or done would have changed the results. The emotional desire of the electorate for any sort of change was not, however, wholly irrational. A new Presidential administration, not associated with the unhappy past four years, would have a better chance to win widespread popular backing regardless of its specific policies and program. Thus it was fortunate for democracy that the American party system, at least every four years, permitted a sweeping transformation in political leadership.

Despite the lack of details, Roosevelt's campaign speeches, with their call for experimentation and action based on careful planning and "a fair and just concert of interests," communicated a faith in democracy as a living and growing idea. In his well-known address before the Commonwealth Club of San Francisco in September 1932, Roosevelt described the concept of limited government which had been at the heart of American democracy and economic expansion. But now in the twentieth century, he suggested, the decline of the frontier and growth of industrial consolidation required the government to step in as an enlightened administrator to preserve both liberty and prosperity. Individual freedom and economic competition no longer operated automatically. In a later review of these years Roosevelt argued that the Republican administrations after the First World War had failed to meet the two great problems facing the United States—the completion of political democracy and the achievement of social justice.

That decade, therefore, can be said to represent a dormant period for democratic processes—a period, nevertheless, which was probably necessary for the revitalizing of any great movement to restore and maintain democracy. The fulfillment of the idea of the very word "democracy" presupposes a national interest on the part of a large percentage of citizens.[5]

Roosevelt's historical analysis depicted the United States as a mature economy in which poverty and depression existed in the middle of abundance. The immediate problem, therefore, he declared in his Inaugural Address, was to institute needed economic reforms and change the pervading defeatist psychology of the country.

The people of the United States have not failed. In their need they have registered a mandate that they want direct, vigorous action. They have asked for discipline and direction under leadership. They have made me the present instrument of their wishes. In the spirit of the gift I take it.[6]

(III)

In the midst of a world-wide rejection of democracy on grounds that it was hopelessly inefficient, simply bad, or gradually dying, the New Deal became a symbol of hope. Its pragmatic program of recovery and reform represented a middle way between the older American individualism and the collectivism of the European dictatorships. In the emergency legislation of the so-called Hundred Days, including the National Recovery Administration, Agricultural Adjustment Administration, and Tennessee Valley Authority, the New Deal adopted a version of national economic planning which, in part, socialized and harmonized varying group and class interests. This program, which Herbert Hoover called fascism and which others likened to a corporate state, owed much to the example of the comprehensive economic planning of the First World War as well as to the associational activities which Hoover himself had urged upon American business in the twenties. Forgotten was the laissez-faire philosophy of free competition or economic individualism. The New Deal was more concerned with advancing the general welfare as represented in the organized group interests of farmers and labor than in protecting the liberties of individuals. The liberalism and democracy of the New Deal accordingly minimized individual freedom in favor of a greater social security and economic equality of the whole people. Roosevelt and the New Deal, Harold J. Laski, the British socialist, later observed in his book *The American Democracy*, "brought into being a positive federal state in America. . . ."[7]

From the standpoint of a number of old-fashioned liberals and conservatives, the New Deal's nationalistic policies marked a startling and tragic departure from a treasured past. Democracy, liberals believed, differed from dictatorship in that it implied a society not content with mere economic security. The chief reason for its defense, a professor of philosophy wrote in a popular magazine, was that "democracy is the only form of government which makes even a pretense of safeguarding what are commonly known as civil liberties. . . ." A conservative economist complained that despite the current avowals of faith in freedom and democracy, the political and social trends of the new deals in Germany and the United States were similar. "They use different catchwords, but are variants of the same theme." Although there was a general feeling among intellectuals that the collective life had indeed arrived, there was also support for T. V. Smith's view that the best of traditional American rugged individualism should be preserved in the midst of its reformation. "*The ideal of rugged individualism*," he declared, "*is right at the bottom, however much correction we must give it at the top*. At the bottom it asserts that the human individual is all that really counts."[8]

Smith spoke of "ragged" as well as rugged individualism. "The wreckage which follows an individualism characterized by chronic unemployment," he noted, "is a raggedness of soul as well as of body."[9] It was the common opinion of the Roosevelt administration that the rebuilding of a sick American society required long-range reforms as well as immediate measures to alleviate the worse effects of the depression. The slogans and shibboleths of the past, to which the President made frequent unfavorable allusions in his speeches, were also treated critically by the pragmatic New Deal lawyer and philosopher Thurman Arnold in his much discussed books *The Symbols of Government* and *The Folklore of Capitalism*.

Arnold subjected the most sacred American political and economic institutions to a searching satirical analysis, duly noting the contrast between actual realities and the myths or folklore accepted by the American people. Prosecution of the trusts, for example, to which most Americans paid lip service, was markedly similar to pious and recurrent crusades against vice or crime. Antitrust laws were "the answer of a society which unconsciously felt the need of great organizations, and at the same time had to deny them a place in the moral and logical ideology of the social structure. They were part of the struggle of a creed of rugged individualism to adapt itself to what was becoming a highly organized society." Arnold recognized that symbols and folklore, even though they were violated and by-passed, were as necessary for governments as for individuals. But these creeds, he observed "*must be false in order to function effectively. This paradoxical statement means that they must express contradictory ideals and must authoritatively suppress any facts which interfere with those ideals.*"[10]

Arnold's books exemplified the pragmatic, amoral, "hard" side of the New Deal—its use of the big city bosses and political machines, its expansion of the federal bureaucracy, and its development of the spending and taxing powers. But there was also another, or "soft" side, more moral, visionary, and hopeful of democracy, which was illustrated in such works as Henry Wallace's *New Frontiers* and David Lilienthal's *TVA: Democracy on the March*. "The greatest need of a modern democracy," Wallace asserted, "is to understand how completely and mathematically moral is the running of a modern state." While precise detailed planning was not necessary except perhaps in the field of natural resources, some measure of centralized planning by government was needed, he believed, to overcome the effects of the various special-interest groups which thought only of their own short-run gains. The New Deal was an effort to restore balance and harmony to the American economy. "If our civilization is to continue on the present complex basis," he wrote, "modern democracy must make rules of the game that go beyond tariffs, monetary policy, freight rate structures, taxation and similar policies which have long concerned the central government. The new rules must also get into fields more directly concerning harmonious relationships between prices, margins, profits and distribution of income." "The keynote of the new frontier," Wallace concluded, "is cooperation just as that of the old frontier was individualistic competition."[11]

Like Wallace, Lilienthal believed that scientific achievements were of no real merit "unless they have a moral purpose, unless they are conceived and carried out for the benefit of the people themselves. Without such a purpose, advances in technology may be disastrous to the human spirit; the industrialization of a raw material may bring to the average man only a new kind of slavery and the destruction of democratic institutions." Democracy was on the march in the Tennessee Valley, not only because of technological progress, but because the people themselves were taken into account. TVA exhibited "an effective combination of the advantages of the *decentralized administration of centralized authority*. . . . Every important administrative decision," Lilienthal observed, "need not be made in Washington. . . ."

> We who believe devoutly in the democratic process should be the first to urge the use of methods that will keep the administration of national functions from becoming so concentrated at the national capital, so distant from the everyday life of ordinary people, as to wither and deaden the average citizen's sense of participation and partnership in government affairs. *For in this citizen participation lies the vitality of democracy.*

Lilienthal was confident that TVA by democratic planning could achieve a harmony of interests—public, private, and individual. In any case, the physical job would be done. If not democratically, he warned that it would be done "in an anti-democratic way" by small groups of private corporations, by a clique of politicians, or by a managerial elite.[12]

Some observers of the whole planned experiment in the Tennessee Valley who were less lyrical in their attitude than Lilienthal questioned how well his grass-roots approach to the TVA worked in practice. As one of the three commissioners who directed the Authority, Lilienthal, with his particular interest in public power, had combined with local agricultural groups to defeat the more radical New Dealers who thought in terms of such original TVA goals as co-ops, subsistence homesteads, rural zoning, and broad regional planning. The democratic tie-in with local sentiment could easily be used to cover concessions to special-interest groups. Thus the original collectivist and cooperative goals of the TVA, which had been stressed by President Roosevelt, were shelved in response to local charges of socialism. Rexford Guy Tugwell, an early member of the New Deal brain trust, who believed that it was precisely these original TVA ideals which justified the venture in planning, summed up his criticism with the assertion that "TVA is more an example of democracy in retreat than democracy on the march."[13]

At the outset of his administration Roosevelt, acting on the theory of government as a harmonizer of interests, tried to pursue the role of a bipartisan national leader. The New Deal, the President told a Wisconsin crowd in August 1934, "seeks to cement our society, rich and poor, manual worker and brain worker, into a voluntary brotherhood of freemen, standing together, striving together, for the common good of all." Earlier that year Roosevelt, in adherence to his nonpartisan strategy, refused to take part in the Jefferson Day celebrations. "Our strongest plea to the country in this particular year of grace," he said, "is that the recovery and reconstruction program is being accomplished by men and women of all parties—that I have repeatedly appealed to Republicans as much as to Democrats to do their part."[14]

The bipartisan approach to politics, however, soon faltered as the first New Deal reform measures lost popularity and became subjected to heavy criticism. The administration was attacked for the way in which the NRA and AAA were dominated by special interests. But as one New Dealer pointed out, the power of such groups could not be separated from the government, even in a democracy. "The truth is," AAA chief George N. Peek said bluntly, "that no democratic government can be very different from the country it governs. If some groups are dominant in the country, they will be dominant in any plan the government undertakes." Despite the bitter attacks of conservatives, Roosevelt's passive technique of responding to the major economic and political pressures of the time was a less radical innovation than a calculated policy of trying to build a new political alignment composed of underprivileged farm, labor, Negro, and minority groups. Roosevelt himself was neither a theorist nor a doctrinaire reformer. Unlike some of the members of his first brain trust, he was not committed to an extreme nationalist philosophy.

For the President national economic planning remained a means to an end and not an end in itself. The New Deal accordingly continued to rest on a large measure of improvisation as it responded to the shifting tides of public opinion.[15]

Midway through Roosevelt's first term, the New Deal underwent a major transition. The achievement of some degree of economic recovery and the failure of the NRA and AAA to pass the Supreme Court's test of constitutionality weakened the case for centralized economic planning. In its place the administration turned to the passage of regulatory measures, more in line with traditional progressive reform, and to stepped-up expenditures for relief and public works. The Social Security Act, increased income and corporation taxes, and new legislation to protect the right of collective bargaining served to broaden the economic base of the New Deal program. At the same time the democratic appeal of these measures helped to check the rise of radical third-party movements, which were being organized with an eye to the forthcoming national elections.

(*IV*)

Roosevelt's easy victory in 1936 muted the clamor of the angry voices which filled the political air in the mid-thirties. In addition to the two traditional major parties and small formal left-wing groups of Socialists and Communists, the political spectrum was colored by an amazing assortment of political evangelists and messiahs ranging from avowed fascists to enthusiastic proponents of old-age pension schemes and other economic panaceas. Father Charles E. Coughlin, Rev. Gerald L. K. Smith, and Dr. Francis E. Townsend together had a popular following numbered in the millions, but the most serious political figure among the right-wing radicals, until his assassination in September 1935, was Senator Huey P. Long. The self-styled Kingfish of Louisiana politics and leader of the Share-Our-Wealth movement, Long as a third-party candidate might have been able to draw away enough of the votes of the discontented to defeat Roosevelt and throw the election to a conservative Republican. The Coughlin, Smith, and Townsend forces did combine in

1936 to form the Union party, but its nominee, the comparatively obscure Congressman from North Dakota, William Lemke, was able to poll fewer than a million votes.[16]

As early as 1929, under the chairmanship of John Dewey, a number of liberals and progressives had launched the League for Independent Political Action, designed to push for a third party along the lines of the old La Follette Progressives of 1924. In the 1932 campaign the League was unable to launch its new party or to transfer much support to Norman Thomas, the Socialist nominee for President. But midway in Roosevelt's first term there seemed some chance that progressive and socialist groups might coalesce around the candidacy of one of the Wisconsin La Follettes or of Governor Floyd B. Olson of Minnesota. However, the New Deal's revived popularity and the danger that any new progressive party would result only in a Republican victory created a general disposition on the part of realistic political leaders to stay with Roosevelt.

Neither farmers nor labor were prepared at this juncture to risk a third party, and the League for Independent Political Action's successor organizations in the field had to admit defeat. In the old Northwest the La Follette Progressive party and the Minnesota Farm-Laborites kept their place as state organizations, safely in the shadow of the New Deal. For their cooperation they were favored in turn with Roosevelt's tacit political blessing. Meanwhile any radical tendencies on the part of organized labor were forestalled by the formation in April 1936 of Labor's Nonpartisan League. The League's chief goal was to further Roosevelt's re-election by preventing the rise of a hostile third party. In New York City the newly organized American Labor party also provided a means by which independent and Democratic voters, reluctant to cast their ballots under the Tammany Hall label, might still support the President.

Thus by 1936 the formal Democratic party was almost being submerged in a New Deal coalition of farmers, labor unions, liberals, progressives, and socialists. At the same time Roosevelt also retained his great mass appeal to the middle-of-the-road voter and to underprivileged minority groups. Neither the American Liberty League, sponsored by disaffected conservative Democrats, nor the Republican party under Governor Alfred M. Landon of Kansas, was able to put together a winning combination, while Lemke's Union party proved even more ineffective in trying to attract the backing of the radical fringe of disgruntled voters.

Roosevelt's great popular majority of over 60 per cent of the total vote and his electoral sweep, in which he carried all but the two states of Maine and Vermont, indicated that his administration had found an acceptable middle way. During the campaign the President's speeches stressed the theme that in a democracy the people were able to shape their own future. "This heritage, my friends," he told an audience at Little Rock, Arkansas, "we owe to Jacksonian democracy—the American doctrine that entrusts the general welfare to no one group or class, but dedicates itself to the end that the American people shall not be thwarted in their high purpose to remain the custodians of their own destiny." The American example of democracy, he noted in his speech accepting renomination, was important for more than the domestic struggle against the depression. "It is not alone a war against want and destitution and economic demoralization. It is more than that; it is a war for the survival of democracy. We are fighting to save a great and precious form of government for ourselves and for the world." In the closing days of the campaign the President again stressed his conviction that the New Deal reforms spelled peace at home and "also peace with other nations. . . . 'Peace on earth, good will toward men'—democracy must cling to that message. For it is my deep conviction," he said, "that democracy cannot live without that true religion which gives a nation a sense of justice and of moral purpose. . . ."[17]

In the face of the Roosevelt personality and policies, extremist groups and parties found it difficult to gain adherents. "Even the representatives of the 'elite' had to admit that the country seemed restored to confidence in its future; that amid a world toying with machinery of totalitarianism, the American form of government had been maintained; that the existence of private enterprise had remained fundamental; that even though the cost of government had risen, the rights of the people had been strengthened."[18]

(V)

Roosevelt's humanistic and pragmatic belief that democratic government was dedicated to carrying forward the will of the people ran counter to the doctrines of a fixed law and natural rights. While support for social and economic reforms through the agency of the federal government had been growing in the twentieth century, the Constitution as interpreted by the Supreme Court over these years had become a symbol of stability and of opposition to change. Among conservatives, and to some extent also among the generality of the people, the Constitution took precedence even over democracy as a prime article of American political faith. Since the Supreme Court was the final arbiter of the Constitution, the Justices were in a position to act as censors of democracy and the majority will. They were not impressed, for the most part, with their colleague Oliver Wendell Holmes' dictum of judicial self-restraint regarding legislation, in which he had stated his belief that "my agreement or disagreement has nothing to do with the right of the majority to embody their opinions in law."[19] Holmes' ultimate ideal was the free individual. So long as man was able to express his ideas, majorities and minorities would continue to trade places to accommodate the new beliefs, interests, and ideals emerging from the competition of the intellectual marketplace. In this way individual freedom was not incompatible with majority rule, and both became equally essential to true democracy.

The failure of the majority of the Supreme Court to accept Holmes' position in its opinions concerning New Deal legislation aroused Roosevelt's ire and reinforced his determination to impose the will of Congress and the President upon the Justices. When Chief Justice Hughes, in administering the oath of office to Roosevelt for his second term, emphasized the words "promise to support the Constitution of the United States," the President in repeating the oath gave the words equal force. But, he said later, at this point he wanted to cry out, "Yes, but it's the Constitution as I understand it. . . ."[20]

A few days before his Inauguration, Roosevelt, in his annual message to Congress, asserted his conviction that "The process of democracy must not be imperiled by the denial of essential powers of free government." In his Inaugural Address he repeated his belief that "The essential democracy of our Nation and the safety of our people depend not upon the absence of power, but upon lodging it with those whom the people can change or continue at stated intervals through an honest and free system of elections. The Constitution of 1787 did not make our democracy impotent," he added. Although the nation had made obvious progress out of the depression, there was still a fundamental challenge to democracy in the low standards of living and poor education of large numbers of the people. The "one-third of a nation, ill-housed, ill-clad, ill-nourished," to which Roosevelt referred, included the bulk of the country's sharecroppers and tenant farmers, migratory workers, unskilled labor, and Negro population.[21] These were the groups for which economic and social democracy, or even political democracy, was often beyond reach. But Roosevelt believed that government, when all those who composed it worked as trustees for the whole people, had the power and the duty to effect needed reforms. Confident that he held this trust, the President two weeks after his Inauguration outlined a revolutionary plan for revamping the Supreme Court by adding new Justices.

Roosevelt's proposal shocked both Congress and the country. It was denounced as a scheme to pack the Supreme Court and establish a dictatorship. Although there had been considerable sympathy for the President in his resentment over the Court's frequent opinions declaring New Deal legislation unconstitutional, the abruptness and secrecy of his specific plan aroused opposition even among those who felt that the powers of the Court should be curbed. Despite Roosevelt's appeals to the country to make popular democracy work, the crescendo of protests which greeted his plan made it apparent that the Constitution and Court were still considered vital parts of the American democratic tradition. While a moderate Court reform bill might have passed, it was clear that the Roosevelt measure commanded little enthusiasm in Congress or in the country at large.

In the middle of the long drawn-out controversy the Supreme Court ruled favorably on several New Deal laws. This sudden change of tactics by the Court, plus the subsequent retirement of several of the Justices, gave Roosevelt an opportunity to claim that he had lost the battle but won the war. But, wherever history might decide that the ultimate victory lay, the struggle had been damaging to the President's prestige as a democratic leader. Even if his plan were regarded as a part of the battle of democracy against a reactionary Court that had failed to keep pace with majority sentiment, the means that the President had used to attain his goal were undemocratic.

Though the Court fight was in some ways a logical culmination of the late Presidential campaign, there were additional factors which Roosevelt failed to confront. It was one thing to win votes for himself as a beloved political leader and another to try to push a controversial bill through Congress. Opponents of the President pointed to the paradox of his calls for more democracy at the same time that he expanded the executive power. Buoyed up by the popular mandate he had received in the 1936 elections, the President became careless in cultivating his relations with Congress. The rank and file of the members felt that they were ignored while a few top leaders alone were consulted.

The deterioration in legislative-executive relations during Roosevelt's second term was measured in the paucity of significant bills which were passed by Congress. A new Agricultural Adjustment Act and a watered-down version of the controversial wages and hours bill were approved in 1938, but Roosevelt's proposal to reorganize the executive agencies of the federal government revived the Supreme Court struggle all over again. Widely dubbed the "dictator bill," the proposal aroused such criticism that it drew from the President a formal denial that he had either the aspirations or qualifications for such a role. After the House of Representatives returned the reorganization bill to committee, the President in a "Fireside Chat on Economic Conditions" told his listeners that "History proves that dictatorships do not grow out of strong and successful governments, but out of weak and helpless ones. . . . Democracy," he warned, "had disappeared in several other great nations–not because the people of those nations disliked democracy, but because they had grown tired of unemployment and insecurity. . . ."[22] Finally, with Congress in open revolt, the President made matters worse by intervening in the Democratic primaries in a largely fruitless effort to defeat conservative members of the House and Senate who had opposed his reform program.

As the President's personal political fortunes sank to a new low point, the administration was also divided by a conflict in basic economic strategy. A group of the original New Dealers, believing that a conciliation of economic and class interests was impossible to attain, favored open warfare upon big business through rigorous enforcement of the antitrust laws. The President in his speeches early in 1938 lashed out at the selfish minorities which were responsible for concentrating economic power in the hands of a few. Congress, pressed into action, established the Temporary National Economic Committee to investigate the effect of monopolistic organizations upon American capitalism. Meanwhile some businessmen urged a form of economic planning and self-regulation reminiscent of the NRA. Despite the depression and New Deal the trend of American life was in the direction of larger units—big business, big labor, big government. But from the welter of confusing counsels and indices, in which Roosevelt took no clearly defined position, the one indisputable fact that emerged was the continuance of a policy of large-scale spending. As James M. Burns points out in his study of the President, "Deficit spending was ideally suited to Roosevelt's ideology and program." Neither a doctrinaire capitalist nor socialist, he found that "Keynesian economics was a true middle way—at a time when New Dealers were groping for a middle way that worked."[23]

Though John Maynard Keynes' direct personal impact upon Roosevelt was never great, the English economist's financial theories became ever more compelling to the New Deal. The large-scale spending, which at first was imperative to cope with the depression, quickly became necessary to assure continued economic recovery. It also, however, was so tied in with both partisan politics and controversial reforms that it could continue to win general approval only after it became part of the nation's rearmament program and wartime budget. As the New Deal approached its ideological limits, Mars came to the rescue, transforming its earlier visions of peaceful reform into a war economy. The argument propounded in the early 1930's—by Henry Wallace and Charles Beard, for example—that a planned economy would avert the need for overseas markets and so help prevent foreign war, now seemed countered by the view of Walter Lippmann and others that all forms of collectivism led inevitably to a war economy, even though they might be masked as social reform.[24]

(VI)

During Roosevelt's second term the administration's primary concern gradually shifted to foreign affairs. In his campaign for re-election in 1936 the President had stressed his interest in world peace and his determination to keep the country out of war. Earlier that year, in an address before the Inter-American Conference for the Maintenance of Peace at Buenos Aires, President Roosevelt linked the two ideals of peace and democracy. Calling democracy "still the hope of the world," he asserted that it could spread from the example of the American nations living in peace with each other. Critical of the rearmament programs of the European dictators, he denounced those nations which used military spending to solve the problems of economic depression and unemployment.[25] But, despite such verbal onslaughts, Roosevelt was reluctant to carry out any retrenchment in the United States military and naval program. Apprehensive of the international situation, and not unmindful of the effects of government spending upon the general economy, the President preferred to continue the nationalistic policy of building up American armed power.

The United States response to the challenge of fascism developed slowly. The President's attack on the so-called aggressor nations in his famous "quarantine" speech at Chicago in October 1937 received what Roosevelt himself complained was a hostile popular reaction. In the uncertain and changing world of the late thirties the American people were confused by the meaning of the world-wide conflict of fascism and democracy. More than anything they were fearful of involvement in another world war. The abandonment of neutrality, isolationists warned, would spell the death of democracy in the United States. Modern war, former President Hoover declared, "means that our country must be mobilized into practically a Fascist state. It would be so organized. It went some distance in the last great war, although we did not use that term at the time."[26]

Though there was little open support for fascism in the United States, thoughtful Americans were alarmed at the spread of such fascist-like societies as the German-American Bund or William Dudley Pelley's Silver Shirts of America. Even more disturbing were the demagogic tactics of such leaders of the extreme right as Father Coughlin, "the radio priest," and the Rev. Gerald L. K. Smith, successor to Huey Long as leader of the Share-Our-Wealth movement. Sinclair Lewis' widely discussed novel, *It Can't Happen Here*, though its alarm seemed exaggerated, pointed nevertheless to the totalitarian tendencies growing in the midst of American democracy. Moreover, it was not forgotten that, as Huey Long was supposed to have remarked, if fascism ever took hold in America, it would arrive in the guise of anti-fascism. According to James Burnham, author of the well-known book *The Managerial Revolution*, United States hostility to fascism was merely resentment of its foreign aspects. "A 100% American totalitarianism would not be objectionable," he concluded.[27] Lawrence Dennis, the leading American exponent of intellectual fascism, argued that a purely American fascism would not have to include all the undesirable features of Hitler's Nazi state.

After the outbreak of the Second World War with the German invasion of Poland, a group of American writers and intellectuals opposed to continued United States neutrality accused their fellows of a failure to understand the world-wide significance of the challenge of fascism to democracy. Working in their ivory towers, these American scholars, whom Archibald MacLeish called "The Irresponsibles," were charged with not having opposed fascism while there was still time to do so without war. In the controversy touched off by MacLeish's declaration, such authors as Sinclair Lewis, H. L. Mencken, and Charles Beard were criticized for having encouraged the American disillusionist spirit of the interwar years. Presumably they had been guilty of undermining the confidence of American youths in American institutions, thus weakening their will to fight the battle of democracy against fascism. "Why has American democracy mislaid its mythology and lost its glamor?" asked Howard Mumford Jones. "If we really want to believe that political democracy is worth fighting for, we need to be told over and over again what pain and suffering it has cost."[28]

Underlying this indictment of American intellectuals by MacLeish and his colleagues was their belief that the values of democracy could be inculcated in American youth by education. Though many persons were repelled by the suggestion that political propaganda should have a place in teaching, an increasing number of educators came to feel that the schools must respond to the double challenge of economic depression and totalitarian government. Followers of John Dewey's philosophy believed that education could not be separated from life. If democracy was to continue to be accepted as a vital part of American freedom and culture, its theory and practice had to be examplified in the school system. Democratic conditions, Dewey warned, did not automatically maintain themselves, nor were they identified merely with prescriptions laid down in formal written constitutions.

> The serious threat to our democracy is not the existence of foreign totalitarian states. It is the existence within our own personal attitudes and within our own institutions of conditions similar to those which have given a victory to external authority, discipline, uniformity and dependence upon The Leader in foreign countries. The battlefield is also accordingly here—within ourselves and our institutions.

"If there is one conclusion to which human experience unmistakably points," Dewey added, "it is that democratic ends demand democratic methods for their realization."[29]

Like Dewey, a number of leading American educators were convinced that the increasingly collectivist character of American society required intelligent social and democratic controls to prevent the assumption of authority by an elite or a dictator. "A Socialized Education for a Socialized Age," was the title of an address which condemned as outmoded the "unsocial idea of success" and the philosophy of laissez faire and individual rights. "In America a socialized education involves the promotion of democracy," the speaker concluded.[30] Professor George S. Counts of Teachers College, Columbia University, in assessing "the prospects of American democracy," pointed out that education had long been a positive and creative force in United States history. As an instrument of politics, education, whether it was realized or not, had always been subjected to social controls. Arguing that "the schools can teach democracy," Counts asserted:

> In the achievement of any program for the defense and advance of democracy, the school, and particularly the public school, must play an important role.
>
> It is therefore proposed that we frankly reject the conception of social and moral neutrality and direct the energies of organized education without reservation to the defense and strengthening of the democratic tradition and way of life.

A symposium by the faculty of Teachers College on "Democracy and Education in the Current Crisis" included in its credo the statements: "Democracy and strong government are compatible. . . . Democracy has faith in intelligence."[31]

(VII)

As the world again plunged into war, the United States reexamined the meaning of its democracy. If fascism threatened the foundations of the Republic, it was important not only to prepare by arms but also to revitalize the people's faith in their institutions. Democracy accordingly became more and more a badge of patriotic loyalty and an almost religious belief. Defending it against communist and left-wing charges that its political freedom did not include social and economic equality, spokesmen for democracy at the same time denied conservative or fascist criticism of democracy as mob rule or anarchy. In a plea for human freedom Jacques Barzun called an absolute and thorough democracy a barbaric ideal akin to the manipulation of the masses by a dictator. True democracy, he declared, "is a balance between popular will and individual rights. It is a civilized society that tries to establish diversity in unity through the guarantee of civil liberties." Seeing an "operative equality as the middle way," T. V. Smith pointed out that American democracy must at least embody an effort to achieve equality. Democracy, the German novelist Thomas Mann told his American lecture audiences in 1938, "is not intellectualistic in an old and outworn sense. Democracy is thought, but it is thought related to life and action. . . . Democracy wishes to elevate mankind, to teach it to think, to set it free. It seeks to remove from culture the stamp of privilege and disseminate it among the people—in a word, it aims at education."[32]

Especially significant were the growing interpretation of democracy as a positive concept and the assumption that to survive it must provide for the social and economic as well as the political needs of the citizenry. Democratic government, it was argued, could no longer be considered solely in terms of a separation of powers and limited authority. The pragmatic democratic ideal was the maximum development of the individual personality, and the democratic state had the function to maintain a climate of individual rights. But the catalogue of those rights was not fixed for all time. In the historian Carl Becker's words, modern democracy required the substitution of "new liberties for old."

As the world crisis mounted and the threat of war spread from Europe, President Roosevelt invoked the ideals of American democracy as an integral part of the national defense. In his official messages to Congress the President depicted a world ravaged by undeclared wars and ready to burst into flames. "There comes a time in the affairs of men," he said, "when they must prepare to defend, not their homes alone, but the tenets of faith and humanity on which their churches, their governments and their very civilization are founded. The defense of religion, of democracy and of good faith among nations is all the same fight. To save one we must now make up our minds to save all. . . . There are many methods short of war, but stronger and more effective than mere words, of bringing home to aggressor governments the aggregate sentiments of our own people." But the President did not spell out these methods beyond calling for the continued rearmament and defense of the United States. The security of the country, he noted, did not depend on arms alone. In a very real and deep sense national unity was "the fundamental safeguard of all democracy. . . . We must as a united people," the President concluded, "keep ablaze on this continent the flames of human liberty, of reason, of democracy, and of fair play as living things to be preserved for the better world that is to come."[33]

In the Presidential election of 1940 Roosevelt ran for an unprecedented third term, but the significance of this issue as a possible threat to the American democratic tradition was largely lost because of the more immediate impact of the European War. In September the Selective Service Act was approved by Congress, and the President announced the exchange with Great Britain of 50 destroyers for naval bases. Although the administration was thus assuming the role of a co-belligerent with England, the continued hold of isolationist sentiments on the people posed a problem for the candidates, both of whom favored an aggressive and interventionist foreign policy. Anxious, however, to win election and gain the peace vote, Roosevelt and Wendell Willkie strove to outdo each other in misleading and demagogic promises to keep the nation out of war. Essentially there was little difference in the position of the two candidates, and Willkie later dismissed his peace speeches as campaign oratory. In a more philosophic vein, toward the close of what had become a bitter and relentless political battle, Roosevelt declared that over the past eight years, "through it all there have been two thoughts uppermost in my mind—to preserve peace in our land; and to make the forces of democracy work for the benefit of the common people of America."[34]

In a year in which more Americans than ever before in the country's history cast their ballots, Roosevelt again won a decisive victory. The popular vote was almost 27 million to over 22 million, and the electoral totals were 449 to 82. But F. D. R.'s plurality in 1940 was the smallest of any winning candidate since 1916, and in New York the margin of victory was only about 225,000. "Unquestionably," one of his biographers writes, "Roosevelt had been lucky in at least two respects: the crisis in Europe and the first flush of returning prosperity. The former took the force out of Willkie's main foreign policy appeal; the latter took the sting out of his main domestic argument, namely the Depression."[35] In his third Inaugural Address the President recalled his past two terms as "fruitful years for the people of this democracy." We know that democracy is not dying, he said, "because democracy alone has constructed an unlimited civilization capable of infinite progress in the improvement of human life."[36]

Interpreting the election as a mandate to carry out his foreign policy, Roosevelt called upon Congress to approve a program for the lend-lease of American military equipment to Great Britain. In a "Fireside Chat on National Security" the President reported that "Democracy's fight against world conquest is being greatly aided, and must be more greatly aided, by the rearmament of the United States and by sending every ounce and every ton of munitions and supplies that we can possibly spare to help the defenders who are in the front lines." Yet, he added, "I would ask no one to defend a democracy which in turn would not defend everyone in the nation against want and privation." "We must be the great arsenal of democracy," the President affirmed in conclusion. "For this is an emergency as serious as war itself." To the White House correspondents at their annual dinner in March 1941, the President pointed out that the enemies of democracy had been wrong in their predictions that the United States could not mobilize its arms and still remain a democracy. In carrying out the task of production "the Nation is calling for the sacrifice of some privileges, not for the sacrifice of fundamental rights," Roosevelt told the members of the press.[37]

The President's lofty phrases, in which he coupled the idealism of democracy and the productive capacities of capitalism, were appealing to an American citizenry which desired to aid the Allies and still stay out of war. But the policy of being an arsenal of democracy involved more risk of involvement than the American people realized or than the President was willing to admit. When the United States began to help convoy lend-lease munitions to Britain, naval incidents with the Nazis in the Atlantic became inevitable. Yet the United States did not become a full-scale belligerent until the Japanese struck at Pearl Harbor. Although the attack in the Pacific united the American people, there was little of the crusading fervor of the First World War. "Morale," Robert Sherwood observed, "was never particularly good nor alarmingly bad. There was a minimum of flag waving and parades. It was the first war in American history in which the general disillusionment preceded the firing of the first shot."[38]

(*VIII*)

The fate of democracy in a nation in arms, the problem of Lincoln and Wilson, now also confronted Franklin Roosevelt. The arbitrary arrests, mass raids, and vindictive prosecutions of the Civil War and First World War were on the whole avoided, but, like his predecessors in wartime, Roosevelt assumed prerogatives akin to those of a dictator. Emergency powers granted to the New Deal in the crisis of the depression were expanded in the course of the war. When Congress failed to pass a measure to stabilize prices, the President announced his intention to assume this authority unless the legislative branch acted promptly. "Here," writes Professor Burns, "was an astonishing usurpation of power in a nation fighting for democratic ideas and processes." Although Roosevelt, like Lincoln, could argue that the life of the nation was at stake, there was ever the danger that in the wartime expansion of the executive power, Congress, as Senator Robert Taft put it in reply to the President, would be reduced to "a mere shell of a legislative body."[39]

Nevertheless the Congress continued to function, and in 1944, in the middle of the war, normal democratic processes were maintained by the holding of the Presidential election. Even though President Roosevelt's popular majority declined to less than 52 per cent of the total vote, Governor Thomas E. Dewey, the Republican candidate, suffered the insuperable disadvantage of not being able to make any effective criticism of his opponent's policies without creating an impression of unpatriotic disloyalty to the country's war leadership.

During World War II the most glaring example of the violation of civil liberties involved the Americans of Japanese ancestry and the Japanese aliens living along the Pacific Coast and in the Hawaiian Islands. Although there was no case of espionage or sabotage by a Japanese-American, all those on the coast were evacuated from their homes, and military government was imposed upon the Hawaiian Islands. Later, after the close of the war, the Supreme Court declared the army rule of Hawaii to have been an illegal invasion of the rights of the inhabitants. But in the case of the West Coast Japanese-Americans, the Court refused to intervene or interfere in a policy that had been carried out under the authority of the Secretary of War and the President.

Apart from the harsh treatment of the Japanese-Americans, there was no concerted official violation of the civil liberties of the citizen in World War II. In part, however, this creditable record is explained by the way in which any significant war opposition had already been forestalled in the months before Pearl Harbor. In 1940 Congress passed the first peacetime sedition act in the United States since 1798. In the rush of legislation in the spring of 1940 few Americans realized that the Alien Registration, or Smith Act, drawn up when Congress was dominated by anti-foreign and anti-alien feelings, went beyond World War I statutes. The clause prohibiting anyone from teaching or advocating the "overthrow or destruction of any government in the United States by force or violence; or to be or become a member of, or affiliate with, any such society, group, or assembly or persons . . ." laid the foundation for the determination of "guilt by association." The only precedent in all American history for this insistence that guilt was not necessarily personal but could be determined by membership or association was in the alien deportations of 1919. Though the Smith Act was largely unworkable during the war, when it was used in the mass sedition trial of a group of alleged Nazi sympathizers, it later became the basis of the anti-Communist and anti-radical prosecutions which followed the war. But in the early 1940's, the Communists and much of the radical left in the United States were glad to be allies of Soviet Russia in the struggle against Hitler Germany.

Except for some 6,000 conscientious objectors who went to prison rather than accept some form of noncombatant duty or alternative service, there was little overt hostility to military conscription. When the Selective Service Act was passed in the summer of 1940, it was widely denounced as a measure that would lead to war and undermine American domestic institutions. In obvious conflict with individual freedom, conscription was also at odds with democracy, except in an interpretation of the latter from an extreme equalitarian point of view. The contradiction between the draft and traditional American ideals was well pointed out in a public statement issued by some 300 educators, authors, clergymen, and business and professional leaders who denounced conscription as a totalitarian device unworthy of the spirit of American democracy.[40] But the comparative toleration extended at least to religious objectors, some 12,000 of whom were assigned to special civilian work, did much to blunt more widespread opposition to the draft law.

If World War II was not destined to be the last large-scale

global conflict in history, it was almost certainly the last war in which the civil liberties of the individual would be taken into account. The most frightening aspect of modern war was not its undemocratic features, but rather the complete and impartial equality with which it treated all men in an indiscriminate bombing of battlefields and cities. Though the continental United States escaped either invasion or attack from the air, the American economy and manpower were almost wholly absorbed in the massive war effort. And in the tremendous scientific feat of fashioning the first atomic bomb, the United States added incalculably to the mass destruction that was already an integral part of modern total war.

In all, a grand total of over 15 million men and women served at some time in the armed forces of the United States during World War II. Of this number there were approximately one million casualties, one third of whom were listed as killed or missing in action. In American history only the Civil War resulted in a comparable sacrifice of life. From an American standpoint, however, much of the war was a battle of production. The great increase in industrial plant capacity strengthened the position of both big business and organized labor. Price controls extending to the retail level brought the war home to every citizen and accomplished an unprecedented regulation of American social and economic life.

As a part of the war, fought in large measure against Hitler's racist doctrines, the American Negro made effective gains in his struggle for equality. During the depression, Negroes, at the bottom of the social and economic scale, suffered cruelly, but under the New Deal economic discrimination, if not social segregation, declined. In 1939 the establishment of a Civil Rights Section in the Department of Justice held out the promise of federal legal support to the Negro. And by executive order in June 1941, President Roosevelt created a Federal Committee on Fair Employment Practices to help eliminate "discrimination in the employment of workers in defense industries or government because of race, creed, color, or national origin." The relative percentage of Negroes in the armed services gradually increased, and some Negroes were allowed to qualify as officers and combat troops. To a greater extent than in World War I, the effects of travel, intermingling, and war service widened the outlook of large numbers of the Negro race.

Even before Pearl Harbor, President Roosevelt and Prime Minister Winston Churchill gave the world an outline of the war aims of the two democracies which expanded upon Roosevelt's earlier announcement of the goal of the Four Freedoms—freedom of speech and worship and freedom from want and fear. On New Year's Day, 1942, the United States took the initiative in drafting and signing a Declaration by the United Nations, reaffirming the Atlantic Charter and cementing the alliance of powers engaged in the war against the Nazis. Although none of these pronouncements had the force of Wilson's Fourteen Points, the United States waged an active struggle to win the ideological war and shape the coming peace. Technique, however, now often seemed more important than content. Whoever controlled the modern mass media ruled men's minds. In the effort to provide public information and sustain popular morale, democratic processes of thought were once again subjected to wartime censorship and propaganda. Even so, the war was seldom real or understandable to the American people except in the concrete terms of their own interests and personal experience. Yet, in the wartime words of a leading American scholar, "One issue cut through everything else. This was the question of whether democracy itself would survive the crisis. . . . There had always been those who distrusted the masses, but faith in democracy as government by all the people had not only survived but grown. Now, however, no one could say with any certainty that this faith could be maintained in the midst of a world torn by the problem of power, a world in which reason and force struggled for equilibrium if not for victory."[41]

Though totalitarianism was not ended by the war, the challenge of fascism to democracy had been met by the defeat of the Axis powers. And, despite the heavy costs of the war in terms of life, liberty, and property, the American people emerged from the struggle more confident of the future of democratic government than they had been in the depths of the depression. "Amid crisis and global war, hope, if not optimism, still lived."

CHAPTER TWELVE

Neither Peace nor War

IF WORLD WAR II was not fought with all the high expectations of the First World War, it was nevertheless a conflict in which the American people believed that the fate and the future of democracy were at stake. In a general way they hoped that, if the world could not be made safe for democracy, it might at least become more susceptible to democratic ideas. In terms of ideologies the war was viewed as a struggle of democracy versus totalitarianism, with the United Nations ranged against the members of the Axis. And, in the task of making good the peace, many Americans felt that the chief continuing problem would be one of translating the wartime unity of the United Nations into a postwar league or confederation of free democracies. Though democracy, unlike totalitarianism, could not be imposed upon a people, the United States attempted to bring about a democratic revolution in occupied Japan and Germany. And the United Nations itself was regarded in the United States as an experiment in democracy on an international scale. As such, it often became a forum for debate and political maneuver rather than a realistic agency of international diplomacy.

Although the American people in the Second World War were less naively optimistic than they had been in the First, they nevertheless failed to appreciate the fact that the outcome of modern war was not likely to be favorable to democratic government. Democracy in both domestic and international matters required freedom and popular control—in a word, a return to the political process. But the heritage of the war, with its emphasis upon force and power, encouraged illiberal tendencies in all nations at the same time that it hampered the peaceful workings of democracy in international affairs.

The period following a war is likely to be disillusioning. If for no other reason, there is the enormous cost of war in terms of human and natural resources, which in the heat of the fighting tends to be overlooked. American losses in World War II, though serious enough, were small compared to those of both its allies and enemies. Europe and extensive areas of the Far East faced enormous problems of physical reconstruction. Almost everywhere political and economic crises placed obstacles in the way of achieving a democratic society. In the regions of the world largely untouched by the war, notably Africa, Latin America, and portions of Asia, strong nationalist feelings had been aroused, while the traditional political and economic leadership of the Western world was much weakened. In the midst of new revolutionary movements in the postwar world, American democracy was also confronted by the challenge of the growing rivalry between Russia and the United States.

(II)

Incomparably the two most powerful nations to emerge from the war, the Soviet Union and the United States each contended for world leadership. Russian expansion along the periphery of its land mass in Europe was countered by an American strategy of containment in which economic and military aid, at a cost of billions of dollars annually, was extended to nations on the edge of the Soviet orbit. As the wartime alliance of the two great powers deteriorated into a state of cold war, the peoples of the world learned to live in an age of uncertainty that exhibited some of the characteristics of both peace and war. As a part of this cold war into which almost all nations were drawn, Russia and the United States waged a bitter conflict for men's minds. In addition to the age-old differences between communism and capitalism, the Soviets and Americans also adhered to contradictory ideas of democracy which they held up to the rest of the world.

In contrast to the explicit enmity of the fascist powers, exemplified in Hitler's contempt for democracy, the Soviet totalitarian regime came to accept democracy as reinterpreted in the light of its own Marxist philosophy. Thus the Soviet hostility of the 1920's gave way to a climate of opinion in which democracy became almost a sacred word. Although nearly all countries showed an increasing concern with democracy by the 1930's, the Russian interest was especially marked.[1] Stalin took up democracy as the opposite of Nazism and encouraged Communist party participation in Popular Front movements. At the Teheran Conference in 1943 he agreed with Roosevelt and Churchill in a pronouncement that looked expectantly to "a world family of democratic nations." And from the time of the Yalta Conference, the invocation of democracy became commonplace as a description of the political organization to be adopted everywhere after the war. It was applied specifically to Poland and the liberation of Europe. The Russians, however, believed that the elimination of the Nazis and their collaborators would insure the institution of democratic governments—apart from the process of elections. Behind this view, which the United States and England rejected, lay the differing conceptions of democracy on the part of Russia and the West.[2]

In the United States these issues provoked a variety of reactions. President Harry S. Truman, in his message to Congress in March 1947 calling for financial aid to the governments of Greece and Turkey, set forth the official American version of the contrast between totalitarian and democratic principles. "One way of life," he said, in outlining what became known as the Truman Doctrine, "is based upon the will of the majority, and is distinguished by free institutions, representative government, free elections, guarantees of individual liberty, freedom of speech and religion and freedom from political oppression. The second way of life is based upon the will of a minority forcibly imposed upon the majority. It relies upon terror and oppression, a controlled press and radio, fixed elections, and the suppression of personal freedoms. . . ."[3]

Earlier, during World War II, in anticipation of coming difficulties, a number of thoughtful Americans had already attempted to work out some sort of plan or forecast discerning the shape of future world problems. In a wise and witty little book, Carl Becker, a respected historian, asked the question "How new will the better world be?" Becker went on to show that the postwar period would continue to be an evolution based on the historical past and not nearly so new as customarily imagined. War and unemployment, which he saw as the two chief faults of modern civilization, were not likely to be eliminated, and the world would also find it difficult to lessen the dangers of nationalism, imperialism, and power politics.

In an editorial in *Life* magazine, which was widely reprinted and later issued as a small book, publisher Henry R. Luce issued a call to arms for American democracy. "We are *not* in a war to defend American territory. We are in a war to defend and even to promote, encourage and incite so-called democratic principles throughout the world." Luce considered that fears of socialism or dictatorship as a result of American participation in World War II were rather silly in the light of the tendencies in such a direction already exhibited in the Roosevelt administration. But the United States, despite what Luce felt were past errors, now had the opportunity to exercise world leadership and make the twentieth century "an American Century." Through its ideals of democracy and free enterprise, through economic and technical assistance, and through American trade, Western civilization would be transformed in the process of its salvation. Luce argued that the only chance to make democracy work was "in terms of a vital international economy and in terms of an international moral order. . . . The fact is," he wrote, "that Franklin Roosevelt failed to make American democracy work successfully on a narrow, materialistic, and nationalistic basis." In his description of the new American mission, Luce was both idealistic and realistic:

> We must undertake now to be the Good Samaritan of the entire world. It is the manifest duty of this country to undertake to feed all the people of the world who as a result of this worldwide collapse of civilization are hungry and destitute—all of them, that is, whom we can from time to time reach consistently with a very tough attitude toward all hostile governments.

At the same time Luce also upbraided American businessmen for the narrowness of their visions in regard to the future of American overseas commerce.

> Our thinking of world trade today is on ridiculously small terms. For example, we think of Asia as being worth only a few hundred million a year to us. Actually, in the decades to come Asia will be worth to us exactly zero—or else it will be worth to us four, five, ten billions a year. And the latter are the terms we must think in, or else confess a pitiful impotence.[4]

If Henry R. Luce stirred the imagination of American conservatives, Vice President Henry A. Wallace performed a like function for American progressives. In their visions of the future both men were willing to discard in considerable measure older American traditions. While Luce called for the abandonment of isolationism, Wallace stressed the broadening of American political democracy through the economic democracy that he saw coming in "The Century of the Common Man." Discussing different types of democracy in a wartime address before the Congress of American Soviet Friendship, the Vice President confessed that "Some in the United States believe that we have overemphasized what might be called political or bill-of-rights democracy. Carried to its extreme form, it leads to rugged individualism, exploitation, impractical emphasis on states' rights, and even to anarchy." Between American political democracy and Russian economic democracy, Wallace believed that it was possible to strike a balance in which the United States would also give added attention to greater equality among races, between the sexes, and in educational opportunities.[5]

Both Luce and Wallace were optimistic in their respective blueprints of the future, but it was also possible, as contributors to a wartime symposium on "The American Idea" pointed out, that democracy in the United States might face a difficult domestic and world situation in the decades ahead. Though America was enormously rich in resources, its war needs could contribute to future scarcities. Racial and social inequalities and prejudices continued to exist despite hasty wartime adjustments. Government controls to regulate and direct the economy, growing constantly more pervasive as a result of the war, were a particular problem in a democracy where the people who lost out in the marketplace could redress their grievances at the polls. "Even the Sphinx must smile," a contributor to the symposium pointed out, "at the irony of a situation in which a people willing to die for democracy willingly lose it in their economic life through its operation in their political life." Finally, despite its great technological achievements so manifest in the war, the United States had no monopoly of science or assurance that its new intellectual leadership would last indefinitely. Instead, the country might suffer a loss of initiative from being an established nation, as well as a decline in the sense of security which it had hitherto enjoyed in its older isolated position.[6]

After 1945 the high degree of military security and of physical freedom from hostile attack or invasion, which had characterized American history from the end of the War of 1812 to the close of World War II, no longer existed. The feeling of power which the explosion of the first atomic bombs gave to the American people proved to be of short duration. In the long run scientific secrecy was impossible to sustain. And as other nations, too, developed nuclear weapons, all notions of national security would become obsolete. In the words of Norbert Wiener, there was now "no distinction between arming ourselves and arming our enemies. Thus each terrifying discovery merely increases our subjection to the need of making a new discovery. . . ."[7] By mid-century, wartime visions of the world-wide advance of democracy through a coming *pax Americana* were subjected to the possibility of a cold war that might at any time spill over into a holocaust of destruction.

(III)

Despite the popular view that American foreign policy must become more democratic and more in accord with public opinion, the conservative nature of United States postwar goals almost precluded the use of democracy as a viable adjunct of American diplomacy. Forced on the defensive, democracy lost its dynamic quality in international relations. Americans, reflecting nostalgically on the security they had enjoyed in the past, could be moved to support the new American foreign policy only in the negative sense of resisting the spread of Russian Communism. As the cold war enforced its demands for national unity, dissent was equated with disloyalty or sedition. People responded reluctantly, though patriotically, to arguments which called for the modification of democracy at home in an effort to save it abroad. While it was true that the political leaders of a democracy had to be beacon lights as well as mirrors of public opinion, their cold-war injunctions of sacrifice and duty were unpleasantly reminiscent of the similar pleas of the fascist dictators in the 1930's. Moreover, if adverse criticism was to be precluded by calls for a bipartisan foreign policy, why, as one commentator pointed out, should Americans condemn the one-party system of Soviet Russia?[8]

It was not the least of the ironies of the postwar years that, in the struggle against communism and Russian expansion, the non-communist forces were often reduced to copying Soviet methods. Liberals or progressives committed to a philosophy of democratic collectivism were reluctant to see in their program any similarities to the collectivism of fascism or communism. Yet, in attacking the Soviets, E. H. Carr noted, the Western world was often denouncing what already existed, in part, in its own area. The contention that modern liberal democracy must not be divorced from the use of force and power, however appealing to many segments of postwar thinking, ran the risk of assuming automatically that democracy meant overwhelming strength and bigness. If luxuries and a high standard of living made Americans physically soft and unwilling to fight for their ideals, it was also true that those ideals could be corrupted by the hard Machiavellian tactics of a cynical and materialist philosophy of international relations. "A president who cannot entrust the people with the truth betrays a certain lack of faith in the basic tenets of democracy," observed diplomatic historian Thomas A. Bailey. "But because the masses are notoriously shortsighted, and generally cannot see danger until it is at their throats, our statesmen are forced to deceive them into an awareness of their own long-run interests."[9]

The very power which enabled America to transmit its ideals and institutions abroad might endanger them at home. Faced by the challenge of communism in much of the world, American democracy was also confronted by still unresolved and formidable domestic problems. While the mass of the American people after the war enjoyed an almost unprecedented degree of prosperity, American Negroes, for example, still had to struggle to gain basic human and civil rights. If the postwar years accordingly seemed a time of troubles for the democratic way of life, it was partly because both national and international conditions had become enormously complex. In this situation real issues were blurred. Much of the confusion and uncertainty of the cold war was carried over into American politics. Demands for national unity left important questions of foreign and domestic affairs undecided, as the two major parties avoided clear-cut stands in favor of appeals to personalities and pressure groups.

For a brief moment in the Presidential campaign of 1948 there seemed to be the possibility that the rise of new third parties might result in a decisive referendum on American postwar policies. In 1948 the Democratic party was split by the defections of both its left and right wings. Conservative Southerners, alienated by planks in the party platform calling for federal government protection of civil rights, formed the States' Rights Democratic party. Meanwhile radical left-wing supporters of former Vice President Wallace's criticism of the Truman administration's foreign policy organized a new American Progressive party. However, Communist influence in the party's councils and the failure of its idealistic program to secure the backing of other radical and progressive groups minimized the significance of Wallace's candidacy. In an election marked by the complacency of the Republican nominee Thomas E. Dewey, President Truman's aggressive campaigning gained him a surprise victory with a popular plurality of slightly more than two million votes. But the relatively small totals of a little over a million votes won by the Wallace and the States' Rights tickets made Truman a minority President.

(IV)

While the Truman administration was able, with only partial success, to expand the domestic social welfare program of the New Deal, its heavy involvement in world affairs, culminating in the Korean War, affected mightily the course of American democracy. In almost every aspect of American life and thought by the 1950's there was important evidence of the impress of the cold war upon the democratic tradition. Increasing militarization of both government and society, the loyalty-security program, and the general conservatism and insistence upon conformity of the postwar period were natural responses to the uncertainty in world conditions. But the militant nationalism and patriotism aroused by the cold war also encouraged manifestations of anti-democratic feeling. If public opinion was seized with hysteria, and people turned into a mob, there could be neither effective self-government nor adequate protection of individual and minority rights. By the same token, rule by a military or industrial elite was the negation of popular democracy. Though none of these conditions actually characterized American society, there was ample reason to be concerned over the illiberal tendencies which seemed to be growing stronger after the war. Popular democracy, particularly in an era of world tensions, placed a premium on consensus and conformity, but the American democratic tradition, it was well to remember, embraced freedom and individuality as well as equality and majority rule.

Over the sweep of American history an integral part of the democratic tradition had been the comparative lack of any significant militarism or undue military influence upon society and government. Although the role of the military had been increasing ever since the war with Spain, there was no precedent in the United States for the tremendous power and prestige which the armed services came to enjoy as a result of the cold-war rivalry with Russia. As a part of the struggle against communism, the American people were won over to the necessity of keeping up the nation's defenses on a virtual wartime basis. Enormous military expenditures, averaging between $40 and $50 billions annually and amounting to well over half the total national budget, peacetime conscription, and the fabrication of weapons of almost unlimited destructive power were only the more obvious examples of the new militarization of the American way of life and economy. For the first time in its peacetime history the United States took on many of the features of a garrison state. Military considerations and thinking became especially marked in American foreign policy. Meanwhile in other branches of the government, as well as in private industry and higher education, military men assumed an increasing range of jobs which had formerly been confined to civilians. As early as 1947, Hanson Baldwin, military analyst of the *New York Times*, declared:

> There is no doubt that since the war the military influence in American government has been increasing, no doubt but that the trend toward greater centralization of federal power has been increasing, no doubt but that our nationalism is, if not rampant, at least feverish. Our unilateral, Pacific-islands policy, the lone-hand MacArthur administration in Japan, our occasional by-passing of the United Nations, the increasing "crisis psychology" of the nation and the prevalence of war talk—above all, the growing American tendency to find solutions for complex problems in physical strength or military force—are perhaps natural consequences of our psychological attitudes.[10]

Democracy, to be sure, was hardly menaced by such popular military figures as Dwight D. Eisenhower, who after his decisive election as President in 1952 followed the example of Andrew Jackson in a generally cautious appraisal of military needs and demands. But there was a threat to democracy in the way in which the military was able to influence public opinion, dominate Congressional committees, and hold a life-or-death sentence over many segments of the American economy. The complex needs of military procurement encouraged the growth of big business, which alone often had the facilities required for the mass production of modern weapons. As David Lilienthal, the first head of the Atomic Energy Commission, observed, the very bigness that was subject to prosecution under the antitrust laws was also desired by the government as part of the process of nuclear rearmament. Lilienthal was typical of the new liberals and modern democrats who had come to feel that bigness on the part of business, government, and labor was now inevitable.[11]

The establishment of the Atomic Energy Commission itself was a dramatic instance of the way in which the tradition of free economic enterprise in American democracy was being subordinated to the interests of modern state capitalism. Congressional legislation gave the Commission a monopoly of nuclear power. And although plans were made for the eventual private use of some forms of atomic energy, considerations of national security required that the military retain essential control over all major developments in the field of nuclear fission. Thus the Atomic Energy Commission closely guarded its work, and the chief fruits of the greatest discovery of modern science were the constant production of instruments of military significance. In no country was atomic energy devoted primarily to the service or improvement of mankind.

The whole idea of a permanent war economy, exemplified in the way in which atomic energy was developed, had frightening implications for a liberal democratic society. As the government entered the realm of private business and industry, it was involved also in practices incompatible with free and responsible self-government. It became a partner and accomplice in some of the illegal, unethical, and monopolistic techniques of big business. Morality in American politics was subject to a new kind of institutionalized graft dependent on securing government contracts. Although the standards of individual government employees were often high, the maze of government-business relations fostered the rise of a new profession of high-powered lobbyists bent on securing federal spoils for their wealthy clients. Shutting the door on fraudulent dealing by Wall Street, the government opened the Treasury portals to another generation of financial buccaneers. In the words of Blair Bolles, the New Dealers' welfare state had become "the rich man's welfare state, aiding those who don't need help or don't deserve it—at public expense."[12]

Even if a war-type economy could be maintained without serious impairment of the American standard of living, it created other problems of no less importance in a democratic society. Likely to be a characteristic feature of the economics of war mobilization was a callous disregard of the individual and the consumer, except as their interests served those of the state. The danger to the individual and to traditional democratic liberties in the postwar economy, however, came not so much from the growth of big government or big business as in the merging of the two under the guise of a war economy or garrison state. The argument that there was a countervailing power between different branches of big business, or between big business, labor, or government, was plausible except when the interests of all such groups were joined in the drive for national security through military preparedness. As the sociologist C. Wright Mills and others demonstrated, there was growing evidence that a new power elite composed of top figures in government, industry, and the armed forces was coming to exercise a dominating influence over American society. Even if this elite did not actually rule, the concentration of political as well as economic powers in its hands had disturbing implications for the future of popular democracy.

In his Farewell Message to the country in 1961, President Eisenhower joined those who were fearful of the possible role of a power elite in the United States. "America's adventure in free government," he warned, could be menaced by the rise of a "military-industrial complex. . . . We must never let the weight of this combination endanger our liberties or democratic processes. We should take nothing for granted. Only an alert and knowledgeable citizenry can compel the proper meshing of the huge industrial and military machinery of defense with our peaceful methods and goals, so that security and liberty may prosper together." Not only was the concentration of vast power among a select few ever a possible corrupting influence in a democracy, but, in a time of stress especially, democracy could succumb to the argument of authority and to pleas of the need for a benevolent despotism.[13]

The sense of fear and insecurity which made Americans willing to support a vast standing military establishment and a wartime economy contributed importantly to the erosion of time-honored rights and liberties. By mid-century the American temper seemed dangerously close to the type of fanaticism from which totalitarian movements derived their chief strength. In such an atmosphere it was well to recall that, on the eve of American entrance into World War II, a distinguished liberal scholar had sounded a warning that was even more apposite to the postwar years. "Let us not," he urged, "in our anxiety to protect ourselves from foreign tyrants imitate some of their worst acts, and sacrifice in the process of national defense the very liberties which we are defending."[14]

After 1945 America's temporary sole possession of the secret of the atomic bomb greatly increased wartime fears of espionage. While such spying, along with intelligence and counter-intelligence, was an obvious corollary of the cold war and the world-wide pursuit of power politics, the presence of a small but dedicated group of Communists in the United States added seriously to the problem. All American Communists were not spies for the Soviets, but their essential loyalty to the United States was certainly open to question. The dilemma facing the American people therefore was how to handle the Communist question without the sacrifice of fundamental American liberties. The federal government, with the support of public opinion and the Courts, held that Communism was a conspiracy and a clear and present danger to the United States. Moreover, Communist sympathizers, though involved in no overt action, were nevertheless condemned by the now officially accepted doctrine of guilt by association. Beginning in the Truman administration, the federal government launched a loyalty-security program to purge the civil service of suspect employees. At the same time state and federal legislation virtually outlawed the Communist party in the United States and excluded its candidates from a place on the ballot in American elections.

Though it was logical to seek safeguards against those whose loyalty to the United States was open to question, the animosities and fears engendered by the cold war and the authoritarian tactics of Senator Joseph McCarthy and various Congressional investigating committees resulted in a far-reaching assault upon minority rights. Not only civil servants concerned directly with the national security but private employees, college teachers, and even clergymen, were dismissed from their positions on the grounds of alleged disloyalty. "McCarthyism," despite the damage it wrought, was primarily a symptom, not a cause, of illiberalism. More dangerous even than its methods, which many deplored, was its assumption that there was a minority group of political lepers in America guilty of so-called wrong thinking. For, in the long run, a majority that created a class of untouchables could do so only at the price of undermining democracy itself. However popular the suppression of dissent might be in the hysteria of the moment, democratic processes of government could not well survive the atmosphere of a police state.[15]

The postwar anti-radical temper of the country also affected American immigration legislation. During the war immigrants, refugees, and displaced persons admitted under emergency quotas contributed importantly to the enrichment of American intellectual and cultural life. Although the McCarran-Walter Act of 1952 ended outright racial discrimination in fixing immigration quotas, discrimination on the basis of nationality and religion remained, and new procedures were adopted to bar the entry of anyone judged likely to engage in so-called subversive activities.

(V)

Both the postwar loyalty program and the new dominating role of military preparedness illustrated America's search for security. This shift of emphasis in American democracy from individual freedom and liberty to the collective security of the group effected broad changes in the whole society. In private corporations as well as in government agencies, it was the organization and the bureaucracy, rather than the individual, which counted. Labor as well as management became highly organized, and union membership soared to new high levels in the years after the war. Even more than the controls fastened on labor in the Taft-Hartley Act of 1947, the bigness of the unions, commensurate with the bigness of industry, insured a conservative middle-class attitude on the part of most workingmen. Meanwhile the economic dependence of individuals upon society was being steadily increased by the forces of modern technology and by the growing volume of social welfare legislation enacted by the federal government. Programs pioneered under the New Deal were continued and expanded in the Fair Deal of the Truman administration and not significantly altered by the Republicans under Eisenhower. No longer radical, social and labor laws were now part of the popular quest for economic and personal security. And, at the same time, in the modern democratic and nationalistic state, the education, health, and well-being of all citizens were becoming ever more matters of common concern.

In the history of the American democratic tradition, education had always been prominent. From the earliest days of the Republic there was widespread recognition of the need of an educated citizenry if self-government was to prevail. For the most part, however, education remained either a private matter or the responsibility of the states, while the role of the federal government was limited to land grants and indirect financial aid. During World War II the normal pattern of higher education was badly disrupted by conscription, even though the armed forces returned many drafted students to the colleges and universities for further specialized in-service training. In 1944 Congress approved the G. I. Bill of Rights, which provided among other benefits the right to a subsidized education for the returning veteran. As Merle Curti pointed out, "The desire for security no less than the traditional commitment to equality of opportunity, figured in the demand for the federal support of education on both the school and college level."[16] Not only was a college education becoming more important to the future social and financial success of the individual, but the nation as well was becoming concerned over the failure of the majority of American youths to realize the full potential of their intellectual talents. Constant developments in the natural sciences, and the less obvious but no less urgent needs in the humanities and social sciences, furthered the demand for more federal support of both education and research. Nevertheless there was also a fundamental danger that the tradition of free inquiry would be lost if universities became almost entirely dependent on government contracts and funds to carry on their research activities.

Following the war, "the task of defining the responsibilities of colleges and universities in American democracy and in international affairs" was entrusted to a Presidential Commission of distinguished educators. In its report the Commission noted that, on the basis of army intelligence tests administered to some 10 million draftees during the war, from one third to one half of the country's college-age population was mentally qualified for a higher education. Yet past experience demonstrated that only about one third of these youths would go on to college. It was therefore proposed by the Commission that college enrollments be doubled over the next decade, largely through the furthering of community colleges and through increased federal funds to public institutions of higher education. If education was to foster a fuller realization of American democracy, the Commission believed that its future role must be "that of critic and leader as well as servant; its task is not merely to meet the demands of the present but to alter those demands if necessary, so as to keep them always suited to democratic ideals." Convinced that America could meet the challenge of totalitarianism only through a heightened appreciation of its own culture and institutions, the Commission stressed the need for a common core of general education.

> A society whose members lack a body of common experience and common knowledge is a society without a fundamental culture; it tends to disintegrate into a mere aggregation of individuals. Some community of values, ideas, and attitudes is essential as a cohesive force in this age of minute division of labor and intense conflict of special interests.[17]

To overcome the marked inferiority of the Southern states in education and to extend the facilities available to Negroes, the Commission recommended that federal aid be disbursed according to the relative needs and financial abilities of the states. The elaborate report of the Commission was a thorough statement of the desirability of equalizing educational opportunities in the United States. Along with this democratic philosophy the Commission also urged what some critics believed was a dangerous degree of nationalism and centralization. Defenders of private and religious education felt that large-scale federal financial support, limited to public institutions, would lead to more governmental authority. In a minority dissent the two Catholic members of the Commission expressed the view that exclusive public control of education "more than any other factor, made the dictatorships of Germany, Italy, and Japan acceptable to an ever-increasing number of their populations. . . . We fear that legislation implementing the Commission's recommendation would go a long way toward establishing an administrative structure for higher education whereby Government in the United States might easily use the Nation's public colleges and universities to promote its political purposes."[18]

In American education, as in religion, diversity with a large measure of responsibility in local and private hands had been a traditional safeguard against statism. Because Americans had always been conspicuous for their generous giving to private charities, they were all the more reluctant to approve a comprehensive program for federal support of education or for medical and health insurance. Although the funds appropriated for indirect federal aid to education mounted steadily after the war, there continued to be strong popular and political opposition to a more equalitarian version of social and intellectual democracy. Meanwhile Americans in ever greater numbers were going to school—some 40 million in grade and high schools, with several million more voluntarily engaged in some form of adult education or registered in a college or university. At the same time church membership and attendance reached a new peak in the years after the war, with over 100 million Americans enrolled in some religious body.

(*VI*)

The schools and the churches were important moral and intellectual influences in American democracy, but by the middle of the twentieth century their traditional leadership was being challenged by new sources of public information. The churches had already lost much of their responsibility for education and social welfare to governmental and secular organizations. Increasingly, standards of taste and morals, social ideas, and intellectual attitudes were being affected by agencies outside the school, home, or church. In this revolution both the government and the commercial mass media played important parts. A wide range of official bureaus performed educational functions through the collection and publication of all sorts of data. Although much of these materials was technical and statistical, a good deal was useful to the average citizen in his own life and work. A growing problem for American democracy, though, was the extent to which the government supplied propaganda as well as facts or withheld information from the people under the guise of national security. Both censorship and propaganda were totalitarian devices which, if continued, could black out the free expression vital to democracy.[19]

Out of his belief that freedom of the press was essential to liberty, publisher Henry R. Luce financed a commission to investigate the role of all the agencies of mass communication–newspapers, radio, motion pictures, magazines, and books. The commission, on which Robert M. Hutchins of the University of Chicago served as chairman, reported in 1947 that a free press was in danger and that those who controlled the mass media were not adequately serving society. Though the danger was a gradual one and though freedom would not be swept away overnight, the commission warned that irresponsibility in the area of popular communication could lead to the demand for government control as an easy, but hardly desirable, solution.

> If modern society requires great agencies of mass communication, if these concentrations become so powerful that they are a threat to democracy, if democracy cannot solve the problem simply by breaking them up–then those agencies must control themselves or be controlled by government. If they are controlled by government, we lose our chief safeguard against totalitarianism–and at the same time take a long step toward it.[20]

In a democracy the media of mass communication were often affected as much by timidity and mediocrity as by positive interference with freedom. From fear of offending powerful minority groups, politicians and businessmen catered to their particular interests or demands. This same tendency was apparent in many of the agencies of public information which censored material deemed offensive. The sheer size and variety of the public audience on which the mass media depended often meant that in the desire to antagonize no group, all controversial issues were automatically barred.

An important question was how to determine what the public

wanted. Were magazine articles and radio programs to be tailored to the least common denominator of popular taste, and the judgment of editors and broadcasters dominated by sponsors and advertisers? The public opinion polls seemed a possible scientific answer to this question, but the polls often reflected only a vague and disembodied general will rather than any real intensity of feeling or conviction. The polls, too, might influence opinion as well as measure it, but after their failure to forecast correctly President Truman's victory in 1948, they tended to lose some of their appeal as an adjunct of democracy, although they continued to be widely used for both commercial and political purposes.

In all the postwar years no issue aroused greater public feeling than the changing status of the American Negro. Gunnar Myrdal, the Swedish sociologist, rightly called his notable wartime study of the Negro problem in the United States *An American Dilemma.* Certainly in no other facet of the American democratic tradition was there such a discrepancy between theory and practice. Even more than the New Deal and the First World War, the Second resulted in far-reaching gains for the Negro population. Although the wartime federal FEPC was not continued, a number of the states, led by New York, passed their own anti-discrimination laws, and Negroes continued to make important economic strides in overcoming job discrimination. During the war, in attacking Nazi persecution of the Jews, the United States opened itself to criticism for its own discriminatory racial policies. After the war the establishment of the United Nations headquarters in the United States focused even greater international attention on American racist practices and "Jim Crow" laws. In 1947 President Truman's Committee on Civil Rights asserted that the "*United States is not so strong, the final triumph of the democrtic ideal is not so inevitable that we can ignore what the world thinks of us or our record.*" It noted that throughout much of the world the American treatment of its Negro population was taken as representative of its attitude toward all dark-skinned persons, making suspect American declarations of support for democracy. Along with recommendations for specific legislation and enforcement of the law, the Committee urged the "elimination of segregation based on race, color, creed or national origin, from American life."[21]

In the meantime the Supreme Court slowly but steadily whittled away at the legal props by which the South in particular maintained its traditional segregation of the races and its discrimination against the Negro. On the eve of the Second World War the Court's decisions had outlawed discrimination in railroad Pullman cars and in state primary elections. Gradually Negroes returned to the polls, with the number of registered voters growing rapidly in each national election, beginning in 1948. Then during the Korean War the armed forces substantially completed the integration of the Negro which had been started in World War II. While little progress was made in breaking down discriminatory racial patterns in private residential housing, public projects were no longer segregated.

In the area of race relations the greatest advance was made in education. In the words of the Supreme Court, "education is perhaps the most important function of state and local governments. Compulsory school attendance laws and the great expenditures for education both demonstrate our recognition of the importance of education to our democratic society." In 1950 the Court held that Negroes must be admitted to the University of Texas Law School and the University of Oklahoma Graduate School. Four years later the Court, in a momentous and far-reaching decision, concluded unanimously that "in the field of public education the doctrine of 'separate but equal' has no place. Separate educational facilities are inherently unequal."[22] While the border states and cities complied with the rulings of the federal courts outlawing segregation in the public schools, in the states of the Lower South, where Negroes were proportionately more numerous, the Supreme Court decision was successfully resisted.

In the bitterness that followed the courts' overthrow of segregation, race relations deteriorated badly in many areas of the South, but in 1957 Congress was able to enact a Civil Rights Act, the first such statute since Reconstruction. This federal measure established a Commission on Civil Rights with authority to investigate the denial of the suffrage and equal protection of the laws to citizens by reason of their color, race, religion, or national origin. Federal attorneys and judges were also empowered to take appropriate action against any persons or officials resisting the law. In the long run it was clear that segregation was doomed and that the Negro would continue to make important progress, not only in gaining his political and civil rights, but also in achieving full social equality. In this regard it was particularly noteworthy that Negroes themselves were taking the initiative in assuming their rightful place within American democracy.

The legal end of segregation was impressive evidence of the living force of the democratic tradition. On the whole, however, it was also true that democracy was being strengthened more in its social relations than in terms of individual rights and liberties. The individual, frustrated in his search for a meaningful personal status, was being compelled to fulfill himself through group activities and loyalties. Under the pressures generated by modern technology, man in his loss of traditional freedoms was finding solace in the community and in a corporate democracy. Happily the diversity of American life and its federal system of government offered the means by which a measure of individual and minority rights might be preserved along with the rule of the majority. In this pluralism lay much of the vitality of American democracy.

Over all American society, and affecting other nations as well, there continued to hover the pressing problems of the world's mounting population and the danger of an atomic war. It was small consolation to reflect that these two problems were not mutually exclusive and that one could cancel the other. Whether or not the world might find a way to avoid eventual catastrophe, it seemed clear that democracy, even in the United States, could hardly survive either a holocaust of nuclear war or the continuing pressure of overpopulation upon limited resources. Thus the future of the American democratic tradition, already some three centuries old, seemed to depend as never before upon the achievement of world peace and international understanding.

Notes

CHAPTER ONE: Colonial Beginnings

1. H. B. Parkes. *The American Experience*. New York: Knopf, 1947, p. 19.
2. Clinton Rossiter. *Seedtime of the Republic*. New York: Harcourt, 1953, p. 9.
3. Charles and Mary Beard. *The Rise of American Civilization*. New York: Macmillan, 1937, I, 88.
4. Charles Borgeaud. *The Rise of Modern Democracy in Old and New England*. New York: Scribner, 1894, p. 107.
5. Roy N. Lokken. "The Concept of Democracy in Colonial Political Thought," *William and Mary Quarterly*, 3rd ser., XVI (Oct. 1959), 568–580.
6. Quoted in Rossiter, *op. cit.*, p. 53; and V. L. Parrington, *Main Currents in American Thought*. New York: Harcourt, 1927–1930, I, 47, 31.

7. T. J. Wertenbaker. *The Puritan Oligarchy*. New York: Scribner, 1947, pp. 44 ff.; R. B. Perry. *Puritanism and Democracy*. New York: Vanguard, 1944, *passim.*
8. Quotations from Merrill Jensen. *American Colonial Documents to 1776*. London: Eyre, 1955, pp. 168, 174, 226.
9. Quoted in Rossiter, *op. cit.*, p. 171. See also Perry Miller. "Thomas Hooker and the Democracy of Early Connecticut," *New England Quarterly*, IV (Oct. 1931), 663–712.
10. Cotton Mather. *Magnalia Christi Americana*. London: Parkhurst, 1702, Book V, p. 46.
11. Quoted in Parrington, *op. cit.*, I, 122. See also Max Savelle. *Seeds of Liberty*. New York: Knopf, 1948, pp. 318 ff.
12. Allan Nevins. *The American States During and After the Revolution*. New York: Macmillan, 1924, p. 6. See also Theodore Thayer. *Pennsylvania Politics and the Growth of Democracy*. Harrisburg: Pa. Hist. and Museum Comm., 1953, *passim.*
13. T. J. Wertenbaker. *The First Americans*. New York: Macmillan, 1927, p. 75.
14. Quoted in T. J. Wertenbaker. *Give Me Liberty: The Struggle for Self-Government in Virginia*. Philadelphia: American Philosophical Society, 1958, p. 3.
15. T. J. Wertenbaker. *The Planters of Colonial Virginia*. Princeton: Princeton U.P., 1922, p. 151.
16. Charles Sydnor. *Gentlemen Freeholders*. Chapel Hill: U. North Carolina P., 1952, pp. 28 ff.
17. A. E. McKinley. *The Suffrage Franchise in the Thirteen English Colonies in America*. Philadelphia, 1905, p. 480.
18. *Ibid.*, p. 488.
19. R. E. Brown. *Middle-Class Democracy and the Revolution in Massachusetts*. Ithaca: Cornell U.P., 1955, chs. 4, 5, 6.
20. Quoted in Gilman Ostrander. *The Rights of Man in America*. Columbia: U. Missouri P., 1960, p. 70.

CHAPTER TWO: Revolutionary Upsurge

1. *The Works of John Adams*, ed. C. F. Adams. Boston: Little, 1850–1856, X, 282. See also *ibid.*, IX, 596; X, 197.
2. *Letters of Benjamin Rush*, ed. L. H. Butterfield. Princeton: Princeton U.P., 1951, I, 388.
3. Robert R. Palmer. *The Age of the Democratic Revolution*. Princeton: Princeton U.P., 1959, *passim.* See also Merrill Jensen. "Democracy and the American Revolution," *Huntington Library Quarterly*, XX (Aug. 1957), 321–341.
4. C. E. Merriam. *A History of American Political Theories*. New York: Macmillan, 1903, pp. 58–59.

5. Quoted in Fletcher Green. *Constitutional Development in the South Atlantic States.* Chapel Hill: U. North Carolina P., 1930, p. 56.
6. Quoted in Elisha Douglass. *Rebels and Democrats.* Chapel Hill: U. North Carolina P., 1955, p. 151.
7. W. F. Dodd. *The Revision and Amendment of State Constitutions.* Baltimore: Johns Hopkins P., 1910, pp. 118–119; W. C. Webster. "Comparative Study of the State Constitutions of the American Revolution," *Annals of the American Academy of Political and Social Science,* IX (May 1897), 385 ff.
8. J. B. McMaster. *The Acquisition of Political, Social and Industrial Rights of Man.* Cleveland: Imperial Press, 1903, pp. 15–21.
9. S. E. Morison and H. S. Commager. *The Growth of the American Republic.* New York: Oxford U.P., 1942, I, 235.
10. Merrill Jensen. *The New Nation.* New York: Knopf, 1950, pp. 23 ff.
11. Allan Nevins. *The American States During and After the Revolution.* New York: Macmillan, 1924, p. 420.
12. *Ibid.*, p. 441.
13. *Ibid.*, pp. 431 ff.
14. *Ibid.*, pp. 445 ff.
15. Chilton Williamson. *American Suffrage.* Princeton: Princeton U.P., 1960, pp. 210–215.
16. *The Writings of Benjamin Franklin,* ed. A. H. Smyth. New York: Macmillan, 1905–1907, VIII, 416.
17. *The Writings of George Washington,* ed. J. C. Fitzpatrick. Washington: G.P.O., 1931–1934, XXVIII, 520; *The Writings of Thomas Jefferson,* ed. A. A. Lipscomb and A. E. Bergh. Washington: Thomas Jefferson Memorial Assoc., 1903, X, 217.

CHAPTER THREE: The First Great Debate

1. *The Writings of Thomas Jefferson,* ed. A. A. Lipscomb and A. E. Bergh. Washington: Thomas Jefferson Memorial Assoc., 1903, XIII, 396.
2. *The Works of Alexander Hamilton,* ed. H. C. Lodge. New York: Putnam, 1904, IX, 71–72.
3. "Thoughts on Government" (1776), in *The Works of John Adams,* ed. C. F. Adams. Boston: Little, 1850–1856, IV, 195–196.
4. Quoted in Merrill Jensen. *The New Nation.* New York: Knopf, 1950, p. 43.
5. Quoted in Charles Warren. *The Making of the Constitution.* Boston: Little, 1928, p. 231.
6. Max Farrand. *The Records of the Federal Convention of 1787.* New Haven: Yale U.P., 1911, I, 26–27, 51.
7. *Ibid.*, I, 48, 132, 299, 430–431, 517; Jensen, *op. cit.*, p. 426.
8. *The Papers of Thomas Jefferson,* ed. J. P. Boyd. Princeton: Princeton U.P., 1950– , XII, 439.
9. Farrand, *op. cit.*, I, 49.

10. Gottfried Dietze. *The Federalist*. Baltimore: Johns Hopkins P., 1960, p. 68.
11. Farrand, *op cit.*, I, 57, 134.
12. C. M. Kenyon. "Men of Little Faith: The Anti-Federalists on the Nature of Representative Government," *William and Mary Quarterly*, 3rd ser., XII (Jan. 1955), 3–43. See also J. T. Main. *The Antifederalists*. Chapel Hill: U. North Carolina P., 1961, pp. 169 ff.
13. Numbers 10, 39, 57, *The Federalist*, ed. B. F. Wright. Cambridge: Harvard U.P., 1961, pp. 133–134, 280–281, 384.
14. *Works of John Adams*, IV, 284, 289, 301, 380; VI, 10, 109.
15. *Ibid.*, VI, 64.
16. *Ibid.*, VI, 477, 483–484.
17. *Papers of Thomas Jefferson* (Boyd), I, 503–504.
18. *Ibid.*, XII, 440.
19. *Ibid.*, XII, 442; XIV, 661.
20. *Writings of Thomas Jefferson* (Lipscomb and Bergh), X, 167–168; XIV, 423; I, 121–122.
21. *Ibid.*, II, 163.
22. J. B. McMaster. *A History of the People of the United States*. New York: Appleton, 1883–1913, III, 149.
23. G. D. Luetscher. *Early Political Machinery in the United States*. Philadelphia, 1903, pp. 12–13, 25; K. H. Porter. *A History of Suffrage in the United States*. Chicago: U. Chicago P., 1918, pp. 22 ff.; Chilton Williamson. *American Suffrage*. Princeton: Princeton U.P., 1960, p. 111.
24. Fletcher Green. *Constitutional Development in the South Atlantic States*. Chapel Hill: U. North Carolina P., 1930, pp. 123 ff.
25. A. A. Ekirch. *The Civilian and the Military*. New York: Oxford U.P., 1956, p. 23.
26. Dixon Wecter. *The Saga of American Society*. New York: Scribner, 1937, pp. 302–303.
27. *The Writings of Thomas Paine*, ed. M. D. Conway. New York: Putnam, 1894–1896, II, 424. See also Howard Penniman. "Thomas Paine–Democrat," *American Political Science Review*, XXXVII (Apr. 1943), 244–262.
28. E. P. Link. *Democratic-Republican Societies*. New York: Columbia U.P., 1942, pp. 20 ff.
29. R. J. Purcell. *Connecticut in Transition*. Washington: American Historical Assoc, 1918, p. 225; *Works of Fisher Ames*, ed. Seth Ames. Boston: Little, 1854, I, 328; II, 347.
30. S. E. Morison. *The Life and Letters of Harrison Gray Otis*. Boston: Houghton, 1913, I, 300.
31. *Works of Alexander Hamilton*, X, 413.
32. John Taylor. *An Inquiry into the Principles and Policy of the Government of the United States*. Fredericksburg: Green, 1814, p. 274.

CHAPTER FOUR: Toward a New Order

1. A. M. Schlesinger, Jr. *The Age of Jackson*. Boston: Little, 1945, p. 312.
2. J. W. Ward. *Andrew Jackson: Symbol for an Age*. New York: Oxford U.P., 1955, p. 213.
3. W. E. Binkley. *American Political Parties*. New York: Knopf, 1943, p. 108.
4. Marvin Meyers. *The Jacksonian Persuasion*. Stanford: Stanford U.P., 1957, pp. 181–182.
5. K. H. Porter. *A History of Suffrage in the United States*. Chicago: U. Chicago P., 1918, pp. 47 ff.; Fletcher Green. "Democracy in the Old South," *Journal of Southern History*, XII (Feb. 1946), 3–23; L. F. Litwack. *North of Slavery*. Chicago: U. Chicago P., 1961, pp. 74 ff.
6. D. R. Fox. *The Decline of Aristocracy in the Politics of New York*. New York, 1918, *passim*. Kent's remarks are in H. S. Commager. *Documents of American History*. New York: Crofts, 1938, I, 232–233.
7. Fox, *op. cit.*, p. 269.
8. J. D. Barnhart. *Valley of Democracy*. Bloomington: Indiana U.P., 1953, pp. 103 ff.; Chilton Williamson. *American Suffrage*. Princeton: Princeton U.P., 1960, ch. 11.
9. *Ibid.*, ch. 10; P. S. Klein. *Pennsylvania Politics 1817–1832*. Philadelphia, 1940, p. 36.
10. J. B. McMaster. *A History of the People of the United States*. New York: Appleton, 1883–1913, V, 380; VII, 162 ff.; C. S. Sydnor. *The Development of Southern Sectionalism*. Baton Rouge: Louisiana State U.P., 1948, pp. 283 ff.
11. Porter, *op. cit.*, pp. 93 ff., 118 ff.
12. McMaster, *op. cit.*, V, 432.
13. H. J. Ford. *The Rise and Growth of American Politics*. New York: Macmillan, 1898, pp. 151 ff.
14. Quoted in Klein, *op. cit.*, p. 78. See also G. D. Luetscher. *Early Political Machinery in the United States*. Philadelphia, 1903, ch. 4.
15. Oscar and Mary Handlin. *Commonwealth*. New York: New York U.P., 1947, p. 173.
16. Charles and Mary Beard. *The Rise of American Civilization*. New York: Macmillan, 1937, I, 737.
17. A. A. Ekirch. *The Idea of Progress in America*. New York: Columbia U.P., 1944, ch. 4.
18. Quoted in *ibid.*, pp. 133–134.
19. Mary P. Mann. *The Life and Works of Horace Mann*. Boston: Lee, 1891, III, 417–418; IV, 251.
20. Quoted in Merle Curti. *The Social Ideas of American Educators*. New York: Scribner, 1935, p. 15.
21. Edward Channing. *A History of the United States*. New York: Macmillan, 1905–1925, V, 250.

22. F. J. Turner. *The United States, 1830–1850*. New York: Holt, 1935, p. 337.
23. House of Representatives, Apr. 23, 1846, *Congressional Globe*, 29th Cong., 1st Sess., p. 714.
24. Turner, *op. cit.*, p. 18.
25. R. H. Gabriel. *The Course of American Democratic Thought*. New York: Ronald, 1940, ch. 2; E. L. Magoon. *Republican Christianity*. Boston: Gould, 1849, p. 7.
26. Calvin Colton. *A Voice from America*. London: Colburn, 1839, p. 57.
27. Quoted in Schlesinger, *op. cit.*, p. 360.
28. *Speeches, Correspondence, and Political Papers of Carl Schurz*, ed. Frederic Bancroft. New York: Putnam, 1913, I, 61–62.

CHAPTER FIVE: Criticism and Commentary

1. *The Writings of Thomas Jefferson*, ed. A. A. Lipscomb and A. E. Bergh. Washington: Thomas Jefferson Memorial Assoc., 1903, IX, 299–300; Albert K. Weinberg. *Manifest Destiny*. Baltimore: Johns Hopkins P., 1935, ch. 4.
2. *Democracy in the Middle West*, ed. J. P. Nichols and J. G. Randall. New York: Appleton, 1941, pp. 65–66.
3. T. L. Nichols. *Forty Years of American Life*. London: Maxwell, 1864, I, 63.
4. George Bancroft. *History of the United States*. Boston: Little, 1834–1874, IV, 5.
5. Quoted in G. D. Lillibridge. *Beacon of Freedom: The Impact of American Democracy upon Great Britain*. Philadelphia: U. Pennsylvania P., 1955, p. 82.
6. *Writings and Speeches of Daniel Webster*, ed. J. W. McIntyre. Boston: Little, 1903, XII, 170.
7. Lillibridge, *op. cit.*, chs. 1–2.
8. W. E. Chace. "The Descent on Democracy: A Study of American Democracy as Observed by British Travellers." MS. Ph.D. thesis (University of North Carolina, 1941), *passim*.
9. Alexis de Tocqueville. *Democracy in America*, ed. Phillips Bradley. New York: Vintage, 1954, I, 15.
10. *Ibid.*, I, 6–7, 11; II, 56, 102, 116, 147.
11. *Ibid.*, I, 53; II, 52.
12. *Ibid.*, II, 169, 171.
13. *Ibid.*, I, 308, 331, 335.
14. *Ibid.*, I, 273; II, 13, 122, 307, 313, 336–337.
15. *Ibid.*, I, 161, 271.
16. *Ibid.*, I, 136.
17. *Ibid.*, I, 142, 203.
18. *Ibid.*, I, 166–167, 177; II, 285.
19. A. M. Schlesinger, Jr. *The Age of Jackson*. Boston: Little, 1945, pp. 369 ff. *Democratic Review*, I (Oct.–Dec. 1837), 14.
20. *Boston Quarterly Review*, **II** (Oct. 1839), 486, 490; **III** (July 1840), 391–392.

21. *Democratic Review*, **XII** (April 1843), 387.
22. Merle Curti. *The Growth of American Thought*. New York: Harper, 1943, p. 304.
23. *Journals of Ralph Waldo Emerson*, ed. E. W. Emerson and W. E. Forbes. Boston: Houghton, 1909–1914, III, 390; IV, 95; *Complete Works of Ralph Waldo Emerson*. Boston: Houghton, 1903–1906, III, 201, 208.
24. *Writings of Henry David Thoreau*. Boston: Houghton, 1906, IV, 356, 358, 387; VI, 210.
25. *The Works of Herman Melville*. London: Constable, 1922–1924, IV, 240.
26. *The Letters of William Gilmore Simms*. Columbia: U. South Carolina P., 1952–1956, I, 167.
27. Quoted in R. H. Gabriel. *The Course of American Democratic Thought*. New York: Ronald, 1940, p. 21.
28. J. F. Cooper. *The American Democrat*. New York: Knopf, 1931, p. 154.
29. Schlesinger, *op. cit*., p. 379; A. A. Ekirch. *The Idea of Progress in America*. New York: Columbia U.P., 1944, pp. 181–182.
30. Quoted in *ibid*., pp. 262–263.
31. Richard Hildreth. *Theory of Politics*. New York: Harper, 1854, pp. 251 ff.
32. Parke, Godwin. *Democracy Constructive and Pacific*. New York: Winchester, 1844, p. 12.
33. G. S. Camp. *Democracy*. New York: Harper, 1841, pp. 20, 178 ff.
34. The discussion of Grimké is based on my documented article, "Frederick Grimké: Advocate of Free Institutions," *Journal of the History of Ideas*, **XI** (Jan. 1950), 75–92.

CHAPTER SIX: Disruption and Disunion

1. H. C. Perkins. *Northern Editorials on Secession*. New York: Appleton, 1942, II, ch. 23; R. H. Gabriel. *The Course of American Democratic Thought*. New York: Ronald, 1940, p. 111.
2. Avery Craven. *The Growth of Southern Nationalism*. Baton Rouge: Louisiana State U.P., 1953, p. 391. See also Craven, "The 1840's and the Democratic Process," *Journal of Southern History*, **XVI** (May 1950), 161–176; and *The Coming of the Civil War*. Chicago: U. Chicago P., 1957, p. x.
3. S. G. Fisher. *The Trial of the Constitution*. Philadelphia: Lippincott, 1862, p. 324.
4. *The Writings of Thomas Paine*, ed. M. D. Conway. New York: Putnam, 1894–1896, I, 7.
5. Quoted in A. F. Tyler. *Freedom's Ferment*. Minneapolis: U. Minnesota P., 1944, p. 466.
6. W. F. Cash. *The Mind of the South*. New York: Knopf, 1941, pp. 60–61.
7. W. P. and F. J. Garrison. *William Lloyd Garrison*. Boston: Houghton, 1894, III, 412.
8. Richard Hildreth. *Despotism in America*. Boston: Jewett, 1854, pp. 7–8, 15–16.
9. Quoted in *Proceedings of the Pennsylvania Yearly Meeting of Progressive*

Friends. New York: Trow, 1855, p. 95. See also H. S. Commager. *Theodore Parker*. Boston: Little, 1936, pp. 185, 266; J. G. Randall. *Lincoln the President*. New York: Dodd, 1945–1955, II, 316.

10. W. E. Channing. *Slavery*. Boston: Munroe, 1836, p. 102. See also R. B. Nye. *Fettered Freedom*. East Lansing: Michigan State College P., 1949, ch. 6.
11. *The Works of John C. Calhoun*, ed. R. K. Crallé. New York: Appleton, 1854–1855, III, 180.
12. *Ibid.*, IV, 551. See also C. M. Wiltse. *John C. Calhoun*. Indianapolis: Bobbs, 1944–1951, II, 268.
13. *Works of John C. Calhoun*, I, 48.
14. Richard Hofstadter. *The American Political Tradition*. New York: Vintage, 1954, ch. 4; Gabriel, *op. cit.*, p. 110; V. L. Parrington. *Main Currents in American Thought*. New York: Harcourt, 1927–1930, II, 82.
15. *Congressional Globe*, 35th Cong., 1st Sess., Appendix, pp. 68, 71.
16. *The Collected Works of Abraham Lincoln*, ed. R. P. Basler. New Brunswick: Rutgers U.P., 1953, II, 266.
17. *Ibid.*, II, 268; Hofstadter, *op. cit.*, p. 114.
18. *Collected Works of Abraham Lincoln*, I, 438–439; II, 461–462.
19. *Ibid.*, IV, 256, 426, 438–439.
20. J. G. Randall. *Lincoln the Liberal Statesman*. New York: Dodd, 1947, p. 86.
21. *Ex parte* Milligan (1866), 4 Wallace, 127.
22. Donaldson Jordan and E. J. Pratt. *Europe and the American Civil War*. Boston: Houghton, 1931, pp. 54 ff.
23. Perkins, *op. cit.*, II, 945; ch. 23.
24. E. L. Pierce. *Memoir and Letters of Charles Sumner*. Boston: Roberts, 1893, IV, 144; Allan Nevins. *The Emergence of Lincoln*. New York: Scribner, 1950, II, 132 ff.
25. David Donald. *Charles Sumner*. New York: Knopf, 1960, p. 388. See also Randall, *Lincoln the President*, II, 152–153.
26. Frederick Grimké. *Considerations upon the Nature and Tendency of Free Institutions*. Cincinnati: Derby, 1848, p. 320.
27. Allan Nevins. *Ordeal of the Union*. New York: Scribner, 1947, I, 518. See also L. F. Litwack. *North of Slavery*. Chicago: U. Chicago P., 1961, pp. 91–92, 263.
28. Walt Whitman. *The Gathering of the Forces*, ed. Cleveland Rodgers and John Black. New York: Putnam, 1920, I, 53 ff.
29. Walt Whitman. *I Sit and Look Out*, ed. Emory Holloway and V. Schwarz. New York: Columbia U.P., 1932, p. 90.
30. Floyd Stovall. *Walt Whitman: Representative Selections*. New York: Am. Bk. Co., 1939, p. 151; Parrington, *op. cit.*, III, 77.
31. Quoted in Walter Lowenfels. *Walt Whitman's Civil War*. New York: Knopf, 1960, p. 144.
32. Stovall, *op. cit.*, pp. 392–393.
33. Quoted in Gabriel, *op. cit.*, p. 129.
34. Stovall, *op. cit.*, pp. 397, 405–406.
35. *Ibid.*, p. 277.

CHAPTER SEVEN: Reconstruction and Revolution

1. Paul H. Buck. *The Road to Reunion.* Boston: Little, 1937, p. viii.
2. J. W. Draper. *History of the American Civil War.* New York: Harper, 1868–1870, III, 669, 671. See also Draper, *Thoughts on the Future Civil Policy of America.* New York: Harper, 1865, pp. 264, 313.
3. Jefferson Davis. *The Rise and Fall of the Confederate Government.* New York: Appleton, 1881, II, 764.
4. Charles and Mary Beard. *The Rise of American Civilization.* New York: Macmillan, 1937, II, 115–116.
5. J. R. Lowell. "Reconstruction" (1865), *Political Essays.* Boston: Houghton, 1888, p. 197.
6. Quoted in Richard Hofstadter. *The American Political Tradition.* New York: Vintage, 1954, p. 155.
7. E. R. Lewis. *A History of American Political Thought.* New York: Macmillan, 1937, p. 46.
8. E. L. Pierce. *Memoir and Letters of Charles Sumner.* Boston: Roberts, 1893, IV, 319.
9. R. H. Gabriel. *The Course of American Democratic Thought.* New York: Ronald, 1940, p. 140.
10. C. Vann Woodward. *Origins of the New South.* Baton Rouge: Louisiana State U.P., 1951, p. 211.
11. *Ibid.*, pp. 342–343. See also Paul Lewinson. *Race, Class, and Party.* New York: Oxford U.P., 1932, *passim.*
12. R. S. Baker. *Following the Color Line.* New York: Doubleday, 1908, p. 261.
13. Herbert Croly. *Progressive Democracy.* New York: Macmillan, 1914, pp. 86 ff.
14. V. L. Parrington. *Main Currents in American Thought.* New York: Harcourt, 1927–1930, III, 9, 21, 23.
15. C. Vann Woodward. *Reunion and Reaction.* Boston: Little, 1951, p. 64.
16. *Life and Labors of Henry W. Grady, His Speeches, Writings.* Atlanta: Hudgins, 1890, p. 113.
17. Woodward, *Origins of the New South*, pp. 61–62, 400.
18. Henry Adams. *The Education of Henry Adams.* Boston: Houghton, 1918, p. 355.
19. A. M. Schlesinger. *The Rise of the City.* New York: Macmillan, 1933, pp. 409–410.
20. C. R. Fish. *The Civil Service and the Patronage.* New York: Longmans, 1905, pp. 224, 229.
21. T. C. Cochran and William Miller. *The Age of Enterprise.* New York: Macmillan, 1942, p. 156.
22. *North American Review*, **CXXVII** (July–Aug. 1878), 1–20.
23. *Atlantic Monthly*, **LXIV** (Nov. 1889), 577–588.

24. E. L. Godkin. *Problems of Modern Democracy*. New York: Scribner, 1896, pp. 39, 90 ff.; "The Moral of the Credit Mobilier Scandal," *Nation*, XVI (Jan. 30, 1873), 68. See also Godkin, *Unforeseen Tendencies of Democracy*. Boston: Houghton, 1898, *passim*.
25. Henry George, Jr. *Life of Henry George*. New York: Doubleday, 1900, pp. 216–217.
26. *Watson's Jeffersonian Magazine*, V (Oct. 1910), 817.

CHAPTER EIGHT: The Triumph of Nationalism and Reform

1. James Bryce. *The American Commonwealth*. New York: Macmillan, 1888, II, 700–701.
2. *Forum*, XXII (Jan. 1897), 579.
3. Eric Goldman. *Rendezvous with Destiny*. New York: Knopf, 1952, pp. 82–83.
4. H. S. Commager. *The American Mind*. New Haven: Yale U.P., 1950, p. 45.
5. Dwight Waldo. *The Administrative State*. New York: Ronald, 1948, p. 40.
6. Charles Beard. *Contemporary American History*. New York: Macmillan, 1914, p. 304.
7. Herbert Croly. *Marcus Alonzo Hanna*. New York: Macmillan, 1919, p. 466.
8. Woodrow Wilson. *Constitutional Government in the United States*. New York: Columbia U.P., 1908, pp. 56–57.
9. E. S. Corwin. "The Impact of the Idea of Evolution on the American Political and Constitutional Tradition," in Stow Persons. *Evolutionary Thought in America*. New Haven: Yale U.P. 1950, pp. 182–199.
10. Louis Filler. *Crusaders for American Liberalism*. New York: Harcourt, 1939, pp. 236 ff.
11. Alfred Kazin. *On Native Grounds*. New York: Reynal, 1942, ch. 4.
12. J. Allen Smith. *The Spirit of American Government*. New York: Macmillan, 1907, p. 355; Bryce, *op. cit.*, I, 608.
13. F. P. Dunne, *Dissertations by Mr. Dooley*. New York: Harper, 1906, p. 281.
14. F. C. Howe. *The City the Hope of Democracy*. New York: Scribner, 1905, p. 86; Tom L. Johnson. *My Story*. New York: Huebsch, 1911, p. xxxv.
15. H. U. Faulkner. *The Quest for Social Justice*. New York: Macmillan, 1931, pp. 91 ff.
16. Bryce, *op. cit.*, II, 73.
17. J. Q. Dealey. *Growth of American State Constitutions*. Boston: Ginn, 1915, ch. 17.
18. C. A. Beard and B. E. Shultz. *Documents on the State-Wide Initiative Referendum and Recall*. New York: Macmillan, 1912, pp. 12, 34.
19. A. L. Lowell. *Public Opinion and Popular Government*. New York: Longmans, 1913, p. 15.
20. Elihu Root. *Addresses on Government and Citizenship*. Cambridge: Harvard U.P., 1916, pp. 252–253.
21. W. H. Taft. *Popular Government*. New Haven: Yale U.P., 1913, pp. 12,

22; *Our Chief Magistrate and His Powers*. New York: Columbia U.P., 1916, pp. 139 ff.
22. Herbert Croly. *The Promise of American Life*. New York: Macmillan, 1909, pp. 333 ff.; *Progressive Democracy*. New York: Macmillan, 1914, pp. 288–290.
23. M. H. Bernstein. *Regulating Business by Independent Commission*. Princeton: Princeton U.P., 1955, p. 36.
24. L. A. Blue. "Recent Tendencies in State Administration," *Annals of the American Academy of Political and Social Science*, XVIII (Nov. 1901), 442–443.
25. Quoted in *ibid*., p. 443.
26. Croly, *Progressive Democracy*, p. 361.
27. Quoted in H. T. Pinkett. "Gifford Pinchot and the Early Conservation Movement in the United States." MS. Ph.D. thesis (American University, 1953), p. 46 and ch. 8.
28. J. H. Tufts. *Our Democracy: Its Origins and Tasks*. New York: Holt, 1917, p. 268.
29. Croly, *Promise of American Life*, pp. 106, 190.
30. *Ibid*., pp. 167–169.
31. Croly, *Progressive Democracy*, pp. 110, 113, 211.
32. Ernst Freund. *Standards of American Legislation*. Chicago: U. Chicago P., 1917, p. 21.
33. George Mowry. *The Era of Theodore Roosevelt*. New York: Harper, 1958, p. 263.
34. Quoted in J. H. Franklin, *From Slavery to Freedom*. New York: Knopf, 1947, p. 438. See also Faulkner, *op. cit*., pp. 10 ff.
35. Croly, *Progressive Democracy*, p. 4.
36. C. W. Eliot. *The Conflict Between Individualism and Collectivism in a Democracy*. New York: Scribner, 1910, p. 129; Croly, *Promise of American Life*, p. 209.
37. Caro Lloyd. *Henry Demarest Lloyd*. New York: Putnam, 1912, I, 295; W. J. Ghent. *Our Benevolent Feudalism*. New York: Macmillan, 1902, p. 8.
38. W. E. Weyl. *The New Democracy*. New York: Macmillan, 1912, p. 193.
39. B. P. DeWitt. *The Progressive Movement*. New York: Macmillan, 1915, p. 99.
40. Mowry, *op. cit*., p. 295; *The Letters of Theodore Roosevelt*, ed. E. E. Morison. Cambridge: Harvard U.P., 1951–1954, VII, 592.
41. Theodore Roosevelt. *The New Nationalism*. New York: Outlook, 1910, p. 11.
42. Chester Rowell, quoted in George Mowry. *The California Progressives*. Berkeley: U. California P., 1951, p. 102.

CHAPTER NINE: American Mission Under Arms

1. Charles and Mary Beard. *The American Spirit*. New York: Macmillan, 1942, p. 550.

2. Merle Curti. *The Growth of American Thought*. New York: Harper, 1943, p. 660.
3. Quoted in C. G. Bowers. *Beveridge and the Progressive Era*. Boston: Houghton, 1932, p. 69.
4. *Forum*, **XXIV** (Dec. 1897), 395.
5. F. H. Harrington. "Literary Aspects of American Anti-Imperialism, 1898–1902," *New England Quarterly*, **X** (Dec. 1937), 650–667; "The Anti-Imperialist Movement in the United States, 1898–1900," *Mississippi Valley Historical Review*, **XXII** (Sept. 1935), 211–230.
6. *Speeches, Correspondence, and Public Papers of Carl Schurz*, ed. Frederic Bancroft. New York: Putnam, 1913, V, 514, 495.
7. *Essays of William Graham Sumner*, ed. A. G. Keller and Maurice Davie. New Haven: Yale U.P., 1934, II, 294; D. S. Jordan. *Imperial Democracy*. New York: Appleton, 1901, p. 141.
8. K. H. Porter. *National Party Platforms*. New York: Macmillan, 1924, p. 211.
9. Schurman Commission, quoted in A. K. Weinberg. *Manifest Destiny*. Baltimore: Johns Hopkins P., 1935, p. 295.
10. National Education Association. *Journal of Proceedings and Addresses*. Chicago: N.E.A., 1899, p. 76.
11. Brooks Adams. *The New Empire*. New York: Macmillan, 1902, p. 211.
12. R. E. Osgood. *Ideals and Self-interest in America's Foreign Policy*. Chicago: U. Chicago P., 1953, p. 47; L. T. Hobhouse. *Democracy and Reaction*. New York: Putnam, 1905, p. 12.
13. W. E. Leuchtenburg. "Progressivism and Imperialism," *Mississippi Valley Historical Review*, **XXXIX** (Dec. 1952), 483–504.
14. H. K. Beale. *Theodore Roosevelt and the Rise of America to World Power*. Baltimore: Johns Hopkins P., 1956, pp. 455–456.
15. C. E. Merriam. *American Political Ideas*. New York: Macmillan, 1929, pp. 253–254.
16. *The Public Papers of Woodrow Wilson*, ed. R. S. Baker and W. E. Dodd. New York: Harper, 1925–1927, III, 225, 410.
17. *Ibid.*, IV, 410–411.
18. *Ibid.*, V, 8, 14, 16.
19. *Congressional Record*, 65th Cong., 1st Sess., p. 208.
20. *Ibid.*, pp. 214, 220, 228.
21. *Public Papers of Woodrow Wilson*, V, 15–16.
22. *Letters of Henry Adams 1892–1918*, ed. W. C. Ford. Boston: Houghton, 1938, p. 643; *Yale Review*, **V** (Jan. 1916), 225–233; *New Republic*, **VI** (March 25, 1916), 205–207.
23. Frederick Palmer. *Our Gallant Madness*. New York: Doubleday, 1937, pp. 111–112, 196; *Congressional Record*, 65th Cong., 1st Sess., p. 996.
24. J. R. Mock and Cedric Larson. *Words That Won the War*. Princeton: Princeton U.P., 1939, p. 4.
25. *Writings and Speeches of Eugene V. Debs*. New York: Hermitage, 1948, pp. 429 ff.; F. L. Paxson. *America at War*. Boston: Houghton, 1939, ch. 13.

26. Daniel Aaron. *Men of Good Hope*. New York: Oxford U.P., 1951, p. 284.
27. *New Republic*, XII (Aug. 18, Sept. 1, 1917), 69, 128–130.
28. *Seven Arts*, II (Sept. 1917), 541; *International Journal of Ethics*, XXVIII (July 1918), 465–484.
29. *Seven Arts*, II (June 1917), 133 ff.
30. *Ibid*., pp. 143 ff.; Randolph Bourne. *Untimely Papers*. New York: Huebsch, 1919, pp. 141 ff.
31. *Public Papers of Woodrow Wilson*, V, 161–162.
32. *Seven Arts*, II (June 1917), 145–146; New York *World*, November 9, 12, 1918.
33. *Nation*, CVII (Dec. 7, 1918), 692.
34. *Public Papers of Woodrow Wilson*, VI, 79; V, 638–639, 439.
35. *Ibid*., VI, 515.

CHAPTER TEN: Disillusionment and Prosperity

1. Harold Stearns. *Liberalism in America*. New York: Boni, 1919, p. 213.
2. *New Republic*, XVII (Nov. 23, 1918), 85–87.
3. J. T. Shotwell. *Intelligence and Politics*. New York: Century, 1921, p. 3.
4. Zechariah Chafee. *Free Speech in the United States*. Cambridge: Harvard U.P., 1948, p. 196.
5. Quoted in *ibid*., p. 317.
6. W. E. Leuchtenburg. *The Perils of Prosperity*. Chicago: U. Chicago P., 1958, p. 81.
7. E. F. Goldman. *Rendezvous with Destiny*. New York: Knopf, 1952, p. 291.
8. W. H. Riker. *Democracy in the United States*. New York: Macmillan, 1953, ch. 2.
9. K. C. MacKay. *The Progressive Movement of 1924*. New York: Columbia U.P., 1947, ch. 4.
10. A. S. Link. *American Epoch*. New York: Knopf, 1955, pp. 300 ff.
11. Leuchtenburg, *op. cit*., p. 187.
12. Quoted in Charles Beard. "The Constitution and States' Rights," *Virginia Quarterly Review*, XI (Oct. 1935), 493.
13. Quoted in J. W. Prothro. *The Dollar Decade: Business Ideas in the 1920's*. Baton Rouge: Louisiana State U.P., 1954, p. 118.
14. Quoted in *ibid*., pp. 63, 117.
15. Gilman Ostrander. *The Rights of Man in America*. Columbia: U. Missouri P., 1960, p. 157.
16. John Higham. *Strangers in the Land*. New Brunswick: Rutgers U.P., 1955, p. 330.
17. H. L. Mencken. *Notes on Democracy*. New York: Knopf, 1926, pp. 22 ff., 181 ff.
18. J. Allen Smith. *The Growth and Decadence of Constitutional Government*. New York: Holt, 1930, p. 197.
19. Quoted in Eric Goldman. "J. Allen Smith," *Pacific Northwest Quarterly*, XXXV (July 1944), 209.

20. F. C. Howe. *The Confessions of a Reformer*. New York: Scribner, 1925, p. 176.
21. Ralph Borsodi. *This Ugly Civilization*. New York: Simon and Schuster, 1929, p. 215.
22. Madison Grant. *The Passing of the Great Race*. New York: Scribner, 1916, p. 5; Introduction to Lothrop Stoddard. *The Rising Tide of Color*. New York: Scribner, 1920, p. xxxii.
23. David Spitz. *Patterns of Anti-Democratic Thought*. New York: Macmillan, 1949, *passim*.
24. *Bulletin of the American Association of University Professors,* **I** (Dec. 1915), 31–32.
25. Walter Lippmann. *Public Opinion*. New York: Penguin, 1922, pp. 34–35, 203; *The Phantom Public*. New York: Harcourt, 1925, pp. 61–62, 185. See also Stow Persons. *American Minds*. New York: Holt, 1958, pp. 374 ff.
26. A. D. Lindsay. *The Essentials of Democracy*. Philadelphia: U. Pennsylvania P., 1929, pp. 8 ff., 31 ff., 62.
27. John Dewey. *Democracy and Education*. New York: Macmillan, 1916, pp. 101, 357, 401.
28. *International Journal of Ethics,* **XXVIII** (July 1918), 499–514; *Scientific Monthly,* **VII** (Dec. 1918), 511–524.
29. E. G. Conklin. *The Direction of Human Evolution*. New York: Scribner, 1921, pp. 111, 116, 126.
30. John Dewey. *The Public and Its Problems*. New York: Holt, 1927, pp. 85 ff., 109, 124.
31. *Ibid*., pp. 212–213; Dewey. *Individualism Old and New*. New York: Minton, Balch, 1930, pp. 28, 35 ff.
32. Dewey, *The Public and Its Problems*, pp. 168–169.

CHAPTER ELEVEN: Challenge and Response

1. Charles and Mary Beard. *America in Midpassage*. New York: Macmillan, 1939, II, 925.
2. *Atlantic Monthly*. **CXLIX** (Jan. 1932), 8.
3. G. S. Ford. *Science and Civilization*. Minneapolis: U. Minnesota P., 1933, p. 23; Herbert Agar. *The People's Choice*. Boston: Houghton, 1933, pp. 128, 197, 312–314.
4. *The Public Papers and Addresses of Franklin D. Roosevelt*, ed. S. I. Rosenman. New York: Random, Macmillan, Harper, 1938–1950, I, 72.
5. *Ibid*., I, x–xi, 627, 646, 752.
6. *Ibid*., II, 15–16.
7. H. J. Laski. *The American Democracy*. New York: Viking, 1948, p. 81.
8. George Boas. "A Defense of Democracy," *Harper's Magazine,* **CLXIX** (Sept. 1934), 425; F. H. Knight. "Social Science and the Political Trend" (1934), in *Freedom and Reform*. New York: Harper, 1947, p. 20; T. V. Smith. *The Promise of American Politics*. Chicago: U. Chicago P., 1936, p. 15.

9. *Ibid.*, p. 6.
10. T. W. Arnold. *The Folklore of Capitalism.* New Haven: Yale U.P., 1937, pp. 211, 356–357.
11. Henry Wallace. *New Frontiers.* New York: Reynal, 1934, pp. 23, 28–32, 274.
12. David Lilienthal. *TVA: Democracy on the March.* New York: Harper, 1944, pp. 5–6, 142, 146, 224.
13. R. G. Tugwell and E. C. Banfield. "Grass Roots Democracy—Myth or Reality," *Public Administration Review,* X (Winter 1950), 49; Philip Selznick. *TVA and the Grass Roots.* Berkeley: U. California P., 1949, pp. 92–93, 262 ff.
14. J. M. Burns. *Roosevelt: The Lion and the Fox.* New York: Harcourt, 1956, pp. 183–184.
15. *Ibid.*, p. 198.
16. D. R. McCoy. *Angry Voices: Left-of-Center Politics in the New Deal Era.* Lawrence: U. Kansas P., 1958, *passim.*
17. *Public Papers and Addresses,* V, 198, 236, 572.
18. E. E. Robinson. *The Roosevelt Leadership.* Philadelphia: Lippincott, 1955, p. 177.
19. Lochner *v.* New York (1905), 198 U.S. 75.
20. Burns, *op. cit.*, p. 291.
21. *Public Papers and Addresses,* VI, 2, 5.
22. *Ibid.*, VII, 242.
23. Burns, *op. cit.*, p. 331.
24. Walter Lippmann. *An Inquiry into the Principles of the Good Society.* Boston: Little, 1937, p. 89.
25. *Public Papers and Addresses,* V, 609.
26. Herbert Hoover. Address, Council on Foreign Relations, Chicago, 1939. Quoted in *Congressional Record,* 76th Cong., 1st Sess., Appendix, pp. 402–404.
27. James Burnham. *The Managerial Revolution.* New York: Day, 1941, p. 152.
28. Herbert Agar *et al. The City of Man: A Declaration on World Democracy.* New York: Viking, 1940; Archibald MacLeish. *The Irresponsibles.* New York: Duell, 1940; H. M. Jones. "Patriotism—but How?" *Atlantic Monthly,* CLXII (Nov. 1938), 586, 592.
29. John Dewey. *Freedom and Culture.* New York: Putnam, 1939, pp. 34, 49, 175.
30. E. B. Wesley. *Annals of the American Academy of Political and Social Science,* CLXXXII (Nov. 1935), 21–29.
31. G. S. Counts. *The Prospects of American Democracy.* New York: Day, 1938, ch. 11; *The Schools Can Teach Democracy.* New York: Day, 1939, pp. 14–15; *Democracy and Education.* New York: Bureau of Publications, Teachers College, 1940, p. 4.
32. Jacques Barzun. *Of Human Freedom.* Boston: Little, 1939, pp. 18–19; T. V. Smith. *The Democratic Tradition in America.* New York: Farrar, 1941, ch.

2; Thomas Mann. *The Coming Victory of Democracy*. New York: Knopf, 1938, p. 25.
33. *Public Papers and Addresses*, VIII, 2–3, IX, 9.
34. *Ibid.*, IX, 552.
35. Burns, *op. cit.*, p. 455.
36. *Public Papers and Addresses*, X, 3–4.
37. *Ibid.*, IX, 641; X, 65.
38. Robert Sherwood. *Roosevelt and Hopkins*. New York: Harper, 1948, p. 438.
39. Burns, *op. cit.*, p. 463; September 7, 1942, *Congressional Record*, 77th Cong., 2nd Sess., pp. 7046–7047.
40. *New York Times*, July 9, 1940, p. 4, col. 1.
41. Merle Curti. *The Growth of American Thought*. New York: Harper, 1943, pp. 752–753.

CHAPTER TWELVE: Neither Peace nor War

1. Ithiel de Sola Pool. *Symbols of Democracy*. Stanford: Stanford U.P., 1952, pp. 67 ff.
2. E. H. Carr. *Democracy in International Affairs*. [Nottingham?]: University College, [1945], *passim.*
3. H. S. Truman. *Memoirs*. Garden City: Doubleday, 1955–1956, II, 105–106.
4. H. R. Luce. *The American Century*. New York: Farrar, 1941, pp. 10–14, 25 ff., 36–37.
5. Henry Wallace. *The Century of the Common Man*. New York: Reynal, 1939, pp. 37 ff.
6. T. H. Robinson. "Democracy in the American Economy," in E. T. Adams *et al. The American Idea*. New York: Harper, 1942, pp. 91–92.
7. Norbert Wiener. *The Human Use of Human Beings*. Boston: Houghton, 1950, pp. 141–142.
8. Felix Morley. *The Foreign Policy of the United States*. New York: Knopf, 1951, p. vii.
9. E. H. Carr. *The Soviet Impact on the Western World*. New York: Macmillan, 1947, *passim;* T. A. Bailey. *The Man in the Street*. New York: Mamillan, 1948, p. 13.
10. H. W. Baldwin. *The Price of Power*. New York: Harper, 1947, p. 136. See also Baldwin, "The Military Move In," *Harper's Magazine*, CXCV (Dec. 1947), 481–489; A. A. Ekirch. *The Civilian and the Military*. New York: Oxford U.P., 1956, ch. 17.
11. David Lilienthal. *Big Business: A New Era*. New York: Harper, 1953, pp. 102–104, ch. 12.
12. Blair Bolles. *How to Get Rich in Washington*. New York: Norton, 1952, p. 12.
13. D. D. Eisenhower. *Public Papers of the Presidents, 1960–1961*. Washington: G.P.O., 1961, pp. 1036, 1038.

14. Zechariah Chafee. *Free Speech in the United States.* Cambridge: Harvard U.P., 1948, p. 566.
15. A. A. Ekirch. *The Decline of American Liberalism.* New York: Longmans, 1955, ch. 18.
16. Merle Curti. *The Growth of American Thought,* 2nd ed. New York: Harper, 1951, p. 784.
17. President's Commission on Higher Education. *Higher Education for American Democracy.* New York: Harper, [1948], I, 6, 49.
18. *Ibid.*, V, 66.
19. F. E. Rourke. *Secrecy and Publicity: Dilemmas of Democracy.* Baltimore: Johns Hopkins P., 1960, *passim.*
20. R. M. Hutchins. *A Free and Responsible Press.* Chicago: U. Chicago P., 1947, p. 5.
21. President's Committee on Civil Rights. *To Secure These Rights.* Washington: G.P.O., 1947, pp. 148, 166.
22. Brown *et al. v.* Board of Education of Topeka *et al.* (1954), 347 U.S. 493, 495.

Bibliography

The following secondary works have been selected for further reference or reading.

GENERAL WORKS

Agar, Herbert. *The People's Choice from Washington to Harding: A Study in Democracy*. Boston: Houghton, 1933.

Agard, Walter R. *What Democracy Meant to the Greeks*. Chapel Hill: U. North Carolina P., 1942.

Baldwin, Leland D. *Best Hope of Earth: A Grammar of Democracy*. Pittsburgh: U. Pittsburgh P., 1948.

Beard, Charles A. *The Republic: Conversations on Fundamentals.* New York: Viking, 1943.

Beard, Charles A. and Mary. *The American Spirit: A Study of the Idea of Civilization in the United States.* New York: Macmillan, 1942.

———. *The Rise of American Civilization*, rev. ed. New York: Macmillan, 1937.

Binkley, Wilfred E. *American Political Parties: Their Natural History.* New York: Knopf, 1943.

Chafee, Zechariah. *Free Speech in the United States.* Cambridge: Harvard U.P., 1948.

Commager, Henry S. *Majority Rule and Minority Rights.* New York: Oxford U.P., 1943.

Curti, Merle. *The Growth of American Thought*, 2nd ed. New York: Harper, 1951.

———. *The Social Ideas of American Educators.* New York: Scribner, 1935.

Edman, Irwin, with the collaboration of Herbert W. Schneider. *Fountainheads of Freedom: The Growth of the Democratic Idea.* New York: Reynal, 1941.

Ekirch, Arthur A. Jr. *The Civilian and the Military.* New York: Oxford U.P., 1956.

———. *The Decline of American Liberalism.* New York: Longmans, 1955.

Franklin, John H. *From Slavery to Freedom: A History of American Negroes.* New York: Knopf, 1947.

Greene, Evarts B. *Religion and the State: The Making and Testing of an American Tradition.* New York: New York U.P., 1941.

Hattersley, Alan F. *A Short History of Democracy.* Cambridge: Cambridge U.P., 1930.

Hayek, F. A. *The Constitution of Liberty.* Chicago: U. Chicago P., 1960.

Hofstadter, Richard. *The American Political Tradition, and the Men Who Made It.* New York: Vintage, 1954.

Morley, Felix. *Freedom and Federalism.* Chicago: Regnery, 1959.

Myrdal, Gunnar *et al. An American Dilemma: The Negro Problem and Modern Democracy*, 2 vols. New York: Harper, 1944.

Parrington, Vernon L. *Main Currents in American Thought.* 3 vols. New York: Harcourt, 1927–1930.

Persons, Stow. *American Minds: A History of Ideas.* New York: Holt, 1958.

Porter, Kirk H. *A History of Suffrage in the United States.* Chicago: U. Chicago P., 1918.

Roseboom, Eugene H. *A History of Presidential Elections.* New York: Macmillan, 1957.

Smith, J. Allen. *The Growth and Decadence of Constitutional Government.* New York: Holt, 1930.

Smith, T. V. *The Democratic Tradition in America.* New York: Farrar, 1941.

Talmon, J. L. *The Rise of Totalitarian Democracy.* Boston: Beacon, 1952.

Van Riper, Paul F. *History of the United States Civil Service.* Evanston: Row, 1958.

Welter, Rush. *Popular Education and Democratic Thought in America.* New York: Columbia U.P., 1962.

FROM COLONIES TO CIVIL WAR

Barnhart, John D. *Valley of Democracy: The Frontier Versus the Plantation in the Ohio Valley, 1775–1818.* Bloomington: Indiana U.P., 1953.

Bates, Ernest S. *American Faith: Its Religious, Political, and Economic Foundations.* New York: Norton, 1940.

Becker, Carl L. *The Declaration of Independence: A Study of the History of Political Ideas.* New York: Harcourt, 1922.

Brown, Robert E. *Middle-Class Democracy and the Revolution in Massachusetts, 1691–1780.* Ithaca: Cornell U.P., 1955.

Carpenter, William S. *Democracy and Representation.* Princeton: Princeton U.P., 1925.

Dietze, Gottfried. *The Federalist: A Classic on Federalism and Free Government.* Baltimore: Johns Hopkins P., 1960.

Douglass, Elisha P. *Rebels and Democrats: The Struggle for Equal Political Rights and Majority Rule During the American Revolution.* Chapel Hill: U. North Carolina P., 1955.

Eaton, Clement. *Freedom of Thought in the Old South.* Durham: Duke U.P., 1940.

Ekirch, Arthur A. Jr. *The Idea of Progress in America, 1815–1860.* New York: Columbia U.P., 1944.

Filler, Louis. *The Crusade Against Slavery, 1830–1860.* New York: Harper, 1960.

Green, Fletcher M. *Constitutional Development in the South Atlantic States, 1776–1860: A Study in the Evolution of Democracy.* Chapel Hill: U. North Carolina P., 1930.

Jensen, Merrill. *The New Nation: A History of the United States During the Confederation, 1781–1789.* New York: Knopf, 1950.

Lillibridge, G. D. *Beacon of Freedom: The Impact of American Democracy upon Great Britain, 1830–1870.* Philadelphia: U. Pennsylvania P., 1955.

Meyers, Marvin. *The Jacksonian Persuasion: Politics and Belief.* Stanford: Stanford U.P., 1957.

Nevins, Allan. *The American States During and After the Revolution.* New York: Macmillan, 1924.

Ostrander, Gilman. *The Rights of Man in America, 1606–1861.* Columbia: U. Missouri P., 1960.

Padover, Saul K. *Democracy by Thomas Jefferson.* New York: Appleton, 1939.

Palmer, Robert R. *The Age of the Democratic Revolution: A Political History of Europe and America, 1760–1800.* Princeton: Princeton U.P., 1959.

Parkes, Henry B. *The American Experience: An Interpretation of the History and Civilization of the American People.* New York: Knopf, 1947.

Perry, Ralph B. *Puritanism and Democracy*. New York: Vanguard, 1944.
Randall, James G. *Lincoln the Liberal Statesman*. New York: Dodd, 1947.
Rossiter, Clinton. *Seedtime of the Republic: The Origins of the American Tradition of Political Liberty*. New York: Harcourt, 1953.
Schlesinger, Arthur M. Jr. *The Age of Jackson*. Boston: Little, 1945.
Smith, T. V. *The American Philosophy of Equality*. Chicago: U. Chicago P., 1927.
Stovall, Floyd. *Walt Whitman: Representative Selections*, rev. ed. New York: Am. Bk. Co., 1939.
Turner, Frederick Jackson. *The United States, 1830–1850*. New York: Holt, 1935.
Tyler, Alice F. *Freedom's Ferment: Phases of American Social History to 1860*. Minneapolis: U. Minnesota P., 1944.
Ward, John W. *Andrew Jackson: Symbol for an Age*. New York: Oxford U.P., 1955.
Weinberg, Albert K. *Manifest Destiny: A Study of Nationalist Expansionism in American History*. Baltimore: Johns Hopkins P., 1935.
Williamson, Chilton. *American Suffrage from Property to Democracy, 1760–1860*. Princeton: Princeton U.P., 1960.
Wiltse, Charles M. *The Jeffersonian Tradition in American Democracy*. Chapel Hill: U. North Carolina P., 1935.

THE LAST HUNDRED YEARS

Aaron, Daniel. *Men of Good Hope: A Story of American Progressivism*. New York: Oxford U.P., 1951.
Bailey, Thomas A. *The Man in the Street: The Impact of American Public Opinion on Foreign Policy*. New York: Macmillan, 1948.
Becker, Carl L. *Modern Democracy*. New Haven: Yale U.P., 1941.
Beloff, Max. *Foreign Policy and the Democratic Process*. Baltimore: Johns Hopkins P., 1955.
Burns, James M. *Roosevelt: The Lion and the Fox*. New York: Harcourt, 1956.
Cochran, Thomas C., and William Miller. *The Age of Enterprise: A Social History of Industrial America*. New York: Macmillan, 1942.
Commager, Henry S. *The American Mind: An Interpretation of American Thought and Character Since the 1880's*. New Haven: Yale U.P., 1950.
Faulkner, Harold U. *The Quest for Social Justice*. New York: Macmillan, 1931.
Filler, Louis. *Crusaders for American Liberalism*. New York: Harcourt, 1939.
Frankel, Charles. *The Democratic Prospect*. New York: Harper, 1962.
Gabriel, Ralph H. *The Course of American Democratic Thought: An Intellectual History Since 1815*. New York: Ronald, 1940.
Goldman, Eric F. *Rendezvous with Destiny: A History of Modern American Reform*. New York: Knopf, 1952.
Higham, John. *Strangers in the Land: Patterns of American Nativism, 1860–1925*. New Brunswick: Rutgers U.P., 1955.

Hofstadter, Richard. *The Age of Reform: From Bryan to F. D. R.* New York: Knopf, 1955.

Kazin, Alfred. *On Native Grounds: An Interpretation of Modern American Prose Literature*. New York: Reynal, 1942.

Laski, Harold J. *The American Democracy: A Commentary and an Interpretation*. New York: Viking, 1948.

Lerner, Max. *America As a Civilization: Life and Thought in the United States Today*. New York: Simon and Schuster, 1957.

Leuchtenburg, William E. *The Perils of Prosperity, 1914–32*. Chicago: U. Chicago P., 1958.

Lewis, Edward R. *A History of American Political Thought from the Civil War to the World War*. New York: Macmillan, 1937.

Lippmann, Walter. *Essays in the Public Philosophy*. Boston: Little, 1955.

Mills, C. Wright. *The Power Elite*. New York: Oxford U.P., 1956.

Mowry, George E. *The Era of Theodore Roosevelt, 1900–1912*. New York: Harper, 1958.

Osgood, Robert E. *Ideals and Self-interest in America's Foreign Relations*. Chicago: U. Chicago P., 1953.

Persons, Stow (ed.). *Evolutionary Thought in America*. New Haven: Yale U.P., 1950.

Pool, Ithiel de Sola. *Symbols of Democracy*. Hoover Institute Studies. Stanford: U.P., 1952.

Riker, William H. *Democracy in the United States*. New York: Macmillan, 1953.

Rourke, Francis E. *Secrecy and Publicity: Dilemmas of Democracy*. Baltimore: Johns Hopkins P., 1960.

Schumpeter, Joseph A. *Capitalism, Socialism, and Democracy*. New York: Harper, 1942.

Spitz, David. *Patterns of Anti-Democratic Thought: An Analysis and a Criticism with Special Reference to the American Political Mind in Recent Times*. New York: Macmillan, 1949.

Waldo, Dwight. *The Administrative State: A Study of the Political Theory of American Public Administration*. New York: Ronald, 1948.

Webb, Walter P. *Divided We Stand: The Crisis of a Frontierless Democracy*. New York: Farrar, 1937.

White, Morton. *Social Thought in America: The Revolt Against Formalism*. New York: Viking, 1949.

Woodward, C. Vann. *Origins of the New South, 1877–1913*. Baton Rouge: Louisiana State U.P., 1951.

Wyllie, Irvin G. *The Self-made Man in America: The Myth of Rags to Riches*. New Brunswick: Rutgers U.P., 1954.

Index

Aaron, Daniel, quoted, 218
Abolitionists, 74, 84, 90, 129–131, 140
Adams, Brooks, 173, 209, 215
Adams, Henry, 162, 164, 215
Adams, James Truslow, 250
Adams, John, 32, 35–36, 51–53, 57–60, 66
Adams, John Quincy, 75, 85, 251
Adams, Samuel, 32–34, 59, 66
Addams, Jane, 175, 197
Administrative agencies, role of, 188–189
Agar, Herbert, 251
Age of Enterprise, The (Cochran and Miller), 164
Age of Jackson, The (Schlesinger), 109
Agreement of the People, English Levellers, 9
Agricultural Adjustment Act (1938), 263
Agricultural Adjustment Administration (AAA), 253, 257–258
Aguinaldo, Emilio, 208
Alabama, 79–80
Aldrich, Thomas Bailey, 205

Alien and Sedition Acts, 68
Alien Registration (Smith) Act, 273
American Association of University Professors (AAUP), 242
American Commonwealth (Bryce), 172–173, 183, 204
American Democracy, The (Laski), 254
American Democrat, The (Cooper), 114–115
"American Democratic Ideal, The" (Adams), 215
American Dilemma, An (Myrdal), 295
American Federation of Labor (AFL), 183
"American Idea, The," World War II symposium, 282
American Journal of Education, 92
American Labor party, New York, 259
American Legion, 238
American Liberty League, 259
American Mercury, 238
American mission, concept of, 100 ff., 112–113, 122, 223. *See also* American Revolution; Fourth of July; Imperialism; Manifest destiny
American Republic (Brownson), 149
American Revolution, 28 ff., 127–128; influence of abroad, 48, 101
Ames, Fisher, 69
An American Dilemma (Myrdal), 295
An Economic Interpretation of the Constitution (Beard), 178
"An Educational Policy for Our New Possessions" (Harris), 208
Anglicans, 11, 24, 43–44
Anglo-Saxon "superiority," 161, 203–204, 241. *See also* Imperialism; White man's burden
Anti-Federalists, 51, 56, 62, 83
Anti-imperialism, 205 ff.
Anti-rent disturbances, New York, 80, 115
Antislavery. *See* Abolitionists
Antitrust laws, 255
Arena, 180
Armistice, World War I, 225–226
Arnold, Thurman, 254–255
Articles of Confederation, 40–41, 47, 54–55, 58
Association, right of: Tocqueville on, 108; guilt by, 289–290
Atlanta *Constitution*, 159
Atlanta Exposition, 156
Atlantic Charter, 275
Atomic Energy Commission (AEC), 287
Autobiography (Steffens), 240
Automobile, 233

Bacon, Nathaniel, 23; Rebellion of, 23, 25
Bacon, Sir Francis, 87
Bailey, Thomas A., quoted, 284
Baker, Newton D., 216
Baker, Ray Stannard, 156
Baldwin, Hanson, quoted, 286
Bancroft, George, 96, 101, 109, 115–116
Baptists, 20, 26, 95
Barnard, Henry, 91–92
Barzun, Jacques, 268
Battle with the Slum, The (Riis), 193
Beard, Charles A., 175, 178, 187, 239, 264, 266; and Mary, quoted, 10, 86–87, 148, 150, 202, 250
Becker, Carl, 269, 280
Bellamy, Edward, 179
Benezet, Anthony, 128
Bentham, Jeremy, 103
Berger, Victor, 228
Beveridge, Albert J., 203–204
Bible and Tract Societies, 89
Binkley, Wilfred, quoted, 76
Bismarck, Prince Otto von, 175
Björnstjerne, Björnson, 206
Bolles, Blair, quoted, 287–288
Borah, William E., 222
Borsodi, Ralph, 240
Boston *Gazette*, 36

Boston Quarterly Review, 109–110
Bourbons, Southern Democrats, 154–155
Bourne, Randolph, 218–219, 221
Bowles, Samuel, 205
Brackenridge, Hugh Henry, 113
Brandeis, Louis D., 196
Brazil, 139
Breckinridge, John C., 138
Brooklyn Daily Eagle, 141
Brown, Robert E., 27
Brownson, Orestes A., 96, 110–111, 149
Bryan, William Jennings, 167–168, 181, 207, 230
Bryant, William Cullen, 109
Bryce, Lord James, 172–173, 183, 185, 204
Buchanan, James, 126
Bureau of Forests, Department of Agriculture, 189
Burgesses, House of, Virginia, 23–24
Burke, Edmund, 33, 67
Burnham, James, quoted, 266
Burns, Anthony, 129
Burns, James M., quoted, 264, 272
Business: and Progressive era, 179, 182–183; in 1920's, 232 ff.

Calhoun, John C., 113, 131–133
California, 100
Calvin, John, 8
Calvinism, 8, 14, 18, 94
Cambridge Platform of 1648, 14
Camp, George Sidney 117–118
Cannibals All! (Fitzhugh), 133
Capitalism: rise of, 9; and Jacksonian democracy, 75–76
Carnegie, Andrew, 160–161, 207
Carr, E. H., 283
Cash, William F., 129
Catholics, 20, 27, 43, 74, 80, 93, 96–97, 111, 236–237
Cato the Elder, 62
Caucus system, 83
Census Bureau, 172
Centralization, trend toward, 148 ff., 174, 239
Channing, Edward, 92
Channing, William Ellery, 130
"Character of Democracy in the United States" (Wilson), 164
Charter of Privileges, Pennsylvania, 21
Chartists, English, 102–103
Child labor, 193, 233
Christianity, and democracy, 94–97, 117. *See also* Church and state; names of churches; Reformation; Social Gospel
Church and state, separation of, 8, 16–20, 43–44, 96, 103
Churches Quarrel Espoused, The (Wise), 19
Churchill, Winston, 275, 279
Cities, misrule of, 183–185
Civil Disobedience (Thoreau), 112
Civil Rights Act: of 1875, 154; of 1957, 296
Civil Rights Section, Department of Justice, 274
Civil service reform, 163–165
Civil War, 125 ff.; significance of Northern victory, 147 ff.; and World War II, 274
Class distinctions, and democracy, 4, 11, 23–24, 172, 245
Clay, Henry, 75, 85, 96
Cleveland, Grover, 163, 206–207
Cleveland, Ohio, as model city, 184–185
Cobb, Frank, 221
Cobbett, William, 67
Cobden, Richard, 139
Collectivism, and economic planning, 250 ff., 282
Colonial assemblies, role of, 10 ff.
Colonization movement, Negro, 65, 129, 142
Colorado, 186
Colton, Calvin, 96
Columbus, Christopher, 162

Commager, Henry Steele, quoted, 174
Commission on Civil Rights, U.S., 296
Committee on Public Information (Creel Committee), 216, 243
Committees of Correspondence, and American Revolution, 32
Common Sense (Paine), 33–34, 44, 67
Commonwealth Club, San Francisco, F. D. R. address before (1932), 252
Communist party, U.S., 228, 273, 284, 289
Conference for Progressive Political Action (CPPA), 231–232
Congregationalism, principle of, 8, 17–20
Congregationalists, 11, 38, 43, 94. *See also* Puritans
Conklin, Edwin Grant, 245
Connecticut: colony, 11, 15–17, 21; state, 35, 45–46, 69, 80, 91; Constitution of 1818, 77, 79, 94
Connecticut Wits, 113
Conquest of the United States by Spain, The (Sumner), 206
Conscientious objectors, in World War II, 273
Conscription. *See* Selective Service
Considerations upon the Nature and Tendency of Free Institutions (Grimké), 100, 118–122, 140
Constitution, U.S., 40, 129, 149, 201, 262
Constitutional Convention, Philadelphia, 46, 52–57, 82
Constitutional Government (Wilson), 177
Constitutions, state: formation of, 35 ff.; revision in Jacksonian era, 77–82. *See also* names of states
Contemporary American History (Beard), 175
Continental Army, 40
Continental Congress, 40
Coolidge, Calvin, 230, 232, 234
Cooper, James Fenimore, 109, 113–115
Cotton, John, 14–15, 17–18
Coughlin, Father Charles E., 258, 266
Council of Revision, New York, 77–78
Counts, George S., 267–268
Crane, Stephen, 179
Craven, Avery, quoted, 126
Crawford, William H., 85
Credit Mobilier, 165
Crisis (Paine), 44
Croly, Herbert, 157, 176, 188 ff.
Cuba, 100, 139, 180, 205, 207, 210
Curti, Merle, quoted, 111, 291

Darwinism, 176–177, 203
Davis, Jefferson, 149
Debs, Eugene V., 196, 217, 227, 232
Declaration of Independence, 34–35, 40, 45, 60, 97, 101, 128–129, 134, 208
Declaration of Rights, Virginia, 37, 43, 46, 60
Defense of the Constitutions (Adams), 57
Deism, 26, 43
De Lancey estate, New York, 42
Delaware, 46
Democracy: changing views of, 1–2; Greek, 2–3, 7; defined, 2, 52; and communism, 4–5; in American colonies, 10 ff.; agrarian, 48, 74–75, 85–86, 250; criticized, 52–54, 67, 113 ff., 238, 241–242; Jeffersonian, 69–71, 190–191, 196; Jacksonian, 74 ff.; direct, 186 ff.; *vs.* representative government, 187 ff.; imperial, 208 ff., 230; and morals legislation, 237–239; and public opinion, 242–243; and World War, II, 268 ff.: Soviet *vs.* American, 279–280
Democracy (Adams), 164
Democracy (Camp), 117
Democracy and Education (Dewey), 244
"Democracy and Education in the Current Crisis," Teachers College,

Columbia University, symposium, 268
Democracy and Empire (Giddings), 209
Democracy and Reaction (Hobhouse), 209
Democracy and the Organization of Political Parties (Ostrogorski), 197
Democracy Constructive and Pacific (Godwin), 117
Democracy in America (Tocqueville), 1, 99, 104–109, 117–118
Democracy Unveiled (Fessenden), 67
Democratic party: of Jacksonians, 75 ff., 84–85, 102, 109–110, 115, 130, 147, 163; after Civil War, 155–156; modern, 206–207, 232, 237, 284
Democratic-Republican Societies, 68
Democratic-Republicans. *See* Democratic party; Republicans, Jeffersonian
Democratic Review, 109
Democratic Vistas (Whitman), 144
Dennie, Joseph, 67
Dennis, Lawrence, 266
Depression of 1930's, 249 ff., 270
Despotism in America (Hildreth), 130
Dewey, Admiral George, 205
Dewey, John, 178, 218, 244 ff., 259, 267
Dewey, Thomas E., 272, 285
De Witt, Benjamin P., 195
Dickinson, John, 40
Dietze, Gottfried, quoted, 55
Dodd, William E., 218
Dollar diplomacy, 210, 212. *See also* Imperialism
Door, Thomas L., 80
Douglas, Stephen A., 139
Draper, John William, 148–150
Du Boris, W. E. B., 193
Dunne, Finley Peter, "Mr. Dooley," 184, 206
Dwight, Timothy, 45
Economic interpretation of history, 177–178
Economic Interpretation of the Constitution, An (Beard), 178
Education, 103; and American Revolution, 44–45; and reform, 90–94; decline in South, 160; and World War II, 291–293
"Educational Policy for Our New Possessions, An" (Harris), 208
Edwards, Jonathan, 26
Eighteenth Amendment, 237. *See also* Prohibition
Eisenhower, Dwight D., 286, 288, 291
Elections, presidential: of 1824–1848, 85; of 1892–1896, 167–168, 230; of 1912, 196–197; of 1920, 230; of 1936, 230, 260–261; of 1940, 270; of 1944, 272; of 1948, 284–285
Electoral College, 56, 81–83
Eliot, Charles W., 195
Ellwood, Charles A., 245
Emancipation Proclamation, 140
Emerson, Ralph Waldo, 109, 111–112, 130, 141
England, 8–9, 91, 102–103, 270–271
Enlightenment, eighteenth century, 44, 89, 128
Epic of America (Adams), 250
Episcopal church, 44. *See also* Anglicans
Equality and equal rights, 4, 75–76, 90, 104–106, 120–121, 245
Era of Good Feelings, 75, 79
Espionage Act, World War I, 217
Essentials of Democracy, The (Lindsay), 243
Eugenics, 241–242
Everett, Edward, 87, 92
Evolution. *See* Darwinism
Ewbank, Thomas, 87
Expansion (Strong), 208

"Failure of Universal Suffrage, The" (Parkman), 164

Fair Deal, Truman administration and, 291
Fair Employment Practices Committee (FEPC), 274, 295
Fairfax, Lord Thomas, 42
Farewell Address, Washington's, 68, 202, 208; Eisenhower's, 288
Farmer-Labor party, Minnesota, 259
Fascism: Italian, 243; threat of in the United States, 247 ff., 258, 265 ff.
Federalism. *See* Limited government; Majority rule *vs.* minority rights
Federalist, The, 56–57
Federalists, 51, 56, 62 ff., 83, 90, 157
Fenno, John, 67
Fessenden, Thomas Green, 67
Feudalism, remnants of in colonies, 11, 22, 24
Fifteenth Amendment, 63, 153
Filler, Louis, quoted, 180
"Fireside Chat on Economic Conditions" (Roosevelt), 263
"Fireside Chat on National Security" (Roosevelt), 271
First Amendment, 217
Fiske, John, 203
Fitzhugh, George, 133
Flower, Benjamin O., 180
Folk, Joseph W., 185
Folklore of Capitalism, The (Arnold), 254
Folkways (Sumner), 176
Ford, Guy Stanton, quoted, 251
Ford, Henry, 233–234
Four Freedoms, Franklin D. Roosevelt's, 275
Fourier, Charles, 90
Fourierism, 116–117
Fourteen Points, Wilson's, 221–222, 275
Fourteenth Amendment, 152–153, 174
Fourth of July, 101, 129
Frame of Government, Pennsylvania, 21
France, 91. *See also* French Revolution
Franklin, Benjamin, 48
Free School Society, New York, 91
French Revolution, 32, 53, 59, 66–69, 101
Freneau, Philip, 45
Frontier and West: colonial, 10, 24–25; in American Revolution, 47–48; in Jacksonian era, 77, 85, 87, 93–95, 100; *vs.* slavery, 134 ff.; after Civil War, 158, 165, 172, 202, 251–252
Fundamental Orders of Connecticut, 17

G.I. Bill of Rights, 291
Gabriel, Ralph H., 95, 114, quoted, 126, 153
Galloway, Joseph, 28
Garland, Hamlin, 179
Garrison, William Lloyd, 90, 129–131, 194
Garvey, Marcus A., 237
General Court. *See* Colonial assemblies
George, Henry, 166–167, 172, 181, 185
Georgia, 26, 46, 64
German-American Bund, 266
Germany, 91, 97, 175, 213–215, 254, 273, 278
Gerry, Elbridge, 54, 66
Gettysburg Address, 2, 137, 208
Ghent, William J., 195
Giddings, Franklin H., 209
Gilded Age, 157 ff.
Gilded Age, The (Twain), 162, 179
Glorious Revolution, in England, 9, 23
Godkin, Edwin Lawrence, 165–166, 181, 206
Godwin, Parke, 116–117
Goldman, Eric, quoted, 173, 230
Gompers, Samuel, 207
Gospel of Wealth, 161

Grady, Henry W., 159
Granger movement, 167
Grant, Madison, 241
Grant, Ulysses S., 161–162, 164, 231
Great Awakening, 25–26
Great Britain. *See* England
Great Community *vs.* Great Society, Dewey on, 246
Greece, ancient, democracy in, 2–3, 127, 132–133
Greeley, Horace, 139
Grimké, Frederick, 100, 140; views on democracy, 118–122
Grimke, Sarah and Angelina, 118
Gronna, Asle J., 214
Growth and Decadence of Constitutional Government, The (Smith), 239

Habeas corpus, writ of, suspended in Civil War, 138
Half-Way Covenant, Puritans', 18
Hamilton, Alexander, 51, 53–56, 62, 66, 234
Hammond, James H., 132–133
Hampton, Wade, 154
Handlin, Oscar and Mary, 86
Hanna, Mark, 175
Harding, Warren G., 228–232, 234
Harper and Brothers, Family Library, 117
Harper's Magazine, 204
Harriman, Edward H., 182
Harris, William T., 208
Harrison, Benjamin, 163
Harrison Narcotic Drug Act, 237
Hawaiian Islands, 205, 272
Hawthorne, Nathaniel, 109, 141
Hay, John, 204
Haymarket affair, 160
Hearst, William Randolph, 180
Hegel, G. W. F., 149
Henry, Patrick, 32, 34, 46
Hildreth, Richard, 116, 130
Hill, James J., 182
History of the American Revolution (Ramsay), 44
History of the People of the United States (McMaster), 63
History of the United States (Bancroft), 101
Hitler, Adolph, 250, 266, 273, 279
Hobhouse, L. T., 209
Hofstadter, Richard, quoted, 135
Holmes, Oliver Wendell, Jr., 177, 217, 261
Home Missionary Society, 89
Homestead Act, 158
Homestead strike, 160
Hooker, Thomas, 15–18, 47
Hoover, Herbert, 229, 234, 251–253, 265
House of Representatives, U.S., 55–56, 59–60, 79, 82, 228, 263
How the Other Half Lives (Riis), 193
Howe, Frederic C., 184–185, 240
Howells, William Dean, 179, 205
Hughes, Charles Evans, 185, 193, 261
Hull House, Chicago, 175
Hutchins, Robert M., 294
Hutchinson, Anne, 16

Idaho, 186
Illinois, 79, 141
Illiteracy, in South and among Negroes, 160, 193
Immigrants and immigration: early, 21–22, 97; after Civil War, 158–159, 164, 193; 1920's, 235–237
Imperialism, 166, 239; rationale of, 201 ff. *See also* Anti-imperialism; Manifest destiny; Militarism; White man's burden
Inaugural Address: Jefferson's, 70; Lincoln's 136; Franklin D. Roosevelt's, 253, 262, 270
Income and wealth, statistics for 1920's, 233

Income tax, 193. *See also* Sixteenth Amendment
Indiana, 79, 93
Indians, 74, 84, 202–203
Individualism: and democracy, 1–4, 8, 74, 117, 190 ff., 246–247, 251 ff., 268, 297; in state constitutions, 37–38; and transcendentalism, 110–112. *See also* Laissez faire; Limited government
Individualism Old and New (Dewey), 246
Industrial Workers of the World (IWW), 228
Industrialism, 74–75, 87–88, 103–104, 133, 158. *See also* Technology
Initiative, referendum, and recall, 186
Inter-American Conference for the Maintenance of Peace, 265
Internal improvements, 85–86
Interstate Commerce Act, 174
Iowa, 141
"Irresponsibles, The" (MacLeish), 266
Irving, Washington, 109
Is America Safe for Democracy? (McDougall), 241
Isolationism, 202–203, 265, 270
It Can't Happen Here (Lewis), 266

Jackson, Andrew, 71, 74 ff., 102–103, 107 ff., 114, 119, 181, 286
Jacksonian democracy, 74 ff., 102–103, 109–110, 113, 132
James, William, 178
Jamestown, 10
Japan, 202, 278, 286
Japanese-Americans, in World War II, 272
Jay, John, 53, 56, 66
Jay, Peter, 78
Jefferson, Thomas, 35, 44, 48, 51 ff., 66, 86, 100, 102, 106, 128, 130–131, 166, 172, 251; views on Constitution, 59–60; philosophy of, 61–62, 69–71, 90
Jeffersonians. *See* Republicans, Jeffersonian
Jews, 27, 236–237, 295
"Jim Crow" laws. *See* Segregation
Johnson, Hiram, 185
Johnson, Tom L., 184–185
Jones, Howard Mumford, 266
Jones, Samuel M., 185
Jordan, David Starr, 207

Kazin, Alfred, 181
Kent, Chancellor James, 78
Kentucky, 63–64, 78–79
Kentucky and Virginia Resolutions, 69
Keynes, John Maynard, 264
King, Rufus, 53
Kipling, Rudyard, 208
Kneeland, Abner, 96
Know Nothing party, 97
Knox, Henry, 54
Korean War, 285, 296
Ku Klux Klan, 229, 236–238, 241

Labor: influence of industrialism on, 87–89; and Progressives, 182–183, 193; after World War II, 290
Labor's Nonpartisan League, 259
Labour party, Britain, 196, 231
La Follette, Robert M., 178, 181, 185, 196, 214, 222, 232, 259
Laissez faire, 75, 86, 121, 159–160, 176–177, 190–192, 253. *See also* Limited government
Landon, Alfred M., 260
Laski, Harold J., 254
Law of Civilization and Decay, The (Adams), 173
League for Independent Political Action, 259
League of Nations, 222–223, 226
Leatherstocking, in Cooper's novels, 114
Lee, Richard Henry, 46
Leisler's Revolt, 25

Lemke, William, 259
Lend-lease, World War II, 271
Letters to John Taylor (Adams), 59
Leuchtenburg, William E., quoted, 209, 229, 234
Levellers, English, 8–9
Lewis, Sinclair, 238, 266
Liberalism. *See* Individualism; Laissez faire; Limited government
Liberator (Garrison), 129, 131
Liberty Bonds, World War I, 220
Lieber, Francis, 117–118
Life, 280
Lilienthal, David, 255–256, 287
Limited government, concept of, 39, 56–57, 85–86, 110, 112, 117, 121, 141–142, 157, 165, 190, 252. *See also* Laissez faire
Lincoln, Abraham, 2, 71, 86, 126, 149, 174, 181, 271; on slavery, 134 ff.; in Civil War, 136 ff.
Lincoln-Johnson plan of reconstruction, 150
Lindsay, A. D., 243
Lippmann, Walter, 243, 265
Lloyd, Henry D., 179–180, 195
Lloyd George, David, 175
Locke, John, 9, 33, 149
Loco-Foco Democrats, 86
Lodge, Henry Cabot, 164, 204, 213
Lodge "force bill," 155
Long, Huey P., 258, 266
Looking Backward (Bellamy), 179
London, Jack, 181
Louisiana, decline of Negro vote in, 155
Louisiana Purchase, 69, 100
Low, Seth, 189
Lowell, A. Lawrence, 187
Lowell, James Russell, 141, 151
Loyalists, in American Revolution, 40, 42, 44
Loyalty-security program, 285, 289–291
Luce, Henry R., 280–282, 294
Lusk, Clayton R., 228; Committee, 228
Luther, Martin, 8
Lynching, 155, 193, 229

MacArthur, Douglas, 286
McCarran-Walter Act, 290
McCarthy, Joseph, 289–290
McClure's, 180
McDougall, William, 241
McKinley, Albert E., quoted, 26–27
McKinley, William, 168, 205–207, 230
MacLeish, Archibald, 266–267
McMaster, John Bach, quoted, 63
Madison, James, 43–44, 46, 51, 54–57, 60, 62, 69
Magna Charta, 37
Magoon, Elias L., 95
Mahan, Alfred Thayer, 204
Main Currents in American Thought (Parrington), 239
Main Street (Lewis), 238
Maine, 140, 260
Majority rule *vs.* minority rights, 3–4, 74, 85, 90, 106–107, 110–111, 116, 119, 148, 154, 227, 297; Jefferson on, 61; Calhoun on, 132; Lincoln on, 135–136
Managerial Revolution, The (Burnham), 266
Manifest destiny, 74, 100–101, 110, 223
"Manifest Destiny" (Fiske), 203
Mann, Horace, 91–93
Mann, Thomas, 268
Mann Act, White Slave Traffic Act, 237
Mardi (Melville), 112–113
Married Women's Property law, New York, 80
Marshall, John, 71
Marxism, 196, 240, 279
Maryland, 20, 39, 63, 80
Mason, George, 37, 43–44, 46, 55
Mass media, and public opinion, 294–295

Massachusetts: colony, 13–19, 27; in American Revolution, 35–36, 46; Constitution of 1780, 38–39, 57; state, 63, 69, 80, 86, 91, 97, 140; constitutional reform in 1820's, 79
Mather, Cotton, 18–20
Mather, Increase, 19–20
Mayflower Compact, 12
Melville, Herman, 112–113
Mencken, H. L., 238, 266
Mercantilism, British, 11, 42
Merriam, Charles E., quoted, 33, 211
Methodists, 95
Mexican War, 132, 142, 202
Meyers, Marvin, quoted, 76
Michigan, 80, 93
Militarism, danger of, 108, 239, 265; Tocqueville on, 108; Grimké on, 122; in Civil War, 137–138; and imperialism, 207, 211; in World War I, 212; post-World War II, 285 ff.
Militia, 215
Mills, C. Wright, 288
Milwaukee Leader, 228
Minnesota, 232, 259
Minority rights. *See* Majority rule *vs.*
Mississippi, Constitution of 1890, 155
Mississsippi Valley, and democracy, 78
Missouri, 79
Mitchell, John, 182
Mobilization: in World War I, 219–220; in World War II, 274
Modern Chivalry (Brackenridge), 113
Monikons, The (Cooper), 115
Monroe, James, 83
Monroe Doctrine, 101, 202
Moody, William Vaughn, 205
Morgan, J. P., 182, 197
Morris, Gouverneur, 53–54
Morris, William, 175
Muckrakers, 179–181
"Mud-sill" theory of democracy, 133–134
Municipal government, reform of. *See* Cities
Munsey, Frank, 180, 197
Myrdal, Gunnar, 295

Nation, 165, 222
National Association for the Advancement of Colored People (NAACP), 194
National Association of Manufacturers (NAM), 234–235
National Education Association (NEA), 208
National Origins Act, 235–236
National Progressive party, Canada, 231–232
National Recovery Administration (NRA), 253, 257–258, 264
National-Republicans. *See* Whig party, U.S.
Nationalism, 99 ff.; in American Revolution, 44–45; and Jacksonian democracy, 74; and reform, 91; *vs.* states' rights, 97; of Whitman in Civil War, 142–145; post-Civil War, 148 ff.; post-World War II, 285 ff. *See also* American mission; Fourth of July
Nation's Business, 235
Natural rights, philosophy of: in American Revolution, 33 ff.; and slavery, 128; following Civil War, 149 ff.
Naturalism, in literature, 179
Naturalization Act (1798), 68–69
Navalism, 204, 207, 211
Nazis, 266, 273, 275, 279, 295
Negro freedmen, 150 ff., 230
Negroes, discrimination against, 103, 140–141, 194, 203, 206; and World War I, 220, 229, 231; in 1920's, 236–237, 245; World War II and after, 274, 284, 292, 295–297
Neutrality, Washington's Proclamation of, 68

Nevins, Allan, quoted, 22, 141
New Deal, 253 ff., 285, 291, 295
New Democracy (Weyl), 195
New England, 11–20, 22–23, 43, 45, 64, 77, 91, 243; towns, 15, 25, 61, 195
New Freedom, Woodrow Wilson and, 182, 198
New Frontiers (Wallace), 255
New Hampshire, 26, 39, 42, 64, 140
New Jersey, 26, 39, 63, 93
New Nationalism, Theodore Roosevelt and, 197
New Republic, 226
New World *vs.* Old, 7–10, 101–103, 208
New York: colony, 11, 26; state, 39, 42, 63, 92–93, 228, 232, 270; constitutional revision in 1820's, 77–79; Constitution of 1846, 80; in Progressive era, 187, 189, 193
New York City, 91, 93, 180, 189, 259
New York Times, 286
New York *World*, 221
Newspaper opinion: and Civil War, 126, 138–139; in 1900's, 180; and mass media, 294
Newton, Sir Isaac, 122
Nichols, Thomas Low, 101
Nineteenth Amendment, 230
Nominating conventions, and political parties, 81, 83–84
Nonpartisan League, 228, 231
Norris, Frank, 179, 181
Norris, George W., 214, 222
North American Review, 118
North Carolina, 22, 25–26, 39, 47, 79–80
North Dakota, 259
Northeastern Confederacy, New England Federalists and, 70
Northern Securities case, 182
Northwest Ordinance, 47, 78
Northwest Territory, 61, 93
Notes on Democracy (Mencken), 238
Notes on Virginia (Jefferson), 45, 62
Notions of America (Cooper), 114
Nuclear war, threat of, 297
Nullification, doctrine of, 132

Oberlin College, 94
"Office of the People in Art, Government, and Religion, The" (Bancroft), 116
Ohio, 64, 79, 93, 118
Ohio Valley, and democracy, 78
Olney, Richard, 206
Olson, Floyd B., 259
On Civil Liberty (Lieber), 117
Ordinance of 1784, 47
Oregon, 100, 141, 186
Osawatomie, Kansas, Theodore Roosevelt address at, 197
Ostrogorski, M., 197
Our Country (Strong), 204
Owen, Robert, 88, 90, 102
Owen, Robert Dale, 88, 92–93

Paine, Thomas, 33–34, 44, 48, 51–52, 57, 59, 128; on French Revolution, 57–68
Palmer, Frederick, 216
Panic of 1819, 76–77
Panic of 1837, 85
Paris Peace Conference, after World War I, 221–222, 227. *See also* League of Nations; Treaty of Versailles
Parker, Theodore, 130
Parkes, Henry B., quoted, 9
Parkman, Francis, 164
Parliament, English, 8
Parrington, Vernon L., 133–134, 157–158, 239–240
Passing of the Great Race, The (Grant), 241
Patroon system, 80
Pax Americana, 204, 283
Pearl Harbor, 271
Peek, George N., 257

Pelley, William Dudley, 266
Pendleton Act, 163
Penn, William, 20–22
Pennsylvania: colony, 21–22; Constitution of 1776, 37, 39; state, 46–47, 63, 79, 83, 92–93; Constitution of 1790, 62, 78–79
"People's War," concept of: Lincoln on, 136; Wilson on, 215
Peoria speech, Lincoln's, 135
Pericles, funeral oration of, 2–3
Perkins, George W., 197
Perry, Matthew C., expedition to Japan, 202
Perry, Ralph Barton, 216
Petition of Rights, England, 37
Philadelphia, 66
Philippines, 201, 205, 208, 210
Philipse estate, New York, 42
Phillips, Wendell, 151
Pilgrims, 12–13
Pilgrim's Progress (Bunyan), 179
Pinchot, Gifford, 189–190
Pinckney, Charles, 54
Plymouth, 12
Poland, 279
Political parties, role of, 103, 108. *See also* names of parties
Politics (Emerson), 111
Polk, James K., 126
Poll taxes, 231
Population growth: colonial, 25; modern, 297
Populists, 155, 166–168, 173, 181, 195, 207
Port Folio, 67
Pragmatism, 178, 244 ff. *See also* John Dewey
"Prayer of Twenty Millions" (Greeley), 139
Preparedness movement, World War I, 212
Presbyterianism, 19–20, 26, 95
President, office of, 81, 107–108, 119–120, 181–182, 238
President's Commission on Education, Report of, 292–293
President's Committee on Civil Rights, 295
Primaries, direct, 186
Primogeniture and entail, 42–43
Prison system, reform of, 46–47, 103
Progress, concept of, 115, 131, 176
Progress and Poverty (George), 166, 172
Progressive Democracy (Croly), 191
Progressive movement, 173 ff.; and imperialism, 209–210; in 1920's, 239–240
Progressive party: in 1912, 196–198; in 1924, 231–232; in 1948, 284–285
Progressivism—and After (Walling), 195
Prohibition movement, 192, 237–238
Promise of American Life, The (Croly), 190–191, 195
Prosperity, 1920's, 232–235
Prussia. *See* Germany
Public and Its Problems, The (Dewey), 246
Public opinion, and democracy, 103, 242–243, 294–295; Tocqueville on, 107; in Progressive era, 187; Lippmann on, 243; Dewey on, 244 ff.; polls, 295
Puerto Rico, 139, 205
Pulitzer, Joseph, 180
Pullman strike, 160
Pure Food and Drug Act, 183
Puritans and Puritanism, 11–20

Quakers, 16, 20–21, 27, 45–46, 128
"Quarantine speech," 265

Radical Republicans, 150 ff.
Ramsay, David, 44
Randall, James G., quoted, 137
Randolph, Edmund, 53–54
Randolph, John, of Roanoke, 71
Red Scare of 1919, 227–229, 238

"Redeemers," of New South, 154, 159–160
Reflections on the French Revolution (Burke), 67
Reformation, Protestant, 8–9
Reform Bill of 1832, 102
Reform movements. *See* Social reform
Regulators, North Carolina, 25
Religion. *See* Christianity; names of church sects and movements
Religious liberty. *See* Church and state, separation of
Republic *vs.* democracy: Madison on, 56–57; John Adams on, 57–59
Republican party: founding, 131; and Civil War, 134; post-Civil War, 156 ff.; and Progressives, 192; modern, 206, 232, 234
Republicans, Jeffersonian, 62 ff., 90, 190–191
Revolution and Democracy (Howe), 240
Revolution of 1688, England, 68
Revolution of 1830, France, 102
Revolutions of 1848, Europe, 97, 101–102
Rhode Island: colony, 11, 15–17, 21, 26; state, 35, 39, 45–46, 53, 79, 91, 141; and Dorr's Rebellion, 80
Rights of Man (Paine), 48, 67
Riis, Jacob, 193
Rise of American Civilization, The (Beard and Beard), 10, 86–87
Rising Tide of Color Against White World Supremacy, The (Stoddard), 241
Rockefeller, John D., 160–161
Roman Catholics. *See* Catholics
Roosevelt, Franklin D., 229, 251 ff., 280–281
Roosevelt, Theodore, 164, 173, 178 ff., 191, 194, 204 ff.
Root, Elihu, 187, 204, 215
Rossiter, Clinton, quoted, 9–10
Rousseau, Jean Jacques, 116
Royal governors *vs.* colonial assemblies, 11, 28
Rush, Benjamin, 32, 45
Ruskin, John, 175
Ruskin College, 175
Russian Revolution (1917), 2, 13
Rutledge, Edward, 53

Sacco, Nicola, 229
Sacco-Venzetti case, 229
Salvation Army, 175
Schlesinger, Arthur M. Jr., quoted, 74, 109
Schurz, Carl, 97, 206
Science, role of, 251. *See also* Technology
Secret ballot, 63, 185
Sedgwick, Theodore, 53
Sedition Act, World War I, 217
Segregation, Negro: following Civil War, 154 ff.; World War II and after, 274, 284, 295–297
Selective Service: in World War I, 215–216, 219; in World War II, 270, 273
Self-culture, 91. *See also* Education
Senate, U.S., 56, 59; direct election of, 186–187, 230
Separatists: in England, 8; in New England, 12–20. *See also* Puritans
Seventeenth Amendment, 186, 230
Share-Our-Wealth movement, 266
Shays' Rebellion, 53, 59
Sherman Antitrust Act, 174
Sherwood, Robert, quoted, 271
Sidney, Algernon, 33
"Significance of the Frontier in American History, The" (Turner), 172
Silver Shirts of America, 266
Simms, William Gilmore, 113
Sinclair, Upton, 181
Single-tax, and Henry George, 166–167
Sixteenth Amendment, 193
Slave trade, African, 42

Slavery: Greek, 3; colonial, 23; and American Revolution, 39, 45–46; antebellum, 127–136; *vs.* free labor, 133 ff., 142–143
Smith, Alfred E., 228, 237, 251–252
Smith, Gerald L. K., 258, 266
Smith, J. Allen, 178, 239
Smith, John, 10
Smith, T. V., 254, 268
Social classes. *See* Class distinctions
Social Contract (Rousseau), 116
Social Gospel, 192
Social reform: in colonies, 65; in Middle Period, 89 ff.; and Progressiveism, 175, 190 ff.
Social Security Act, 258
Socialist party, 195–196, 228, 231–232, 259
"Socialized Education for a Socialized Age, A," 267
Society of the Cincinnati, 65–66
Sons of Liberty, 68
South: in Jacksonian era, 77, 93; and Civil War, 125 ff.; New, 154 ff.
South American republics, independence of, 101
South Carolina, 39, 46, 64, 80, 83, 118, 154
Soviet Russia, U.S.S.R., 240, 273; and cold war, 278 ff.
Spain, 202, 205, 207
Spanish-American War, 166, 168, 201, 204 ff.
Spencer, Herbert, 176
Spirit of American Government, The (Smith), 178
Spoils system, Jacksonian, 84; after Civil War, 163–165
Square Deal, Theodore Roosevelt and, 182–183
Stalin, Joseph, 279
Stamp Act, 33
Standard Oil Co., 180
States' rights, 97, 127, 132–133, 147–149
States' Rights Democratic party, 284–285
Steffens, Lincoln, 180, 184–185, 240; *Autobiography*, 240
Stephens, Alexander H., 149
Stevens, Thaddeus, 93
Stoddard, Lothrop, 241
Stowe, Calvin, 93
Strong, Josiah, 204, 208
Stuart kings, 8–9
Suffrage: in colonies, 14–28; religious tests, 14, 27, 39, 64, 80; property qualifications, 16, 24, 39, 52, 64, 77 ff.; following American Revolution, 63–64; universal manhood, 64, 120; in Jacksonian era, 77 ff.; Negro, 77–78, 140–141, 151 ff.; education or literacy tests, 80, 152–153; women's, 230–231. *See also* Fifteenth and Nineteenth Amendments
Sumner, Charles, 139–140, 153
Sumner, William Graham, 176, 206–207
Sunday School Union, 89
Supreme Court, U.S., 71, 81; in Civil War, 137–138; post-Civil War, 154–155, 174, 193, 217, 228, 232; and New Deal, 261–263; in civil-rights cases, 296
Symbols of Government, The (Arnold), 255

TVA: Democracy on the March (Lilienthal), 255
Taft, Robert A., 272
Taft, William Howard, 183, 188, 196
Taft-Hartley Act, 290
Tammany Hall, 259
Taney, Roger B., 137
Tarbell, Ida, 180
Taylor, John, of Caroline, 59, 71, 121
Teachers College, Columbia University, 267–268
Technology, 86–88
Teheran Conference, 279

Temporary National Economic Committee (TNEC), 264
Tennessee, 64, 80
Tennessee Valley Authority (TVA), 253, 256–257
Texas, 100
Theory of Politics (Hildreth), 116
Thirteenth Amendment, 151–152
This Ugly Civilization (Borsodi), 240
Thomas, Norman, 259
Thoreau, Henry David, 109, 111–112, 130, 133
Tocqueville, Alexis de, 1–2, 74, 89, 99–100, 117–118, 122, 215; views on American democracy, 104–109
Toleration Act, Maryland, 20
Tories. *See* Loyalists
Totalitarianism *vs.* democracy, 275 ff., 292
Townsend, Francis E., 258
Toynbee Hall, London, 175
Trade unions. *See* Labor
Transcendentalism, 111–112. *See also* Emerson; Thoreau
Travelers, European, views of American democracy, 99, 103 ff.
Traveller from Altruria, A (Howells), 179
Treaty of Versailles, 222–223, 226
Triumphant Democracy (Carnegie), 161
Truman, Harry S., 280, 284–285, 289, 291, 295
Truman Doctrine, 280
Tufts, James H., 190
Tugwell, Rexford Guy, 257
Turner, Frederick Jackson, quoted, 8–9, 93, 95, 172–173
Turner, Nat, slave revolt, 131
Tuskegee Institute, 156
Twain, Mark, 162, 179, 205
Tweed Ring, 164, 183

Union party, 260
Unitarianism, 94
United Nations, 275–277, 295
United States Gazette, 67
University of Oklahoma Graduate School, and segregation, 296
University of Texas Law School, and segregation, 296
Utah, 186
Utopian Socialism, 88, 90, 92, 95–96

Vallandigham, Clement L., 138
Van Buren, Martin, 109
Vanzetti, Bartolomeo, 229
Vermont: Constitution of 1777, 39, 46; state, 47, 64, 140, 260
Veto power, 81
Villard, Oswald Garrison, 194
Vindication of the Government of New-England Churches, A (Wise), 19
Virginia: colony, 22–24, 26; Constitution of 1776, 37, 39; state, 42–44, 47, 59–63, 79–80, 83, 90; Constitutional Convention, 1829, 77, 131
Voice from America to England, A (Colton), 96

Wages and hours bill (1938), 263
Walden (Thoreau), 112
Wallace, Henry A., 255–256, 265, 281–282, 284–285
Walling, William E., 195
"War and the Intellectuals, The" (Bourne), 219
War Industries Board, 220
War Message, Wilson's, 213–214
War of 1812, 69–70, 73, 75, 78
Ward, John William, quoted, 76
Warren, Mercy, 45
Washington, Booker T., 156, 193
Washington, George, 46, 66; and Martha, 66
Washington Benevolent Societies, 70
Watauga settlements, 47
Watson, Thomas E., 168

Wealth Against Commonwealth (Lloyd), 180
Wealth and Misery (Owen), 88
Webb, Sidney and Beatrice, 175
Webster, Daniel, 87, 92, 102, 149
Webster, Noah, 69
Wentworth, Benning, 42
West. *See* Frontier and West
Weyl, Walter, 195
Wheeler, Burton K., 232
Whig party, U.S., 75, 84, 102, 109–110, 115, 147, 157–158
Whigs, English, 33, 36, 48
Whiskey, excise tax on, 66
White man's burden, 206 ff. *See also* Anglo-Saxon "superiority"; Imperialism
Whitman, Walt, 109, 126, 141–145
Wiener, Norbert, 282
Williams, Roger, 15–18, 47
Willkie, Wendell, 270
Wilmot Proviso, 142
Wilson, James, 55
Wilson, Woodrow, 164, 176, 181, 196–198, 211 ff., 243–244, 271
Winthrop, John, 13–15, 18
Wisconsin, 80, 186, 232, 257, 259
Wise, John, 19–20
Women's rights movement, 90, 193
Women's suffrage, 186, 230–231. *See also* Nineteenth Amendment
Woodward, C. Vann, 159
Working Man's Advocate, 86, 88
World War I, 211 ff.
World War II, 268 ff.
Wright, Frances, 92
Wyoming, 186

Yalta Conference, 279

Zionism, 236